Dear Shawn

We are extremely
pleased to have
you joining the

EA-RS Group.

Sincerely

Mark Wheeler

Catastrophe and Systemic Change

PERSPECTIVES

SERIES EDITOR: DIANE COYLE

Catastrophe and Systemic Change

Learning from the Grenfell Tower Fire
and Other Disasters

Gill Kernick

LONDON PUBLISHING PARTNERSHIP

Published by London Publishing Partnership
www.londonpublishingpartnership.co.uk

Published in association with
Enlightenment Economics
www.enlightenmenteconomics.com

ISBN: 978-1-913019-29-7 (hbk)

A catalogue record for this book is
available from the British Library

This book has been composed in Candara

Copy-edited and typeset by
T&T Productions Ltd, London
www.tandtproductions.com

Back cover author photograph taken by
Mike Reynolds (rocky.m.reynolds@gmail.com)

Printed and bound by TJ Books Ltd, Padstow

To the 72 souls lost in the Grenfell Tower Fire, including
my former neighbours from the twenty-first floor:
Abdulaziz El Wahabi (52)
Faouzia El Wahabi (42)
Yasin El Wahabi (20)
Nur Huda El Wahabi (15)
Mehdi El Wahabi (8)
Logan Isaac Gomes (stillborn at seven months)
Ligaya Moore (78)

And to my beloved father
Louis Auret Kernick
(7 August 1930–24 June 2017)

Contents

Introduction: the book I wish I'd never had to write

We used to play in the hallways because it was pretty big. We had a nice little group on that floor.

Lulya, 12, survivor from the twenty-first floor of Grenfell Tower[1]

It was like a burnt matchbox in the sky.
It was black and long and burnt in the sky.

Ben Okri, Grenfell Tower, June 2017[2]

WHY THIS BOOK?

I lived on the twenty-first floor of Grenfell Tower from 2011 to 2014. On 14 June 2017, seven of my former neighbours died in the fire. This book is dedicated to them.

But my interest in Grenfell is not only personal. Professionally I work in high-hazard industries, partnering with organizations to build their leadership capabilities and culture in order to prevent catastrophic events. As I watched the tower burn, I promised to ensure that we learned – to make those lost lives count in some way.

In the immediate aftermath I was hopeful.

Catastrophic events have the power to be disruptive and bring about lasting change. I worked in the oil and gas industry in the aftermath of the explosions at the Texas City refinery (2005; fifteen deaths) and the Gulf of Mexico Macondo well (2010; eleven deaths and the industry's biggest ever environmental disaster). I travelled the world – from Australia to Algeria, from Jakarta to Oman – delivering training to help embed the cultural and leadership lessons from those tragedies. I have spent my career working with people who are courageous enough to look at themselves in the mirror and confront their own failings as leaders. I've heard too many stories of loss, of pain. And I've witnessed what is possible when people come together, authentically, willing to show their vulnerability and to learn and build robust cultures, in order to prevent more suffering.

I therefore naively imagined that the worst residential fire in London since World War II – a fire that killed seventy-two people in the UK's richest borough – would engender a desire to learn and change.

I was wrong.

I went from being hopeful, to discovering there had been multiple failed opportunities to learn, to realizing that, far from being an isolated 'bad building', Grenfell revealed systemic failures in building safety and construction across the country, leaving thousands of people living in unsafe homes.

History predicted that we'd find out what happened, identify lessons and then fail to learn them.

Rather than focus only on Grenfell, I needed to understand why we don't learn from catastrophic events more broadly. Whether it be the Covid-19 pandemic or the Boeing Max air disasters, there is an 'awful sameness' to these tragedies, a horrific unifying failure to heed plentiful warnings and change.

In an attempt to understand why our failure to learn makes sense, this book explores two questions.

- Why don't we learn?
- What would it take to enable systemic change?

Both a personal and a professional account of my own investigations and reflections, its intent is to promote enquiry and debate in the hope that it will help us learn from – and therefore prevent – catastrophic events. I offer a model of systemic change, not as a definitive solution but rather as a framework to evoke reflection.

But first, let's step back in time.

IT WAS THE SKY THAT DECIDED US

In 2011 my husband, Keith, and I had returned to London after living abroad, and we wanted to rent in North Kensington for a couple of years while we saved for a deposit. Sick of looking at ridiculously overpriced basement flats with no light or space, a high-rise apartment caught my eye.

It was on the twenty-first floor of Grenfell Tower.

I remember the precise moment I walked in: the first view of the bedroom and then down the hall to the open-plan living area, the dual-aspect windows, the light, the sky ... the space. Breathtaking. Keith and I looked at each other, nodded, then turned to the agent: where do we sign?

It remains one of the most beautiful places I've lived, with the indescribably exquisite colours of the sunsets visible from its windows, and the views of the fireworks on New Year's Eve and bonfire night – little jewels lighting up the horizon. Perched high, watching the slinky movements of the Tube trains as they pulled into and out of Latimer Road station. The jumbled network of cars and roads, and little stick figures walking around. We'd imagine it was a model railway set, like my grandad used to build. One of our windows looked directly onto the (in)famous brutalist 'streets in the sky' Trellick Tower. Falling in love with high-rise living, we'd dream of buying a flat there.

There were six flats on each floor at Grenfell. Three families lived on our floor; we'd chat in the lift, and always take in parcels for one another. The children used to play in the lift lobby, screeching and laughing. Sometimes we'd leave the door open and they'd sneak in, giggling, before running away as soon as they saw us. Teenager Yasin was curious about my work, and he used to tell me how he wanted to start his own business. He'd knock on the door to borrow our bicycle pump. Once, Andreia discovered it was Keith's birthday and showed up with a cake.

Yasin is dead. Andreia's son Logan Isaac was stillborn.

On 4 April 2014 we moved into an apartment on the fifteenth floor of Trellick. Huge windows, stunning views. Grenfell in the middle: a rectangular block of warm lights and memories.

14 JUNE 2017

It had been a great day at work. We ate dinner outside on Golborne Road on that hot summer evening. We were happy. It feels like another life.

Later I was struggling to sleep, lying on the sofa in the living room, annoyed at the sirens and the helicopter, making assumptions about drugs and gangs. Then I walked into the bedroom.

The flames... A diagonal line of yellow and orange... Disbelief. Grenfell. Engulfed.

Sitting on the bed with Keith, watching. Helpless. Work-related images ran through my mind: Piper Alpha, Macondo, fire, explosions, death.

And, the next morning, wandering the streets and sorting clothes. Staring at the tower, watching the astonishing bursts of intense multicoloured flames still coming from windows. People searching for families and friends, desperate, hopeful, hopeless. There were edgy and angry confrontations. Posters and pictures appeared, and thousands of people gathered. Flowers, grief, solidarity, love, pain.

Later that day I sat on our balcony with Matthew Price, a journalist covering the fire for the BBC, who had been interviewing my husband. Looking at the burning building, I thought again of Piper Alpha: on 6 July 1988, 167 people died in what is still the worst industrial accident in the UK. During a refurbishment of the platform, the original principle of ensuring that a North Sea oil rig's accommodation block and muster point was as far as possible from the operating facility was compromised.[3] Those who survived did so by jumping off the platform into the sea – defying policies that claimed that doing so would mean certain death.

I turned to Matthew and said, 'I will do whatever it takes to make sure we learn, to make those lost lives count.' That moment is as vivid for me as when I first saw the fire.

THE REALIZATION OF SYSTEMIC FAILURE

Over the coming months it became clear that, far from being an isolated incident, Grenfell was symptomatic of deeper failures. A failure to build safe homes. A failure to learn from past incidents. A failure to effectively respond to low-probability, high-consequence risk.

I recall the moment I discovered that there is no process to ensure that recommendations from public inquiries or other public investigations are implemented, or to assess their effectiveness.[4] And the moment when, through tears, I read evidence given to a Select

Committee in June 1999. Set up to investigate a fire in Scotland that killed Alexander Linton, the Fire Brigade Union said:[5]

> The primary risk therefore of a cladding system is that of pro-viding a vehicle for assisting uncontrolled fire spread up the outer face of the building, with the strong possibility of the fire re-entering the building at higher levels via windows or other unprotected areas in the face of the building. This in turn poses a threat to the life safety of the residents above the fire floor.

Later I discovered the other failed opportunities to learn, such as the Lakanal House fire in 2009, where a refurbishment wrapped the building in flammable cladding. Fire spread from the flat of origin in four minutes. Six people died, including three-week-old Michelle Udoaka.[6]

Perhaps most heartbreaking was reading a blog written by Grenfell residents and campaigners Francis O'Connor and Eddie Daffarn, written eight months before the fire:

> Only a catastrophic event will expose the ineptitude and incom-petence of our landlord ... and bring an end to the dangerous living conditions and neglect of health and safety legislation that they inflict upon their tenants and leaseholders.[7]

Eddie was rescued while escaping from the sixteenth floor of the tower.

Three years after Grenfell, the scale of the building safety crisis was becoming evident.

- Four hundred and fifty-five high-rise residential buildings have been identified as having similar ACM cladding to that on Gren-fell: 155 social sector residential buildings, 206 private-sector res-idential buildings, 54 student accommodation blocks, 30 hotels and 10 other publicly owned buildings. As of June 2020, 246 (54%) had not had the cladding removed.[8]
- The government has estimated that a further 1,700 high-rise buildings have other unsafe cladding; it has no data yet on mater-ials on the 85,000 lower-rise buildings (those between 11 metres and 18 metres tall) and had no specific data on care homes under

18 metres. These are of particular concern as elderly and vulnerable residents exacerbate the risks associated with dangerous cladding.[9]

- More than 500,000 people in the UK could be living in buildings with unsafe cladding.[10] In addition to the issue of cladding, post-Grenfell inspections have revealed systemic failings regarding issues such as non-compliant fire doors and missing or incorrectly fitted cavity barriers that can compromise compartmentation. Social housing landlords estimate that the cost of making their buildings safe will exceed £10 billion.[11] The government estimates it will cost £15 billion to remediate all fire safety defects in England alone.[12]

Learning from Grenfell would require a much broader focus than the tower itself: the problem is systemic. This book maps and structures my observations and reflections about why we don't learn from catastrophic events and how we might do so, beginning with Grenfell and extending out into other contexts.

Much of what I discovered was unsurprising. I had anticipated issues such as weak regulations, poor procurement and supply chain management practices, and a failure to understand low-probability, high-consequence risk.

But I had not anticipated concluding that we should not rely on those in power to affect change. I had not foreseen that the system is perfectly designed to ensure we do *not* learn. I had not envisaged the depths of the failings of governance and accountability, or how entangled political agendas and power are with our failure to learn. I had not anticipated how much an obsession with blame or blame avoidance drove the lack of political intent or will to ensure meaningful and systemic change.

But I have found hope. Not in the traditional hallowed halls of political, industrial or financial power but rather through the democratization of change that provides us all with the opportunity (or perhaps duty) to be change-makers – to positively disrupt the status quo.

We can create meaningful systemic change by moving beyond our reliance on simplistic, bureaucratic, command-and-control ways of operating and instead embracing complexity and ambiguity; by campaigning to ensure that consequences are fairly borne by those that contribute to disasters; by tapping diverse and distributed knowledge and by creating spaces for genuine enquiry and reflection.

For, it is in the thousands of tiny steps we take, whether individually or collectively – steps towards goodness – that hope lives. As we have witnessed living through a global pandemic in 2020/21, catastrophes, in all of their horror, do offer something unique. As Rebecca Solnit, author of *A Paradise Built in Hell: The Extraordinary Communities that Arise in Disaster*, says: 'When all the ordinary divides and patterns are shattered, people step up to become their brothers' [and sisters'] keepers. ... And that purposefulness and connectedness' is where the seeds of change are sown.[13] My wish is that we will all become seed sowers, for what matters to us, for a world we cannot yet see.

INTENT, BOUNDARIES AND PRINCIPLES

While grateful for the opportunity to write this book, and thankful to those who read it, this will always be 'the book I wish I didn't have to write'.

To help navigate the complexities of doing so, especially before the official Public Inquiry and the inquests are completed, I've had to create some boundaries and principles.

My intent is simple: to offer my reflections in the hope that they will contribute to enquiry and debate that leads to meaningful change.

I finished writing three-and-a-half years after the fire, and it is yet to be determined how (or if) many of the issues I raise will be resolved. The book should be read as a 'moment in time' reflection, rather than as a definitive summary of what happened and the response.

- The book is not intended to share the story of those most impacted by Grenfell. The grief of those directly affected is incomprehensible. It is not my place to share their story. Where I do provide examples from Grenfell, they are in the public domain and are shared for the intent of learning.
- I don't try to replicate or second-guess the work of the Public Inquiry. At the time of writing, the inquiry is ongoing and is

unlikely to be completed for a number of years. While prompted to write by Grenfell, my intent is to reflect on the broader issue of why we don't learn from catastrophic events.

- I have not set out to provide a detailed technical account of what happened at Grenfell. I am not a technical expert and I therefore articulate what happened in a non-technical way. The broad scope of the book has necessitated delving into areas beyond my normal expertise. Any resulting errors are mine alone.
- Likewise I have not attempted to cover every issue associated with Grenfell. I have made judgments on what to exclude based on whether it is critical to the overall picture and whether sufficient official and independent evidence is available.
- I don't seek to blame anyone. While I am critical of some actions, they need to be understood in context, and they are presented to illustrate points rather than to blame individuals. As discussed in chapters 3 and 5, blame fixes nothing.
- And finally, I don't present a party-political view. I am critical of both local and central government, but not in a party political way. All political parties – as well as the political system itself – contribute to our failure to learn.

I have included examples from my work in high-hazard industries; they have been adapted to ensure confidentiality.

When I lead workshops, I'm not so concerned about the workshop itself: rather, I'm interested in and intrigued by what participants might do once they leave it! I'm curious to discover how the conversations we have while together might spark new thoughts, insights and action later.

And the same is true for this book. My hope is that it will spark something in you, the reader, that might help those lost lives count. I'm curious about what you might do after reading the book.

THE BOOK'S STRUCTURE

'Part 1: The Grenfell Tower fire' explores what we currently know about the fire and why it happened. Chapter 1, 'The Grenfell Tower fire: not just the cladding', summarizes what happened on the night. Chapter 2, 'Before, during and after: getting in the tunnel', summarizes what we know at the time of writing about the failed opportunities to learn before the fire, the emergency response on the night, and the response since then.

'Part 2: Analysis and reflections' seeks to understand why our failure to learn makes sense by exploring two questions: why don't we learn, and what would it take to enable systemic change? As a starting point, chapter 3, 'Complexity, safety and systemic change: making the water visible', is intended both to create a shared language and to make transparent my own thinking and biases. I define what I mean by systemic change and explore the three lenses used in the analysis: complexity, safety and leadership.

Chapters 4–7 are structured around four elements: foundational, behavioural, relational and contextual. I share stories of other catastrophic events, consider widely held myths, reflect on insights from Grenfell, propose the conditions that prevent change, and look at the key opportunities to positively disrupt the status quo.

Chapter 4, 'The foundational elements: of bricke or stone', asks what foundational structures are in place to prevent catastrophic events, exploring issues such as known weaknesses in regulations. Chapter 5, 'Behavioural elements: blame fixes nothing', considers what mechanisms are in place to prevent and respond to catastrophic events; issues such as human error and failures to respond to concerns raised through government scrutiny mechanisms are explored. Chapter 6, 'Relational elements: I thought I would make happy both of them', considers how relational issues contribute to catastrophic events, arguing that our unwillingness to address power imbalances is central to our inability to effect change. Chapter 7, 'Contextual elements: the patronizing disposition of unaccountable power', explores issues such as trust and the impact of bias on decision making.

The concluding chapter, 'The democratization of change: of despair and hope', draws together the four elements – foundational, behavioural, relational and contextual – into the Grenfell Model for Systemic Change, creating a compelling picture about why our failure to prevent and respond to catastrophic events makes sense.

After sharing some personal reflections on grief and change, the book ends by suggesting some actions for organizations, the media, government, think tanks, and citizens and communities. I also offer up four areas of disruption for us all to focus on: developing our capacity to deal with complexity and ambiguity; ensuring fairly borne consequences; tapping diverse and distributed knowledge; and creating the space to challenge deeply held, and often invisible, assumptions and biases.

Finally, I conclude that the biggest hope lies in the democratization of change, in individual and community actions that, as Rebecca Solnit says, 'remake the world, and ... do so mostly by the accretion of small gestures and statements and the embracing of new visions of what can be and should be'.[14]

Thank you for reading.

PART I

THE GRENFELL TOWER FIRE

Chapter 1

The Grenfell Tower fire: not just the cladding

In the event of any internal fire starting near a window, there was a disproportionately high probability of fire spread into the rainscreen cladding system.

Dr Barbara Lane, Grenfell Inquiry Expert Witness[1]

If a fire is ignited in a cladding system such as this made of these materials under any circumstances, we have to expect it to spread quickly and catastrophically because of the nature of the materials involved.

Professor Luke Bisby, Grenfell Inquiry Expert Witness[2]

THE FIRE

Two-hundred and ninety-seven people were in the tower on the night of the fire, including sixty-seven children under the age of eighteen. Two-hundred and twenty-seven escaped.[3]

Twenty-five men, twenty-nine women and eighteen children died.[4] The youngest victim was Logan Isaac Gomes, stillborn at seven months. The seventy-second victim of the fire, Pili Burton, never recovered from her escape and died some months later.[5] The median age was forty, the oldest victim was eighty-four, the youngest (after Logan Isaac) was six months.[6]

Based largely on expert evidence heard during Phase 1 of the Grenfell Tower Inquiry, and on the Phase 1 report, this chapter describes what happened on 14 June 2017. After providing some background about the building, it explains the key aspects of the 2012–16 refurbishment and explores their consequences.

Background[7]

Grenfell Tower was built in 1974 in North Kensington, a culturally diverse area famous for Portobello Market and the Notting Hill Carnival, the largest event of its kind outside of Rio de Janeiro.

Figure 1. Grenfell Tower prior to the refurbishment.[8]

The occupants of the tower in 2017 reflected the diversity of the surrounding area. Some had grown up locally, some came from Europe for work, others came as refugees from North Africa, the Middle East, Afghanistan or further afield. Many were employed in the local area and some ran their own businesses.[9] There were architectural students, consultants, artists, teachers and hospital porters. At the time of the fire there were 129 flats:[10] 115 were home to social housing tenants and the other 14 were privately owned.[11]

The tower (figure 1) itself was just over sixty-seven metres tall. It had a basement, a ground floor and twenty-three further storeys. The floor area was approximately 22 metres by 22 metres. It had a central reinforced concrete core and four concrete columns, one at each corner. At the time of construction, the exterior building comprised horizontal structural concrete panels, sliding aluminium-framed windows and a number of non-structural white window infill panels.[12]

Floors 4–23 were designated for accommodation, with six flats on each floor. The lower levels were designed to provide more flexible community space, such as a nursery and a community health centre.[13] Nine accommodation units were added to these lower levels during the 2012–16 refurbishment.[14]

The tower was owned by the local authority, the Royal Borough of Kensington and Chelsea (RBKC), a small but densely populated borough[15] that contained some of the country's most sought-after and expensive properties as well as some of its largest social housing estates. It was managed by the Kensington & Chelsea Tenant Management Organisation (the KCTMO) and governed by a 'modular management agreement' that was entered into in 1996.[16] Under this agreement the RBKC delegated responsibility to the KCTMO for maintenance and major works as well as giving it responsibility for health and safety and fire safety.[17] The KCTMO was, in essence, a 'managing agent'. The RBKC continued to own properties, including Grenfell, and was accountable for strategic housing policies.

As an 'arm's length management organisation', the KCTMO was owned by its resident members and was managed by a board of directors comprising eight elected tenant and leaseholder members, four appointed councillor members and three other independent members.[18] Ironically, the original idea behind such TMOs was that they would give residents power over how their buildings were managed.

Following the fire, all housing stock was handed back to the RBKC in December 2017 for management. The KCTMO still exists but only as a 'shell', in order to participate in the Public Inquiry.[19]

As well as the major refurbishment that was carried out between 2012 and 2016, a number of other works took place that are relevant to the fire.[20] These included the refurbishment of the lifts in 2005–6 and the replacement of all entrance doors in local authority tenant flats in 2011–13.

Finally, between 2012 and 2015, a new leisure centre and an academy school were built next to the tower, limiting the primary access route for vehicles.[21]

THE 2012–16 REFURBISHMENT

Between 2012 and 2016, major work was done on the tower. The building was overclad externally, and internally there was a full refurbishment of the lowest floors. In addition, building services work was carried out within every floor and in every flat, including the fitting of new heating systems.[22]

Buildings are generally overclad to improve their appearance and/or environmental performance. The 2012 planning application for Grenfell stated that 'the over-cladding works are an integral part of the upgrade to the heating of the building, while also being a complete overhaul to its appearance'.[23] Effectively, a new external wall was created by attaching a number of components to the concrete facades: a cladding system was added, the windows were moved outwards, and the architectural crown was clad.

The chairman of the Grenfell Tower Inquiry, Sir Martin Moore-Bick, concluded in the Phase 1 Report (2019) that after the refurbishment: 'The external walls of the building failed to comply with ... the Building Regulations 2010, in that they did not adequately resist the spread of fire. ... On the contrary, they actively promoted it.'[24] The report did not reach any conclusions about why it was decided to reclad the building, saying that this would need further examination during Phase 2.[25]

During Phase 1 of the inquiry we did learn that those changes to the cladding system, the windows and the architectural crown were significant.

The cladding system[26]

The system implemented at Grenfell, called a ventilated rainscreen system, is designed to shelter the building from the majority of direct rainfall while having gaps to permit the ventilation of the cavity behind the panels and ensure that water is collected and drained away.[27]

The cladding system (figure 2) that was added to the building comprised one or two layers of polyisocyanurate (PIR) foam insulation against the original concrete wall, then a cavity which separated the insulation from the outer layer of aluminium composite material (ACM) panels, which were comprised of two thin aluminium panels with a polyethylene (PE) core.[28]

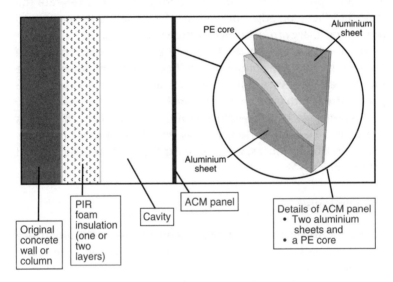

Figure 2. The cladding system and ACM panels.[29]

This PE core of the ACM cladding panels was the main cause of the fire spread. It melts, drips and burns. The dangers of such materials were well known and had been documented over several decades, so, according to expert witness Luke Bisby, any competent fire professional could have been expected to be aware of these dangers.[30]

The ACM panels – manufactured as plain sheets by the company Arconic Architectural Products SAS (referred to as Arconic) – were fabricated into cassettes, or three-dimensional shapes, and hung on steel or aluminium supports or rails fixed to the concrete structure.[31] This meant that each cladding panel was cut and folded to hang on the rails, thereby exposing more of the flammable PE core, resulting in multiple routes where the PE was exposed directly to heat and flames. The metal rails themselves enabled pooling of melted PE.

Fixed directly to the building was a layer of insulation, mostly comprised of Celotex PIR foam insulation, with smaller quantities of Kingspan phenolic polymer foam also present.[32] PIR and phenolic foams are synthetic thermosetting polymers that have low thermal inertia, meaning the surface temperature increases rapidly when heated. As a result, they have comparatively low times to ignition and can support rapid flame spread; they can also accelerate the spread of flame on adjacent materials by insulating the cavity and preventing energy from being lost from the system.[33]

Both vertical and horizontal cavity barriers should have been installed to stop the spread of fire, but inspections after the fire found that they were not continuous and, in many cases, were poorly fitted, with gaps between them.[34]

According to expert witness Professor Luke Bisby: 'If a fire is ignited in a cladding system such as this made of these materials under any circumstances, we have to expect it to spread quickly and catastrophically.'[35]

The windows[36]

During the tower's refurbishment, windows were reduced in size and moved outwards to sit flush with the new cladding system. The new window frames and their inset extractor fans were made of unplasticized polyvinyl chloride (uPVC), and they were glued, rather than fixed, into position. uPVC melts at a low temperature, losing stiffness at around 60 °C and melting at 90 °C.

Building regulations required that cavity barriers be placed around the windows to stop the spread of fire, but none were present at Grenfell, in either the design drawings or the building itself.[37] Materials that were used around the windows included extruded polystyrene, which melts rapidly, forming burning droplets; flammable phenolate foam and spray foam; and EPDM (ethylene propylene diene monomer) rubber. Most of these materials had no potential fire-resisting performance and led directly into the cladding system on the outside of the building.[38]

Expert witness Dr Barbara Lane, said: 'Once a fire inside a flat within Grenfell Tower was close to the window, there was a real likelihood that fire would break out of that flat and into the cladding.'[39]

The architectural crown

The refurbishment involved changes to the precast concrete crown at the top of the building. The columns and beams there were wrapped in a band of tall ACM cassettes, or 'fins', folded into 'C shapes.' The crown's purpose was purely aesthetic.[40] Exposed edges of PE were found everywhere.

THE CONSEQUENCES

The refurbishment had catastrophic consequences that can be explored by considering the start of the fire, the breaking of compartmentation, the external fire spread, the internal failures and conditions, and the smoke and toxicity.

The start of the fire[41]

The fire began in the kitchen of flat 16 on the fourth floor: Behailu Kebede's home. He called the fire service at 12.54 a.m. to report the fire. As he left his flat, he turned the main fuse box off, providing a 'frozen moment' that pointed to the area where the fire started: a fridge-freezer. UK and EU regulations allow plastic covers at the rear of these appliances; in the US, steel covers are required. A steel cover would likely have slowed the spread of the fire. The fire was initially the size of a waste-paper basket, or half an armchair. Fires of this size are not uncommon, and a building should be expected to contain it. The cause of the fire was accidental.

The breaking of compartmentation[42] and the 'stay put' strategy[43]

Compartmentation refers to a design by which fire is contained within a single unit or a single floor. According to Professor Jose Torero, expert witness to the Grenfell Tower Inquiry, it is the primary defence mechanism and forms the basis of the fire-fighting strategy of stay put, which advises residents to remain in flats that are not in the immediate vicinity of the fire. Compartmentation is not the first layer of protection, but it is the only one that brings robustness. Once it was breached, no secondary defence (such as fire doors) could have been expected to withstand the fire. Egress (escape) or rescue is the preferred option once compartmentation is breached.[44]

Compartmentation was breached at around 1.14 a.m., when the fire entered the cladding. This was twenty minutes after Mr Kebede had called the emergency services, and before firefighters had opened the kitchen door in flat 16.[45] From this point, the stay put strategy was not viable. It was reversed at 2.47 a.m., nearly two hours after the first 999 call and more than ninety minutes after compartmentation was breached.

At the stage that compartmentation was breached, the ignition of other components of the facade and external flame spread was inevitable.

It is likely that the fire entered the cladding through the uPVC window frames and/or the extractor fans and surrounding materials. uPVC loses mechanical strength at relatively low temperatures. The heat from the smoke of the fairly small fire was capable of causing the uPVC to fail, providing an opening into the cavity between the insulation and the ACM cladding panels through which flames and hot gas could pass. The flames would have spread across the ceiling, reaching the inside of the window and then igniting any of the components exposed by the melted uPVC, such as the PIR window insulation or the rubber damp-proof membrane.

As the fire spread, the intensity of the heat was such that the glass in the tower's windows failed, allowing fire to re-enter flats. The entire Grenfell fire-fighting strategy assumed compartmentation would work.

External fire spread[46]

The fire at Grenfell acted differently to other cladding fires in that once it entered the cladding it engulfed the entire building.

Within fifteen minutes the fire had spread vertically up nineteen floors to the top of the east face of the tower, accelerating as it rose. The materials on the tower fed off one another, further fuelling the fire – as if a flame was spreading up a solid-fuel surface. The materials, the numerous cavities and the metal railings created routes for the fire to spread both vertically (up and down) and horizontally. As expert witness Barbara Lane said: 'At every turn … there's something there that can participate in a combustion process. So, all the time, the flame front has something that will allow it to carry on.'[47]

A distinguishing feature at Grenfell seems to have been the architectural crown. The fire rapidly spread laterally around the crown and engulfed the building, as the exposed PE from the folded ACM cassettes melted and dripped, starting new fires, and as the lower fires made their way up the building. Helicopter footage shows the flame front progressing and causing extensive pools of burning PE, which could then flow down the spandrels and columns. This pooling and dripping of the PE together with falling burning debris enabled the fire to spread down below the upper floors.

The rapid internal penetration (ingress) of the fire above level 20 (where most people died) can be attributed to the progression in the crown. Glass smashed, extractor fans broke, uPVC frames melted; smoke and fire would have travelled through open windows. Smoke may well also have entered through gaps around the windows. When asked if there was anything that could have been done to stop the spread of fire in the crown, Dr Lane said: 'The only way to stop the crown from being a flame front on its own is to not clad it in a combustible material.'[48]

Internal control failures[49]

In the event of a fire, the lobbies and the central enclosed stairwell should have provided a safe way for occupants to escape. The stairwell, built within the thick concrete core of the building, was designed to be a protected escape route: the last place to which smoke and fire could spread. The lobbies should have been similarly protected from smoke and fire to enable access to the stairwell. However, there were several internal control failures that compromised both the lobbies and the stairwell, inhibiting both escape and rescue.

Firstly, front doors were replaced in 106 homes between 2011 and 2013. The vast majority of these doors did not close automatically, as they should have done, and they resisted fire for just fifteen minutes, instead of the required thirty.[50] The initial density of the smoke in the lobbies was probably caused by front doors being left open, either as people escaped or as they were rescued.

In addition to the doors of the flats, firefighters propped open the stairwell doors,[51] from the lobbies into the stairs, to rescue people or run firefighting hoses into lobbies and flats. In one instance, a body reportedly propped a door open.[52] The primary cause of smoke and heat entering the stairwell was these open doors.

New services has been installed in the lobbies as part of the refurbishment that could cause them to become uncomfortably warm under normal conditions; this had led to the existing environmental smoke and ventilation system being modified. The failure of ventilation in the common corridors and the lobby, coupled with doors being propped open, failed to protect the stairwells from smoke.

In 2005–6 the lifts were replaced but they were not upgraded to firefighting lifts, as was the management company's policy and regulation at the time of the fire.[53] Firefighting lifts carry more people and have their own power source and escape hatch. Even though they had not been upgraded, firefighters should have been able to take control of them to carry equipment and conduct rescues. However, the override mechanism did not work on the night. This meant that the escape route for people with limited mobility was compromised, that the firefighters could only access the twenty-three-storey building via the stairs, and that the lift quickly filled with smoke as residents attempted to use it to escape – something that, at times, had fatal consequences.

Grenfell had a dry riser rather than the wet riser required by regulations at the time Grenfell was built. A wet riser means that water is available in pipes within the building that are connected directly to the mains; they should allow two pipes to operate at full pressure at the top of the building. By contrast, dry risers require the fire brigade to connect water to the mains, which takes time and makes it more difficult to get sufficient pressure on higher floors.

There was also an issue with the floor numbering in the stairwell not being clearly visible, or even accurate. Floor numbers had been changed but not clearly marked during the refurbishment. This would have contributed to orientation difficulties both for residents and firefighters.

The result[54]

The combination of the external fire spread engulfing the building and the internal control failures had devastating consequences.

The fire spread quickly up the east column of the tower, setting fire to the homes on that side of the building: the flat 6 on each level. All of these residents managed to escape their flats, if not the tower. Many would have left their doors open as they fled, and with missing or ineffective door-closers this opened a path for the rapid spread of smoke.

There is a golden early period in a fire when people can make an easy escape. Conditions tend to get worse at an exponential rate, so if you delay escape you can get caught by rapidly deteriorating conditions. Half of the people between floor 6 and floor 11 had started to escape by 1.30 a.m. (thirty-six minutes after the first 999 call). The rate of escape decreased rapidly thereafter. The internal control failures created conditions in both the lobbies and the stairwell that inhibited escape and rescue, as well as the ability to fight the fire. Thick black smoke created a barrier – both physical and psychological – to residents and hindered their ability to move from their flats. Poor visibility and irritants in the smoke when they opened doors were a significant deterrent to escape.[55]

Conditions inside the tower changed rapidly. At some times it was safer for some people to escape than others. Thick black smoke was reported in some lobbies between 1.30 a.m. and 2.00 a.m. Rania Ibrahim was at home on the twenty-third floor with her two daughters, Fethia and Hania Hassan. Her husband was away on business. At approximately 1.40 a.m., less than an hour after the first emergency call, she livestreamed a Facebook video[56] as she opened her front door. It showed thick black smoke, with the lobby light only faintly visible. Rania and her daughters died in the fire.

A 'hot zone' was reported between floors 13 and 16, reaching 150 °C. Between 1.45 a.m. and 2.25 a.m., nobody exited the tower from above that zone. A group of people who were descending the stairs turned back for some reason, mostly retreating to the twenty-third floor, where many died. It's possible the 'hot zone' contributed to this. There are reports of someone, assumed to be a fireman, shouting 'go back'.

Meron Mekonnen, who was on the stairs when those around her suddenly turned around, said:

> It changed everything once we heard 'go back' – we were panicked but on our way down – when we heard go back I assumed something terrible, something worse was happening below us

– I assumed maybe it was another resident – probably seeing flames in the stairways – who could say go back – you know in a fire who could possibly say go back unless there was something worse – it changed everything.[57]

The higher up the tower you were, the more likely you were to die. No one who lived on or below the tenth floor died. Sixteen people who originally resided between floor 11 and floor 17 died: thirteen in their flats and three whose bodies were recovered outside the tower. Fifty-four residents who originally lived between floor 18 and floor 23 died. There was significant internal movement among this last group, with twenty-four people dying on the top floor, nine of whom resided there and fifteen of whom had moved up the building to the twenty-third floor.[58]

Smoke and toxicity[59]

The dense thick smoke that was present in the tower indicates a high concentration of two key toxic gases: carbon monoxide and hydrogen cyanide. Exposure to these can be deadly, but people who are inhaling them are often unaware. They act both cumulatively and additively. The PIR insulation produced high quantities of carbon monoxide. As it was enclosed in a cavity between the wall and the ACM cladding, it probably burned ineffectively, thus increasing the amount of gas released. uPVC (which was used around the windows) produces high yields of carbon monoxide as it burns, and it also affects how surrounding materials burn, further increasing the yield of both carbon monoxide and cyanide. Cyanide fires tend not to be fatal as it is initially incapacitating rather than deadly. If you're exposed to cyanide, it will make you collapse before you can escape. If people die in fires, they usually have a lethal dose of carbon monoxide in their blood.

The outcomes for individuals depended on their exposure in their flats. The hazardous conditions in the lobbies led to occupants experiencing zero visibility, breathing difficulties and pain. Ironically, it was the least-affected flats that became the most dangerous, because when people took refuge in the southwest corner of the block, which was the last place to be affected by fire spread, they remained there for an hour or more before they were forced to evacuate as the fire reached them. These people were therefore the most exposed to toxic gases. Most of the people who died in Grenfell Tower died from carbon monoxide inhalation. Expert witness Professor David Purser said: 'Dying from carbon monoxide, even if there's cyanide in the mixture, is not a painful death. You basically faint then go slowly into a coma and die.'[60]

REFLECTIONS

My intent in this chapter has been to tell the story of 14 June 2017. To show that the events of the night were not just down to the cladding, but rather the result of multiple factors. This lethal combination of failures is a characteristic of major accidents (see more in chapter 3.)

The chapter is not intended as a technical summary of all the factors at play.[61]

People often ask about my experience as a former resident of the tower, often imagining that I'm traumatized by imagining what it would have been like if I'd been living there at the time of the fire. That is not the case. What is hard is that I know the building so I can picture the lobbies and the stairwells, and imagine what it might have been like for those in the tower: residents, visitors and firefighters alike. Rather than shy away from this, I believe it is important to visualize and imagine the experiences of those most impacted that night. While no one will ever know the true horror, thinking about it might reinforce our resolve to prevent anyone from experiencing that level of suffering again. For this reason, I have attempted to put the occupants of the tower at the centre of the unfolding events.

Let us now turn to looking at a broader analysis of Grenfell, considering events before, during and after the fire.

Chapter 2

Before, during and after: getting in the tunnel

> If those materials had been known – the building shouldn't have been occupied, because the Fire Brigade would have then also known what was facing them.
>
> Dr Barbara Lane, expert witness, Grenfell Tower Inquiry[1]

> There was no support in the immediate aftermath. It was absolutely crazy. Three days of wandering around hospitals trying to find some answers. Different hospitals wouldn't let us in.
>
> INQUEST report, 'Family Reflections on Grenfell'[2]

This chapter lays out key events before, during and after the fire. It explores missed opportunities to learn before the fire, and it highlights some near misses since Grenfell that, fortunately, have not led to further loss of life.

The London Fire Brigade's response during the fire is then considered. I am a fierce defender of the firefighters who risked their lives that night but there were significant failings holding important lessons.

Two key phases after the fire are considered: the Grenfell Tower Inquiry and the government response. Not intended as a comprehensive summary of the response to Grenfell, I provide a snapshot by laying out some key events from the three-and-a-half years since the fire that are important when considering why we don't learn from catastrophic events.

Many of the issues raised here are revisited in part II.

Getting in the tunnel

Hindsight changes how we look at past decisions. It is easy with the information we have now to judge actions retrospectively, and to construct simplistic narratives to explain what happened and who is to blame. It turns complexity into linear cause-and-effect chains and binary decisions. To learn from events such as Grenfell we need to guard against this by 'getting in the tunnel' and attempting to understand why decisions made sense rather than judging them with information that wasn't available to people at the time. As the human factors and system safety specialist Professor Sidney Dekker states, 'the point is not to see where people went wrong, but why what they did made sense'. It will help you to see mistakes 'as interesting windows on the functioning of the entire system of which people were part'.[3]

Without this perspective, we cannot learn.

My invitation is to read, not to judge, but to try to understand the point of view of those in the unfolding situation. Dekker again: 'To them the outcome was not known (or they would have done something else). They contributed to the direction of the sequence of events on the basis of what they saw on the *inside* of the unfolding situation.'[4]

BEFORE: MISSED OPPORTUNITIES TO LEARN

A story sticks in my mind as an illustration of the fine line between a near miss and a catastrophe. A floating production storage and off-loading (FPSO) unit is a large floating vessel used by the offshore oil and gas industry for the production and processing of hydrocarbons, and for the storage of oil. The crew of one of these units once shared with me how, after a large gas release, they had been forced to muster for four hours with flammable gas surrounding them while sitting on top of tonnes of stored oil, until the wind dispersed the gas. Some welding work scheduled for that day had been delayed. Favourable wind conditions and the lack of an ignition source marked the fine line between an uncomfortable four hours and a catastrophic event that would likely have cost all of their lives.

The difference between near misses such as this and a catastrophic event is often a matter of luck or chance. Paying as much attention to learning from these high-potential near misses as to incidents that result in serious injuries or fatalities is critical and indicates a strong safety culture.

Before the Grenfell Tower fire[5]

Stretching back to 1973, there have been numerous opportunities to learn from other fires and prevent a future catastrophe.

Summerland, Isle of Man (1973). In August 1973 a fire at an indoor holiday complex for 5,000 holidaymakers on the Isle of Man claimed fifty lives. The building had been coated with an acrylic substance called Oroglas, enabling the building to be climate controlled. It was so flammable that a police officer who attended the blaze took some shards home with him to use as firelighters. In order to save on costs, sprinklers had not been installed. As the fire started, people were told not to panic and to stay inside.

Ruth McQuillan-Wilson recalls the fire. She was five years old at the time, and on holiday with her family:

> Dad had spotted smoke coming out through a ventilation shaft and an announcement was made from the floor. It was smelting and burning lumps from the roof. It fell on people's backs, a lot of people had back injuries. Dad's hair was on fire. And then we had to run through the flames.
>
> I was badly burnt at that point and I thought 'I'm going to die in front of all these people'.
>
> We had to escape over bodies, and I looked down at my hands and I couldn't understand what was wrong. The fingers were webbed, like a duck's feet. The skin was just all melted.

An inquiry recommended that sprinklers be installed in all large buildings and that large buildings' external walls should be fire resistant.

Knowsley Heights, Merseyside (1991). In April 1991 newly installed cladding on a block in Merseyside caught fire when some youths set a pile of furniture at the base of the tower alight. Residents reported thick black smoke and melting windows. The stairwell acted as a chimney. Nobody died in the fire and the subsequent investigation found that the cladding was legal.

Garnock Court, Irvine (1999). In June 1999, there was another cladding fire, this time in Scotland. Before the cladding was installed at Garnock Court, fires in the block had been contained, but when Alexander Linton dropped a cigarette in his fifth-floor flat, the flames broke through a window and into the external cladding. Mr Linton, a wheelchair user, was incinerated in the fire. A Select Committee report said the danger of cladding systems was that fire might exit a building at one floor, spread up the building and re-enter on another floor.

Harrow Court, Stevenage (2005). In February 2005 three people died in a fire in Harrow Court. The man who lived in the apartment where the fire started was rescued, but the woman he shared the flat with, Natalie Close, died, as did the firefighters Michael Miller and Jeff Wornham during the rescue attempt. Residents had been given advice to stay put. In the wake of the fire, the Fire Brigades Union called for a review of the stay put policy and the installation of sprinklers in all high-rise blocks.

Lakanal House, London (2009). In 2009 six people died in a fire in Lakanal House in London. Two years before the fire, the local council had refurbished the building, wrapping it in flammable cladding and installing false ceilings – all of which helped the flames spread. There was no sprinkler system.

Rather than containing fire for an hour as per requirements, the blaze spread beyond the compartment of origin in four minutes.

Rasheed Nuhu and his family took shelter with their neighbours and another family, obeying instructions to shut themselves in the bathroom and hold damp towels over their faces. Then smoke started coming through a vent in the bathroom wall. Mr Nuhu and his family ran to the balcony. They were rescued after forty minutes and led down the blackened and smoke-filled stairwell. Their neighbours stayed behind and died in the bathroom. The youngest, Michelle Udoaka, was three weeks old.

The coroner who investigated the deaths, Frances Kirkham, recommended the retrofitting of sprinklers, that stay put advice should be reviewed, and that the advice given during fire survival calls (when someone says they are trapped by smoke or fire) be reconsidered.

Shepherd's Bush fire, London (2016). **On 19 August 2016, within walk-ing distance of Grenfell Tower, a fire 'ripped through five storeys' of a high-rise residential block.**[6] In May 2017 the London Fire Brigade wrote to the chief executives of all London boroughs warning that the facade at Shepherd's Bush had not met building regulations in terms of limiting the speed of fire spread. It encouraged local authorities to include considering the extent to which external panels complied with building regulations in their risk assessment process.[7]

And further afield. A London Fire Brigade presentation titled 'Tall building facades', dated 13 July 2016, included numerous examples of global facade fires, including the three below.[8]

- The 2012 Tamweel Tower fire in Dubai. The fire spread up the sides of the building, through its highly flammable aluminium and fibreglass cladding, before reaching the roof.[9] All occupants were evacuated.
- The April 2013 Grozny Fire, where a forty-storey skyscraper in the Chechen capital caught fire and flames spread rapidly from the fourth floor. More than 100 firefighters battled the flames; no one was killed or injured.[10]
- The 31 December 2015 Address fire, also in Dubai, began on the twentieth floor and rapidly spread up the exterior of the building. Occupants were safely evacuated.[11]

The fire brigade report concluded that:

New construction material and method of construction are being used in facades and with a limited understanding of their fire behaviour/ performance.

There is a need to understand:
- What products are being used in the facade system and their fire behaviour; and
- If they are used appropriately and meet the relevant guidance

These could affect the way fires develop and spread in a building.

Despite this, very few (if any) of the incident commanders at Grenfell Tower were aware of the risks posed by exterior cladding. The London Fire Brigade Commissioner Dany Cotton – who was in charge of safety and assurance at the time of the production of the 'Tall building facades' slide presentation – has said she was unfamiliar with it at the time of the Grenfell Tower fire and could not explain why its circulation was limited to a small number of fire engineers.[12]

And the near misses continue

We have also seen many concerning near misses since 2017.[13]

- The Barking Fire, on 9 June 2019, saw a huge fire rip through timber cladding on balconies at Samuel Garside House. It later emerged that low-rated 'class D' timber cladding had been used and a fire risk assessment had identified the balconies as a significant hazard.
- On 9 August 2019 Crew Care Home burned to the ground, although luckily all residents escaped. The building was timber framed.
- A timber-framed apartment block in Worcester Park, southwest London, burned to the ground on 9 September 2019.
- On 18 November 2019 a student accommodation block, known as the Bolton Cube, was seriously damaged by fire. It was clad in 'high-pressure laminate' panels.[14]

Fortunately, nobody died in these fires. We tend to brush off these events, failing to treat them as the learning opportunities they represented. In the months after Grenfell I was mentored by Jim Wetherbee, a retired former Navy test pilot and NASA astronaut. I recall him saying: 'You can either take the view that we are "post-Grenfell" or the view that we are "pre the next Grenfell".' Which view you take determines your sense of urgency regarding learning and change.

DURING: THE LONDON FIRE BRIGADE RESPONSE

The following section highlights key findings from Phase 1 of the Grenfell Tower Inquiry regarding the response of the London Fire Brigade (LFB).

Expert witness Dr Barbara Lane said:

> If those materials had been known – the building shouldn't have
> been occupied, because the Fire Brigade would have then also
> known what was facing them.[15]

The bravery and courage of both control room staff and firefighters on the night is beyond question, and while it is true that the LFB
should never have had to respond to such a fire, we need to learn
from both the cause and the response.

In his report, the inquiry chair Sir Martin Moore-Bick said that
while mass evacuation of the tower would have posed serious risks
due to the internal layout of the building and the lack of any kind of
communication system:

> It is likely that, in the face of a rapidly developing fire on the
> exterior of the building and an increasingly pervasive spread
> of smoke and fire throughout the interior, prompt evacuation
> would have resulted in the saving of many more lives.[16]

The inquiry report highlighted key failings regarding preparation and planning, the incident ground and the control room. After
describing how the fire brigade operates, each of these is expanded
upon. Dany Cotton was the LFB commissioner at the time of Grenfell. She has since retired and been replaced by Andy Roe, who was
assistant commissioner in attendance at Grenfell. Andy Roe is the
officer who reversed the stay put policy.

How the LFB operates[17]

The LFB is the fire and rescue authority for Greater London. The head
of the brigade, the commissioner, is responsible for overseeing 5,500
employees, 4,600 of whom were full-time operational firefighters.
Below the commissioner, in a hierarchical structure, sit a number of
assistant commissioners and deputy assistant commissioners. Protocols are in place to escalate the level of command as an incident
becomes more severe.

There are two broad spheres of activity.

- The control room takes emergency calls, deploys resources, communicates with the incident ground, and conducts 'fire survival guidance calls', which kick in when someone says they are trapped by smoke or fire. Per policy, the operator should remain on the phone until the caller is rescued or leaves the building.
- The incident ground is where firefighters under the direction of the incident commander and other officers work to extinguish fires and, where necessary, carry out rescue operations.

The control room[18]

This is usually located in a custom-built facility in Merton, south London. On the night of the fire it was operating from its fallback facility in Stratford. While similar in layout, Stratford was smaller (which some say helped communication) and it did not have the two large television screens that the Merton facility had, which would normally be tuned into a 24-hour news channel and the helicopter downloads (when in use). The intent of these screens is to give the control room an overview of what is happening at an incident.

Responsibility for control room operations lies with the deputy assistant commissioner for operations, who is supported by principal and senior operations managers. The senior operations managers have overall responsibility for managing the control room. They are not required to be in the control room out of normal working hours, although they must respond to pager communications and are automatically mobilized to the control room when (i) an incident requires between nine and twelve appliances, (ii) a major incident is declared by the LFB, or (iii) several lengthy fire survival guidance calls are in progress.

'Officers of the watch' manage the control room during their shift. Control room operators deal with two key types of call: emergency calls and fire survival guidance calls.

On each shift, one operator is assigned as paging operator, giving them the responsibility for notifying brigade officers about an incident using a paging system and ensuring that more senior officers are contacted and attend when an incident escalates.

Two operators are assigned as radio operators. They are the key link between the control room and the incident ground.

There are two integrated control systems that enable the operators to manage emergency calls and mobilize resources.

The incident ground

Firefighting operations are organized around fire stations located across the various London boroughs, each under the direction of a borough commander. Each fire station is staffed with a station manager, a watch manager, a crew manager and firefighters. Stations have either one or two appliances, and each appliance has a crew of three or four firefighters under the direction of a crew manager. In stations with one appliance, the crew manager is also the watch manager. The most senior officer attending the incident ground becomes the incident commander, and an escalation in the severity of an incident prompts an escalation in the seniority of the incident commander.

There are two basic appliances: a pump and a pump ladder. They are similar, but the pump ladder has a 13.5 metre ladder rather than a 9 metre one. Some fire stations also have fire and rescue units, which have more complex equipment including double-cylinder extended breathing apparatus, weighing 23 kilogrammes and providing a working time of forty-seven minutes. Standard appliances have standard breathing apparatus: a single-cylinder system weighing 15 kilogrammes and providing a working time of thirty-one minutes. During an incident, a control officer at the incident ground manages an electronic log that provides real-time information in relation to each breathing apparatus wearer. In addition to the basic appliances, the LFB has eleven aerial appliances.

During an incident, a key role is incident command support, which provides the primary link between the incident ground and the control room, communicating via radio with the two radio operators in the control room. This role is initially provided by the first pump in attendance; at larger incidents, specialist command units are used.

At the ground itself, key communication systems are the airwave radio system, which is primarily for communication between the control room and senior officers, and a high-frequency analogue radio system for use on the incident ground. All firefighters have their own handheld analogue radio. The main drawback of these is that any given channel can only transmit or receive one voice transmission at a time.

The forward command post at an incident is called the bridgehead, from which firefighters are deployed. It must be established in clean air, and in a high-rise building the standard is to establish it two floors below the fire.

Key failures[19]

The Grenfell Inquiry found that the LFB had key failings in its planning and preparation, at the incident ground and in the control room. Some of these are detailed below.

Planning and preparation
LFB's preparation and planning for a fire such as Grenfell were inadequate.

Contingency evacuation plans for fires in high-rise buildings were required by both national and LFB policy. The policy clearly envisages that evacuation may be necessary should compartmentation be breached and stay put become untenable. It suggests that officers consider how evacuation could be conducted during familiarization visits. No such plan was in place at Grenfell. The LFB incident commanders had received no training in how to recognize the need for an evacuation or how to organize one.

The risks of facade fires were known by the LFB, as evidenced by the 2016 'Tall building facades' presentation. But – at most – only one of the firefighters on the ground at Grenfell had seen it. No training was given to incident commanders or senior officers on the dangers of combustible cladding or on how to recognize a cladding fire.[20]

Basic information held by the LFB on Grenfell was out of date, wrong or missing altogether, and crews were not trained to gather critical information during regular inspections, as was required by both national guidance and LFB policy.[21] They should have collected information specific to Grenfell relating to the likelihood and impact of fire spread beyond compartmentation, the need for evacuation, the functioning of fire lifts, and potential communication problems. This information should have been included in the documentation available to those attending the event.[22]

At the incident ground[23]
The first incident commanders, although experienced, were of relatively junior rank. None of the initial incident commanders or senior officers had been able to conceive of the possibility of mass compartmentation failure or, therefore, the need to order a total evacuation of the building.

The inquiry found that the evidence 'taken as a whole strongly suggests that the "stay put" concept had become an article of faith within the LFB so powerful that to depart from it was to all intents and purposes unthinkable'.[24]

Between 1.30 a.m. and 1.50 a.m., as the fire engulfed the building, it should have been obvious that only a supervised mass evacuation would minimize the number of casualties. Stay put was eventually reversed at 2.47 a.m. when Assistant Commissioner Roe took over as incident commander. By this time, it was too late to carry out a managed evacuation.[25]

There were serious failings of command, the report found.[26] The first incident commander was the watch manager, who responded to the first emergency call at 12.54 a.m. and handed over command at 1.50 a.m. A watch manager is trained to manage an incident up to six pumps. By the time he handed over command, twenty-two pumps were in attendance.

While giving evidence he said that by 1.31 a.m.:

There were probably moments where I did feel hopeless. It's a very, very difficult place to be as an incident commander when it's just – it's just relentless. ... This was like nothing else I had ever experienced before. The ferocity, the way that fire was developing, it was just relentless.[27]

More senior officers failed to provide him with sufficient support. The principal failure prior to the reversal of stay put was one of command. None of the officers seized control.[28]

Handovers in command were problematic in their brevity. At one point, two officers were, unwittingly, in command in parallel. At times there were two or three separate lines of communication between the control unit and the ground floor lobby. The chain of command had too many links. At no stage was the bridgehead directly in communication with the command unit. Information was captured on walls and paper, and by radio. The reliability of the information was inaccurate.

Many of the physical and electronic systems and communications did not work properly.[29]

At 2.44 a.m., when Assistant Commissioner Roe took command, he immediately reversed the stay put strategy (at 2.47 a.m.), saying it was 'absolutely unsustainable'. His strategy was to flood the building with extended breathing apparatus wearers and provide as much assistance as possible to the remaining occupants. This was outside of policy as the firefighters were in the building with no firefighting equipment and at considerable personal risk. Thirty-six occupants escaped between 2:53 a.m. and 8.07 a.m., including eight from floors 21 and 22 and eight from floor 18.[30]

In the control room[31]
Control room operators (CROs) were overwhelmed by the number of emergency and fire survival guidance (FSG) calls they received. There were policy shortcomings regarding how to deal with multiple FSG calls, the application of stay put, and the requirements that needed to be followed if an FSG caller has to escape from a burning building.

Operators did not always obtain the necessary information, such as flat number, the number of people present, or whether any were disabled. Nor did they always assess conditions or the possibility of escape.[32]

In many cases, operators assumed that firefighters would arrive quickly, and assured callers that that was the case, when it wasn't true and they had no basis to think it was. They had not been aware of the danger of assuming crews would reach callers, which was one of the lessons from the fire at Lakanal House in 2009, which killed six people.[33]

In his written evidence, Marcio Gomes (who eventually escaped from the twenty-first floor with his pregnant wife and two daughters but whose son Logan Isaac was stillborn) said: 'I wish the operators had been honest and more knowledgeable about the situation from the first phone call as, had I known that no help was coming, I would have handled the situation differently.'[34]

Channels of communication between the control room and the incident ground were improvised and prone to error. Likewise, there was no organized means of sharing information among the CROs, and they had little access to information from other sources. They had no overall picture of the speed or pattern of the fire spread, and in some instances they dismissed information from callers: at one point they were telling people that the fire was on the fourth floor when in fact it had already reached the top of the tower.[35] The lack of the large television monitors in the fallback control room that was used on the night probably contributed to this.

LFB policy requires that operators stay on an FSG call until the person is either rescued or leaves the building, but there were too many calls for this to be possible, putting operators in a difficult position. Some did stay on calls for a long time, while others hung up to take other calls. No plan was made to call people back. Operators had not received sufficient training in handling multiple FSG calls and there were weaknesses in supervision.

When the stay put advice was revoked, the instruction to use blunt and forceful language to ensure callers did not retain any lingering hope that they would be rescued was not passed on clearly to all CROs. This led to differing tones being used.

For example, a CRO in a call at 2.43 a.m. told Bassem Choukair: 'Well, we are trying to get to you but it's very difficult. ... You make the decision whether you think you need to leave or not.'[36] Bassem, his mother-in-law Sirra, his wife Nadia and his children Meirna, Fatima and Zaynab all died on the twenty-second floor.[37]

Another CRO shortly after 2.58 a.m., in a call with Alemishet Demissie, said: 'If you don't do what I tell you, you're going to die in that flat. Okay? I know it's really harsh but that's the truth.'[38] Alemishet was rescued by firefighters, leaving the building after 3.30 a.m.[39]

While there were many failings, the chair of the inquiry, Sir Martin Moore-Bick, reminded us that 'we should remember that the Control Room Operators bore the personal consequences of the night with remarkable fortitude and the psychological cost to them must not be underestimated'.[40]

One operator stayed on a call with twelve-year-old Jessica Urbano Rameriz for fifty-four minutes, starting at 1.29 a.m. Between 1.35 a.m and 1.47 a.m, Jessica was in the bedroom and told the operator that smoke was coming in through the window, that she was with a group of eleven people including a two-year-old child, and that she was struggling to breathe. The operator advised Jessica to make sure the window was shut and the door blocked, and said that firefighters were coming to get her. Jessica said people had tried to leave but couldn't because of the smoke. A few minutes before the call ended Jessica stopped responding. The operator could hear the sound of breathing for some time after that and ended the call when the line went silent.[41]

AFTER: THE GRENFELL TOWER INQUIRY

The day after the fire, the prime minister, Theresa May, announced a Public Inquiry. Chaired by retired judge Sir Martin Moore-Bick, the terms of reference[42] are to 'examine the circumstances surrounding the fire at Grenfell Tower on 14 June 2017'.

The inquiry is divided into two phases. Phase 1 looked at what happened on the night of the fire and published its final report in October 2019. Phase 2 is considering why it happened. It began in January 2020 and hearings are expected to continue through to February 2022,[43] with the final report published sometime after that.

It is arguably the most complex inquiry ever undertaken. By January 2020 the inquiry had received more than 757,300 documents. It disclosed 20,752 documents in Phase 1, and at the time of writing had disclosed 210,848 documents in Phase 2. There were 639 individual and 39 organizational core participants,[44] a status that confers rights such as access to evidence prior to hearings and being able to suggest lines of inquiry.[45]

Phase 1: what happened?

The Phase 1 hearings began in May 2018 with the bereaved giving pen portraits of those who lost their lives and ended with closing statements in December 2018. Evidence was heard from expert witnesses, LFB firefighters and CROs and survivors.[46]

One significant finding of the Phase 1 report (2019) was that:

> The external walls of the building failed to comply with the Requirement B4(1) of Schedule 1 of the Building Regulations 2010, in that they did not adequately resist the spread of fire having regard to the height, use and position of the building. On the contrary, they actively promoted it.[47]

The chair had not expected to rule on this in Phase 1 but said that the evidence was compelling and that Phase 2 would now focus on why and how it ended up on the building.

The report was critical of the preparation and response of the LFB, raising concerns about whether the LFB was capable of learning from its mistakes. It made several recommendations, including the following.[48]

- Owners and managers of high-rise residential buildings should have certain legal obligations, including providing local emergency services with information about the construction of the external walls of their building.
- Improvements in the training of all personnel of fire and rescue services, to ensure they know the risk of fire taking hold in such external walls.
- Improvements in the LFB policies and training for the control room, to ensure better handling of larger volumes of calls, as well as improving communication between the control room and the incident ground.
- The government should develop national guidelines for carrying out evacuations of high-rise residential buildings.

Phase 2: why the fire happened

Intended to uncover why the fire happened, the second phase of the inquiry has been broken down into a number of modules (see table 1[49]). At the time of writing, module 2 hearings are in progress.

Opening statements were heard in January 2020, with hearings originally intended to be completed by June 2021.[50] But, beset by delays, these are now expected to continue till at least February 2022.[51]

Initial delays were due to the Attorney General considering a late request by some core participants and witnesses for privilege from self-incrimination, which provides witnesses protection from their oral evidence being used against them in any further prosecution.[52] The request was granted for individuals.

The onset of Covid-19 then brought about a pause in proceedings from March to July 2020,[53] when they resumed with limited-attendance hearings, meaning that the bereaved and survivors could not attend in person. Covid-19 again halted proceedings in mid December; they resumed on 8 February 2021, this time with hearings being conducted via remote video links.[54] These moves to limited and remote hearings angered some of the bereaved and survivors.

Table 1. The Grenfell Tower Inquiry, Phase 2 modules.

MODULE	TOPIC
Module 1	**The primary refurbishment: overview and cladding.** Examining the role, acts and omissions of the professionals and others involved in the refurbishment from 2012 to its sign-off in July 2016.
Module 2	**Cladding products: testing/certification, product marketing.** A close examination of the testing, classification, certification and marketing of key products used in the external wall.
Module 3	There are three aspects to module 3: **Complaints and communication with residents**, investigating complaints made by residents before the fire regarding fire safety, fire doors and workmanship. The responses of the TMO and RBKC to the complaints and the TMO engagement with residents during the refurbishment. **Compliance with the Fire Safety Order 2005**, considering compliance by the TMO, RBKC and LFB with obligations under law with a focus on the fire assessments carried out. **Active and passive fire safety systems** inside the tower will explore the lifts, fire doors, smoke extraction system together with the gas supply system.
Module 4	**Aftermath of the fire.*** The performance of local and central government in the immediate aftermath of the fire.
Module 5	**Firefighting.** Considering the adequacy of the firefighting response on the night. Issues not covered in Phase 1 include the adequacy of the training of firefighters and communications and equipment.
Module 6	**Government.** Considering the role of central and local governments. In particular, the responses to previous incidents and reports including building regulations and guidance.
Module 7	**Further evidence from expert witnesses.**
Module 8	**The circumstances in which each deceased met their death.** Presentation of evidence to enable the finding of facts necessary for the purposes of the Coroners and Justice Act 2009.

* The GTI announced in January 2021 that module 4 hearings would take place after module 7, likely in January and February 2022. This decision was deemed to be in the public interest so as not to further delay modules 5 and 6. (GTI. 2021. Update on Inquiry. 28 January (https://www.grenfelltowerinquiry.org.uk/news/update-inquiry-47).)

Karim Mussilhy, vice-chair of the families group Grenfell United, said: 'For us, a part of the justice process is being able to be in the room when people who are responsible for what happened to our loved ones face questions.'[55]

While in no way intended to speculate on findings or comprehensively summarize what has been heard to date, the following attempts to give a flavour of what is emerging. The opening statements were characterized by 'the merry-go-round of buck-passing', module 1 by 'questionable competency and missed opportunities', and module 2 perhaps represents 'the greatest corporate scandal of our time', as we learn about the gaming of the testing system by product manufacturers.

Phase 2 opening statements: the merry-go-round of buck-passing
During opening statements, Chief Council to the Inquiry Richard Millet (QC) said that with the exception of the RBKC, and to a lesser extent the insulation manufacturer Celotex:

> Each core participant who played a material part in the refurbishment of Grenfell Tower has laid out a detailed case for how it relied on the work of others, and how in no way was the work it did either substandard or non-compliant. In every case, what happened was, as each of them would have it, someone else's fault.[56]

The RBKC had admitted to significant failures in building control: it apologized for issuing the completion certificate on 7 July 2016, which it said it should not have done.[57]

Celotex, whose insulation was on most of the building, had previously admitted that, in a 2014 test, fire-resistant boards had been placed between temperature monitors in order to pass the test and the company had failed to disclose this. These test results led to it advertising the insulation as suitable for use on high-rise buildings.[58] In its written opening statement, Celotex said that these matters involved 'unacceptable conduct on the part of a number of employees'.[59]

During the inquiry's opening statement, QC Millett, recalling his Phase 1 opening statements where he 'invited the core participants not to indulge in a merry-go-round of buck-passing', added:

> Any member of the public reading these statements and taking them all at face value would be forced to conclude that everyone involved in the refurbishment of Grenfell Tower did what they were supposed to do and nobody made any serious or causative mistakes. ... The notion that Grenfell Tower was not compliant

with functional requirement B4.(1) [to adequately resist the spread of fire over the external walls] without anyone being at fault is unlikely.[60]

This merry-go-round of buck-passing is brilliantly captured in the *Guardian* graphic in figure 3.[61]

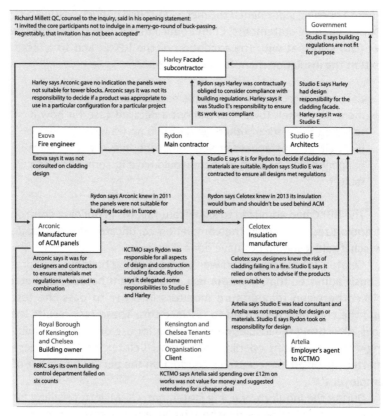

Figure 3. The merry-go-round of buck-passing.
(Copyright Guardian News & Media Ltd 2021.)

Module 1: questionable competency and missed opportunities
The Grenfell supply chain included more than ten contractors and subcontractors, not including the manufacturers and suppliers of the materials.[62] The RBKC was the local authority owner of the

building and it initiated and paid for the 2012–16 refurbishment. The KCTMO procured and oversaw the refurbishment work, appointing Rydon as the 'design and build' contractor in 2014. The advantages of design and build are that the mobilization of contracts can occur in parallel with the design, speeding things up, and the client only has one contract/person to liaise with. However, the client does relinquish a degree of control and quality as they do not have influence over who are selected as subcontractors.

We have heard that Grenfell was the first time the KCTMO were given the opportunity to carry out major capital works on RBKC's behalf, having previously carried out only relatively minor projects.[63] One witness said that the property services department 'hadn't been performing to the standards that either KCTMO or the RBKC wanted'.[64] Additionally, Studio E, the architects, had no experience of refurbishing high-rises or cladding residential buildings,[65] and only very limited knowledge of fire safety building regulations.[66]

Before Rydon was awarded the design and build contract for the refurbishment, it had been told by the KCTMO that cost savings were needed. The KCTMO's target for savings was circa £800,000.[67] An internal error in the bid meant that Rydon had budgeted £212,000 too low, in essence meaning they needed to find more than a million pounds in value engineering.

It was during this value engineering process that the original design for zinc cladding was substituted for ACM cladding with a PE core.[68] Rydon estimated the switch would lead to savings of approximately £420,000, but in an attempt to recover some of the savings for itself, it told the KCTMO that savings would be around £300,000.[69]

Rydon's contract manager, Mr Lawrence, had given 'his hardest sales pitch' to persuade planners to switch to the cheaper ACM cladding.[70] The RBKC planners did accept the change but opted for a more expensive installation method that involved hanging cassette panels off rails rather than riveting them directly onto the building. Driven by aesthetics, this installation method has a far worse fire performance than the cheaper riveted solution.[71]

Mr Lawrence also seemingly failed to respond to an email from KCTMO project manager Claire Williams, who had asked for 'clarification on the fire retardance of the new cladding' and said 'I just had a "Lacknall" moment' (referring to the Lakanal House fire).[72] We also heard that Daniel Anketell-Jones, the design manager from the cladding contractor, Harley Facades, said in an email discussing the need for cavity barriers around the windows: 'There is no point in "fire stopping", as we all know, the ACM will be gone rather quickly in a fire!'[73]

It emerged that the KCTMO had briefed Rydon's Mr Lawrence that there were several vocal residents. Lawrence said: 'I think there were several very vocal, dare I say aggressive residents that, in my opinion, regardless of what work was being carried out or not, they still would have had reason for complaint.'[74]

Expert witness Beryl Menzies said that the plans for Grenfell should have been rejected by RBKC building control before construction work ever started, saying that the failure to ask for detailed information about the cladding was a 'fundamental failing'.[75] The RBKC building control inspector, Mr Hoban, who resigned ten weeks before the fire, told how a 2013 restructure of the department involved shutting down the 'special projects' team that had previously taken on the inspection of more difficult jobs.[76] At the end of his evidence, an openly sobbing Mr Hoban addressed the bereaved directly, saying:

> I am truly heartbroken by what happened that night, particularly for those who lost their lives, you know, the children, the brothers and sisters, sons and daughters, fathers, mothers, grandfathers and grandmothers that lost their life. I also have never forgotten the people that night that got out with their lives. Their lives have changed so dramatically since then, and likewise the people or the families that lost loved ones that night. You know, their lives will never be the same, and I just want to say that I'm truly heartbroken for them.[77]

Module 2: a great corporate scandal[78]
Module 2 is dealing with the certification, testing and marketing of materials involved in the refurbishment. The evidence already provided has prompted the journalist Peter Apps, writing in *The Spectator*, to say: 'The picture the inquiry is painting is not yet complete. But it is already starting to look like one of the great corporate scandals of our time.'[79]

There were three key product manufacturers:

- Arconic, a large multinational aluminium company that manufactured and sold the ACM cladding panels with a PE core (Reynobond PE 55);
- Kingspan Insulation Ltd (referred to as Kingspan), which manufactured the K15 insulation used on a small portion of the tower (Kingspan did not know its product had been used until after the fire); and
- Celotex Ltd (owned by French company Saint Gobain), which manufactured the insulation (RS5000) used on most of the tower.

Evidence suggests that Arconic, Kingspan and Celotex were aware their products posed fire risks, and it points to gaming of UK testing regimes and questionable marketing practices.

We have heard how, despite a 2005 French test during which Arconic's PE-cored ACM cladding burned fiercely, achieving a low (European 'Class E') classification, the company continued to market its product in the UK as the much safer European 'Class B', based on an earlier British certification.[80] A string of emails shows how some of the technical team seem to have agonized about the morality of continuing to sell the cladding. In 2015, Claude Wehrle, a senior member of Arconic's technical team, wrote: 'PE is DANGEROUS on facades, and everything should be transferred to FRI [fire resistant] as a matter of urgency.'[81] But internal emails record the firm resolving to continue selling in countries where 'national regulations are not as restrictive'. The UK was one of those countries.

In 2002 a path to the use of combustible insulation on high-rises was opened, providing it passed a large-scale fire test: this meant that the insulation could be used on high-rises only in the same combination as in the system that was tested (see chapter 4).

In December 2007, Kingspan, the market leader, used this method to test the fire safety of its Kooltherm K15 product. The rig was mocked up like a building, with aluminium cladding panels on a steel frame. It created a 'raging inferno'. The BRE, the certification body conducting the tests, had to stop it early as it risked setting fire to the laboratory.[82] But Kingspan kept selling the product as safe to use on high-rise buildings using a previously successful 2005 test. The inquiry has heard how this 2005 test was 'wholly invalid' as its rig products (or system) used materials such as cement fibre cladding and steel and graphite cavity barriers that were not freely commercially available or widely used, making it unlikely it would be used in the same combination as was being tested.[83] It also emerged that after the 2005 test, Kingspan changed the composition of the insulation so that, according to a former employee, it was no longer the same product. The market was not told of the 2007 'raging inferno' tests or that the product composition had changed.[84]

Celotex, whose insulation was used on the majority of Grenfell Tower, was envious of Kingspan's monopoly on the high-rise market and sought to catch up.[85] As previously mentioned, it emerged that fire-resistant boards were used around the temperature monitors during a test in 2014, distorting the result.[86] Jon Roper, a twenty-two-year-old graduate in charge of Celotex's efforts to break into the high-rise market, said during evidence:

> I went along with a lot of actions at Celotex that, looking back on reflection, were completely unethical, and that I probably didn't potentially consider the impact of at the time. I was, as we've said, I was 22, 23, first job. I thought this was standard practice, albeit it did sit very uncomfortably with me.[87]

All three firms have denied responsibility for the disaster. Arconic says its cladding should not have been used on the tower in the way it was and has pointed to other issues such as the insulation and inadequate fire barriers. Kingspan said it did not pursue Grenfell, knew nothing of the specific design, and has now passed numerous tests with K15 insulation that support its historic marketing claims. Celotex says it had no design responsibility, and that compliance was a matter for those involved in the refurbishment. It said it had repeated the distorted test in 2018 and its materials had passed.[88]

At the time of writing, the inquiry has not heard evidence from the certification or testing bodies.

AFTER: THE GOVERNMENT'S RESPONSE

As we have seen, Grenfell revealed *systemic* issues with fire and building safety in the UK. We will look first at the local government response to the fire and then go on to explore central government's response to the broader issues.

The local government response

The immediate aftermath
In the days after the fire, with thousands of volunteers descending on the area and amidst overwhelming donations, strong criticisms were voiced about the local government response. A 2019 report published by INQUEST, a charity providing expertise on state related deaths and their investigation, found that support, information and communication in the immediate aftermath was chaotic and inconsistent.[89]

The haphazard nature of the emergency response increased anxiety and trauma – families felt abandoned. The inadequacy of the response meant the local community, non-governmental organizations and families were all forced to assume the role of advocates, carers and sources of information. In the words of those impacted:

> There was no support in the immediate aftermath. It was absolutely crazy. Three days of wandering around hospitals trying to find some answers. Different hospitals wouldn't let us in.

> We have a perception that the Government will always look after us, [we] thought there would have been an organised response, but there wasn't. It was chaotic and people didn't know where to go.

> There was no central register of who was safe, who was in which hospital. The next of kin should have been told.[90]

The Independent Grenfell Recovery Taskforce
Responding to criticism about its response, central government established the Independent Grenfell Recovery Taskforce to ensure that the local council, the RBKC, had the capacity and capability to deliver an effective long-term recovery plan for its residents. It was disbanded after producing five reports, the last of which came in March 2020.[91] This final report, nearly three years after the fire, acknowledged that progress had been made, but concluded:

We remain concerned about the pace of change; the culture across the council; and the quality of the relationship with the bereaved and survivors and the wider affected community.

Consequently, we remain unable to give you unequivocal assurance that RBKC is effectively delivering a recovery for the bereaved and survivors and the wider community in north Kensington.[92]

Central government's response

The Building Safety Programme
In the wake of the fire, the Ministry of Housing, Communities & Local Government established the Building Safety Programme to 'ensure that residents of high-rise residential buildings are safe, and feel safe from the risk of fire, now and in the future'.[93]

As of May 2020, it has provided £600,000 for the remediation of ACM cladding on private and public-sector high-rise buildings and £1 billion for the remediation of buildings with dangerous non-ACM cladding. A further £3.5 billion was announced in February 2021.

As part of the Building Safety Programme's main work,

- an Independent Review of Building Regulations and Fire Safety was conducted;
- combustible cladding was banned and new legislation proposed;
- a new building safety regulator was established; and
- in light of 'the dishonest practice by some manufacturers of construction products, including deliberate attempts to game the system and rig the results of safety tests',[94] plans for a new construction products regulator were announced in January 2021.

Let us consider some of these measures in more detail.

The Independent Review of Building Regulations and Fire Safety
In July 2017 the government announced that an independent review would be conducted by Dame Judith Hackitt, a former chief executive of the Health and Safety Executive. It was tasked with addressing 'systemic failings in the regulatory system and deeper problems in the industry'.

The review's interim report,[95] published six months after the fire, found that 'the current regulatory system for ensuring fire safety in high-rise and complex buildings is not fit for purpose'. [96] Hackitt said: 'I have been shocked by some of the practices. ... A cultural and behavioural change ... is now required across the whole sector.' She added that the 'mindset of doing things as cheaply as possible and passing on responsibility for problems and shortcomings to others must stop'.[97]

The final report,[98] published in May 2018, describes the culture as a 'race to the bottom' and identifies ignorance, indifference, a lack of clarity on roles and responsibilities, and inadequate regulatory oversight and enforcement tools as having underpinned the systemic failure. It called for a principled – rather than prescriptive – approach. Some of the report's recommendations are included below.[99]

- Improve the focus on building safety during design, construction and refurbishment by, for example, creating a set of duty holder roles and responsibilities, and establishing a series of gateway points to strengthen regulatory and change control oversight.
- Improve the focus on building safety through the occupation phase by establishing a duty holder responsible for building safety for the whole building, with a requirement that they present a safety case at regular intervals.
- Give residents a voice by providing reassurance and recourse, including greater transparency of information, better involvement in decision making and a no-risk route to escalate concerns.
- Tackle poor procurement practices and ensure continuous improvements and best-practice learning.

Banning combustible cladding
Controversially, the independent review did not recommend a ban on combustible cladding. Relatives of those who died said this was akin to allowing the sale of 'poisoned water'; industry experts said it marked a failure to protect life safety and politicians branded it a 'whitewash'.[100]

Dame Hackitt argued that:

Simply banning something from happening is no guarantee of compliance. If people attach too much reliance upon banning activities and particular materials as being a solution to this problem, it will create a false sense of security.[101]

Within hours of the final building safety report being published, the government announced it would open a consultation on the banning of combustible cladding,[102] and in December 2018 (eighteen months after the Grenfell Tower fire) combustible cladding was banned on new high-rise buildings containing flats, new hospitals, residential care premises, dormitories in boarding schools and student accommodation.[103]

Primary legislation: the building safety and fire safety bills[104]
Expected to be read into law in 2021, the Building Safety Bill brings into law many of the Hackitt review recommendations, and the Fire Safety Bill provides a foundation for secondary legislation that can take forward recommendations from Phase 1 of the Grenfell Tower Inquiry.

Both of the bills have met with criticism[105] – about how they interact with one another, for example – and there have been calls for both to explicitly exclude historical remediation costs from being passed on to leaseholders.[106]

The effectiveness of the government's response

If effectiveness were measured by the number of official reports, committees and consultations produced since Grenfell, the scorecard would be very different from that which considers practical steps such as rehousing survivors, remediating buildings with ACM cladding, and dealing with broader issues in the UK's building safety crisis.

Rehousing survivors
In the aftermath of the fire, the prime minster said that residents would be rehoused as soon as possible, and within three weeks at the latest.[107]

But a year after the fire, of the 203 households that needed housing, only 83 were in permanent homes and 64 were still in emergency accommodation (usually a hotel).[108] Two years after the fire, 15 households had still not been permanently rehoused.[109]

Remediating buildings with ACM cladding
The government has identified and tracked the progress of remediation of high-rise buildings with ACM cladding. Within a year of the fire, 15 buildings had completed remediation,[110] and by June 2020, three years after the fire, of the 455 buildings identified as needing remediation, 158 (35%) had completed it.[111] This number rose to 216 (45%) by December 2020,[112] giving an average of 62 buildings per year.

The building safety crisis

The scale of the issues. The scale of the building safety issues extends far beyond the issues of remediating ACM cladding. Since Grenfell, we have seen numerous instances of residents being asked to evacuate their homes due to other safety concerns.[113] For example, nearly 900 residents, mainly students, were asked to immediately leave their six-floor development in London in October 2020. The housing association owner said the problem was 'wider than a cladding issue' and that a series of safety checks undertaken by technical consultants had revealed further problems with the development.[114]

In addition to the 455 high-rise residential buildings (taller than 18 metres) with ACM cladding that need remediation, the government estimates that a further 11,300 such buildings have other forms of flammable cladding, 1,700 of which are likely to be high risk and require urgent remediation.[115] If remediated at the same rate as ACM-clad buildings since Grenfell (sixty-two per year), this work would take twenty-seven years to complete. (It is not known how many buildings below 18 metres have dangerous cladding.)

The House of Commons report 'Cladding: progress of remediation', published in June 2020, was critical of the government's response, saying:

> It is deeply shocking and completely unacceptable that three years after the Grenfell Tower Fire, there are still 2,000[116] high-risk residential building with dangerous cladding.[117]

It also expressed concern that, given the amount of time since the fire, the government did not yet have reliable data about the number of buildings with dangerous non-ACM cladding.[118] The report also pointed out that limiting access to the Building Safety Fund to high-rise buildings excluded a potentially significant number of high-risk buildings, referencing recent fires at a student accommodation block (the) and a residential block (Samuel Garside House) that were both below 18 metres.[119]

The need to move beyond a focus on cladding and address other fire safety issues, such as fire doors and poorly installed or missing cavity barriers, was also highlighted. The report estimated that it would cost £15 billion to remediate all fire safety defects in England alone.[120]

Unintended consequences and the cladding scandal. As the extent of the building safety issues became clearer, sales began to fall through on high-rise flats as lenders and insurers wanted assurance on building safety.[121] In an attempt to unblock the market, an advice notice[122] was issued by the independent expert advisory panel, and this led to an External Fire Wall Review Form (EWS1)[123] being introduced. Obtaining an EWS1 requires an intrusive test, meaning that it is expensive and potentially difficult to obtain. This problem has been exacerbated by a shortage of surveyors, many of whom, in the wake of Grenfell, have been unable to acquire professional indemnity insurance.[124]

While the EWS1 process was designed for buildings over 18 metres in height, there has been 'scope creep', with some mortgage lenders asking for these forms before offering a mortgage for buildings of any height. *The Times* has estimated that up to 1.5 million flats could be un-mortgageable for years to come as residents cannot prove their buildings are safe.[125]

Stating that the government should have been more aware that its advice notices were likely to have serious consequences for residents, the House of Commons cladding report said that the requirement for an EWS1 form had effectively paused mortgage applications and the sale of affected properties.[126]

Who should pay? The Ministry of Housing, Communities & Local Government has maintained that building owners are responsible for ensuring their buildings are safe and has said that residents and leaseholders should not be the ones to bear costs.[127] But leaseholder law means that many are liable for remediation costs and interim fire safety measures such as 'waking watch', where buildings are patrolled to alert and help evacuate residents if needed,[128] as well as being liable for inflated insurance costs.[129]

A typical cladding bills is £30,000 per flat, and in one block the cost reached £115,000.[130] The House of Commons cladding report cited an example of a service charge increasing from £90 per month to £400 to cover the installation of alarms and a 24-hour waking watch.[131] One building saw its insurance premium rise from £36,379 per year to £194,285: an increase of 434%. Another was quoted £530,000 to renew: an increase of 1,133% over their previous insurance premium.[132]

The stories of those impacted by the cladding scandal are devastating, in terms of both the financial costs of interim fire safety measures and the toll on people's physical and mental health.[133] Rituparna Saha, from the UK Cladding Action Group, said: 'There are people who have had to put off having a family, having babies, because they cannot move. There are people who have been forced out of retirement back into work to pay for bills for remediation.'[134]

One affected resident, giving evidence to the committee, said:

> I package it up into three things. It is the fear of living in an unsafe building. It is the fear of living in the unknown; a fire could happen at any point and it is compressed with these bills that we simply cannot afford as well. It is the feeling that we are trapped; we cannot sell and we cannot move. It is the fear of the unknown and the fact that we are trapped.[135]

The conclusion of the House of Commons report reads: 'We have heard clear evidence of the physical and mental health toll that this crisis has had on residents. We view this as a public health crisis and the Government must do so as well.'[136]

On 10 February 2021, under increasing pressure, the government announced a further £3.5 billion to fully fund the removal of dangerous cladding in buildings over 18 metres and a long-term, low-interest, government-backed financing arrangement for leaseholders in buildings of 11–18 metres in height (under the scheme no leaseholder would pay more than £50 per month for the removal of unsafe cladding).[137] It also announced a levy for developers who wanted to build certain high-rise buildings, and a tax on the UK residential property sector that would raise £2 billion over a decade to pay for the removal of cladding.

While further funding was welcomed, the scheme was criticized for paying for the removal of cladding only in high-rise buildings and for failing to deal with issues other than cladding. It also left lease-holders liable for the cost of some of the remediation of historic building failures and for interim safety measures, as well as their increased insurance costs.

Writing in the *Sunday Times*, Martina Lees pointed out that five of the top housing developers had made £10 billion in profit since Grenfell.[138]

PART 1 CONCLUSIONS: FROM HOPE TO DESPAIR

My intent in this section has been to present facts and steer away from analysis. To conclude, though, I offer some personal reflections.

Having worked in high-hazard industries and witnessed first-hand both the impact of and the response to catastrophic events, in the days and months after Grenfell I was hopeful. Despite the shock and grief, I knew that catastrophes could lead to rapid and much-needed change. Grenfell offered the opportunity for both industry and the government to provide collaborative, courageous and bold leadership.

It shocks and frightens me that three and a half years after the fire we don't even know the scale of the issues. We don't have a clear, transparent, risk-based approach to identifying and remediating unsafe buildings. Our response seems siloed and focused on cladding rather than considering risk holistically and identifying and remediating those buildings most in danger first.

It still surprises and saddens me that we didn't immediately see the building industry and government collectively take responsibility for the state of our buildings, for the years of terrible practice that left thousands living in unsafe homes. The fact that, more than three and a half years after the fire, key stakeholders in both government and industry have not put aside their commercial and legal interests, to collaborate and find solutions to make homes safe, indicates a devastating lack of leadership.

In the state of Victoria, in Australia, faced with similar problems with cladding but thankfully no fatalities, the government has set up both a fund for repairs and a holistic risk-based approach to prior-itizing remediation. The government pays 50% and the remainder is funded by increased building permit levies, ensuring costs are borne by the industry that created them rather than by residents.[139]

It enrages me that innocent leaseholders and residents are bearing the financial and emotional costs of making buildings safe. Any future moves in the direction of fairness regarding funding remediation will be down to tireless campaigning by those impacted, not to the type of leadership by government and industry that I'd expected to see in the wake of Grenfell.

It infuriates me that those involved in the refurbishment of Grenfell and those who supplied the materials used on the tower have, for the most part, not accepted responsibility. They appear more interested in blaming others than learning, and for many of them Grenfell appears to have had little financial impact.[140]

Giving evidence during Phase 2 of the inquiry, expert witness Dr Barbara Lane said that what she had seen 'reflects culture and behaviour I have experienced and observed elsewhere in the construction industry through my own professional work'. She went on:

> I think for me fire safety engineering is about protecting people. It's a massive responsibility. But when you forget that, and you get caught up in the game of, you know, making things work, getting things through, you forget about your primary responsibility, which is protecting people, and that has been a problem in the construction industry, based on my own experience.[141]

This book was borne out of a despair that is eloquently captured in those words. But it was also motivated by a desire to understand why these decisions and behaviours make sense. To move beyond my anger and my instinctive response to blame and judge. To get in the tunnel and begin to understand the systemic issues at play that maintain our inability to learn or respond effectively to tragedies.

Part II articulates what I discovered.

PART II

ANALYSIS AND REFLECTIONS

Chapter 3

Complexity, safety and systemic change: 'making the water visible'

I would rather have questions that can't be answered than answers that can't be questioned.

Richard Feynman, Nobel-winning physicist[1]

All models are wrong, but some are useful.

George Box, statistician[2]

My journey post-Grenfell has, in many ways, been existential. It eroded my belief and trust in government to operate with good intent and forced me to expand my views of change and my role in enabling it.

In the months after Grenfell, naively and with no authority, I made submissions to the Public Inquiry and met and emailed key stakeholders, wanting to bring people together to share learnings. A chief executive from an organization central to the refurbishment said, 'Gill, no one wants to learn'. A senior researcher at a prestigious thinktank told me that what matters to politicians is retaining power – there is no incentive to admit mistakes or learn. Hiding and brushing things under the carpet is, politically, a better strategy. When a respected leader in construction confirmed my fears that the industry had relegated Grenfell to a narrow housing and high-rise-building issue, everything I knew about change from my long career experience felt irrelevant.

I knew about creating change when people are committed to it, with executives and organizations willing to shift their own thinking, to work collaboratively, to sit with the unknown, to experiment and fail, to welcome challenge. I didn't know about creating change in a highly political environment, where preserving the status quo and avoiding blame seemed to be the primary interests.

I have therefore spent much time since Grenfell observing, and reflecting on two questions.

- Why don't we learn from catastrophic events?
- What might enable systemic change?

Immediately after Grenfell I considered that there were two primary failings. Firstly, having a narrow view of safety and not considering low-probability, high-consequence (catastrophic) risks distinctly; and secondly, a lack of leadership. I have since added a third: a failure to understand how to operate effectively in an increasingly complex world.

Watching the Covid-19 pandemic unfold while writing this has confirmed my view that failings in these three areas are core to our inability to effectively prevent and respond to catastrophic events. These form the three primary lenses for my reflections and analysis.

In this chapter, to create some shared language, and to make my own biases transparent, after defining what I mean by systemic change I explore each of these lenses. I then end by explaining the methodology used in subsequent chapters.

SYSTEMIC CHANGE

A couple of days after the fire, in an interview for the BBC, I said: 'We have to get beyond blame to the systemic, cultural and leadership issues that actually led to decisions being made.'[3]

I've heard the many calls for systemic change since, and seen the myriad explanations of what was wrong and how to fix it. I've watched the tireless campaigning by those most impacted, and seen the impassioned pleas for swift action – and the snail's pace response. I came to realize that there was little clarity or shared understanding about what we meant by systemic change.

Piecemeal versus systemic change

Distinguishing between piecemeal change and systemic change[4,5] is helpful. The former impacts parts of the system: building regulations, for example, or technical competency. Systemic change, by contrast, requires 'shifting the conditions that are holding the problem in place'.[6]

Most of the responses to Grenfell and other disasters are piecemeal: changing parts of the system but not the system itself. Piecemeal change will happen post Grenfell, and it is absolutely critical that it does. We will see changes to regulations and to firefighting practice, we will see changes to what materials are used when buildings are erected and to how they are tested and certified. I am not at all confident, though, that we will see systemic change.

Will we shift the conditions holding in place our failure to listen to residents, care workers, NHS staff and others operating at the sharp end? Will we shift the conditions holding in place our failure to understand catastrophic risk? Will we shift the conditions holding in place our over-reliance on regulations and ivory tower expertise? Will we shift the conditions holding in place our deep, and often unconscious, biases, beliefs and assumptions?

The Stephen Lawrence case provides good insight into the difference between piecemeal change and systemic change. On 22 April 1993, Stephen was murdered in an unprovoked racial attack while waiting for a bus. In February 1999, the Macpherson Inquiry report into his death and the allegedly corrupt police investigation that followed labelled the police as 'institutionally racist' – defined as 'the collective failure of an organisation to provide an appropriate and professional service to people because of their colour, culture or ethnic origin'.[7]

There has undoubtedly been piecemeal change in the wake of these findings. For example, detailed targets for the recruitment, retention and promotion of black and Asian officers have been introduced, and an Independent Police Complaints Commission, with the power to appoint its own investigators, has been created.[8] However, it is less obvious that there has been significant systemic change, i.e. that the conditions holding in place institutional racism have shifted.

Twenty years after the inquiry, Macpherson said that the report had allowed the police to take a step in the right direction but stressed that 'there's obviously a great deal more to be done'. Leroy Logan, a former chair of the National Black Police Association, maintains that the force remains institutionally racist, saying that while improvements have been made, 'We still don't have the promotion of equality and justice in the organisation. Black officers are disproportionately subjected to discipline compared to their white counterparts. You still see black staff hugging the lower ranks and they aren't breaking through to the upper levels of the organisation.' He went on:

> We still have disproportionality in stop and search, where a black person is five times more likely to be stopped by police than their white counterparts. They are 20 times more likely to be stopped under section 60 roadblocks and you are more likely to be Tasered if you are black. So even if this is unconscious bias, the fact the police force knows these figures but have not decided to question why this is happening and haven't addressed it – it is institutionally racist.[9]

Piecemeal change is relatively easy: you identify what went wrong and then put plans in place to correct it. For systemic change, though, we need a different perspective.

Making the water visible

'The water of systems change', co-authored by one of the great systems thinkers Peter Senge, recounts a story to illustrate why the concept of systemic change is so challenging:

> A fish is swimming along one day when another fish comes up and says, 'Hey, how's the water?' The first fish stares back blankly at the second fish and then says, 'What's water?'[10]

Systemic change requires *making the water visible* – illuminating the systemic forces at play and 'grappling with this messy kaleidoscope of factors'.[11]

Let us consider the issue of building materials, which we know contributed to Grenfell (see chapters 2 and 3). A piecemeal approach might control what specific materials were used on high-rise buildings, whereas a systemic approach would require grappling with some messy issues. Issues such as the role of political lobbying by product manufacturers; the independence of self-funding testing and certification bodies; the trade-off's being made under the guise of sustainability; and the limitations of siloed governance and regulations. We'd need to assume that these issues were at play beyond the narrow scope of Grenfell and consider what other dangerous products might be being used both in buildings and in other industries.

This would reveal far more complex challenges than banning certain building materials or tightening up construction product testing and classification. It would require a rethinking of which behaviours we consider acceptable and which we do not.

Piecemeal change requires looking at what is wrong with the system; systemic change needs a different approach. Such problems 'are entrenched and perpetuated by the status quo of power, institutional culture, social expectations, myth and narrative'.[12] The first step is to reveal the conditions holding the problems in place: to make the water visible, to grapple with this 'messy kaleidoscope'. Rather than asking what is wrong with the system (which gives you piecemeal answers), this is best done by considering that the system is functioning perfectly and to observe and discover *what* it is perfectly designed to produce.

The analysis and reflections in part II are, in essence, my attempt to make the water visible.

COMPLEXITY

I was fortunate, in the months after Grenfell, to be mentored by Jim Wetherbee. Jim is a former American naval officer, test pilot and NASA astronaut. He is a veteran of six Space Shuttle missions and worked to implement the corrective actions developed after four major accidents: two Space Shuttle disasters – *Challenger* in 1986 and *Columbia* in 2003, both of which resulted in seven deaths – and, in the oil and gas industry, the Texas City Refinery explosion (2005, 15 deaths) and the Deepwater Horizon disaster (2010, 11 deaths and the industry's largest marine oil spill).

I recall Jim saying, on a day when I felt particularly helpless: 'The doors of the people who should be talking to you will likely be closed, stop knocking on them. Look for the open doors.' This took me out of linear thinking, into the emergent maze of change and complexity. I've stopped knocking on closed doors. I've stopped engaging in activities or conversations that will do nothing but maintain the status quo. I've learned that systemic change requires disruption – that I too need to shift how I think and act. I've come to see that kindness can be more disruptive than aggression, that compassion can be more impactful than taking positions. I've learned to plant seeds, and not to worry about which ones live and which ones die.

That is the nature of complex change.

The characteristics of complexity

Many of our traditional, top-down, bureaucratic and mechanistic ways of thinking – grounded in mythical cause-and-effect narratives such as 'we'll roll out this regulation and it will change behaviour' – are becoming redundant. And yet, as we'll explore in future chapters, our responses to catastrophes come from this paradigm.

As the limitations of traditional approaches have become more apparent, I've become interested in the field of complexity. The prevalence of frameworks such as VUCA (volatile, uncertain, complex and ambiguous) environments, wicked (seemingly unsolvable) problems and complex adaptive systems are all examples of a growing awareness and understanding of how to operate effectively in an increasingly complex world.

Resulting from the interconnectivity of and the interrelationships and interactions between elements within a system and between a system and its environment,[13] complexity is 'more a way of thinking about the world than a new way of working with mathematical models'.[14]

Some characteristics of complex systems are given below.[15,16]

- Change is *emergent*, rather than directed or controlled in a linear fashion; interactions are nonlinear and minor changes can produce major consequences.
- Complex systems are *not predictable*. Cause and effect are not 'tightly coupled': we can't predict outcomes or retrospectively understand cause.

- They involve a large number of *interacting elements* with *distributed control* – the digital world has increased the number of interactions exponentially.
- And they are *adaptive* and *co-evolve*. Elements in a system can change based on their interactions with one another and with the environment.

These characteristics are highlighted by events such as the killing of George Floyd in America leading to the removal of the statue of Cecil Rhodes at Oxford University,[17] or the creation of a global youth movement for climate change stemming from one young girl's protest outside the Swedish parliament.[18] Witness also how local communities created support networks in response to Covid-19 far more rapidly and effectively than government interventions were rolled out.

Our ability to learn to operate effectively with increasing complexity is critical. Consider that a simple tablet (of the technical, not medicinal, kind) possesses the processing power of 5,000 desktop computers from thirty years ago. Pause and reflect on the fact that the human genome project cost US$2.7 billion and took more than a decade to complete, but we can now sequence a genome in a few hours for less than a thousand dollars.[19] A 2015 study predicted – with 76.4% certainty – that by 2025, the first 3D-printed liver transplant will take place.[20] Some predict that 90% of news will be generated by artificial intelligence by the mid 2020s.[21,22]

The boundaries between the physical, biological and digital worlds are blurring and merging, challenging and confronting what it means to be human: what are our rights and responsibilities?[23] We are changing not only '"what" and "how" we do things, but also "who" we are'.[24] Sometimes referred to as the age of disruption, we are on the cusp of the next Industrial Revolution.

The Fourth Industrial Revolution

Unlike incremental evolutionary change, revolutionary change is dramatic and forced. Driven by external circumstances, it disrupts normal operations and requires innovative approaches.

'In its scale, scope and complexity, the transformation will be unlike anything humankind has experienced before,' says Klaus

Schwab, founder and CEO of the World Economic Forum.[25] The coming revolution will differ from previous ones by its velocity, enabled by the deeply interconnected world, and by its breadth and depth, as it disrupts almost every industry in every country, leading to paradigm shifts at all levels: economic, business, societal and individual. This will require the transformation of entire systems.[26]

Skills such as complex problem solving, critical thinking, creativity, emotional intelligence and cognitive flexibility will become increasingly important.[27,28] Social tensions will likely increase as the job market segments into low-skill/low-pay and high-skill/high-pay work, with a hollowing out in the middle, leading to an increasingly disenfranchised middle class.[29]

Covid-19 has amplified these tensions and highlighted the agile, adaptive, collaborative approaches that will be needed during this revolution. Overnight it disrupted the way we worked, forcing rapid innovation and highlighting the chasms and inequalities in society. It has underscored the limitations of traditional approaches by governments, businesses and citizens alike.

To operate effectively in an increasingly complex world, governments will need to change how they approach public engagement, as the central role of conducting policy diminishes and linear, mechanistic, 'top-down' approaches become increasingly unfeasible in a time of unprecedented change and innovation. Issues of national security will be critical as cyber security and biological warfare create new risks, and cyberwarfare blurs the lines between war and peace.[30]

While technology gives governments the ability to increase control, it also enables the redistribution of power by enabling citizens to engage, voice their opinions and coordinate actions. Governments will 'have to learn to collaborate and adapt, while ensuring that human beings remain at the centre of all decisions'.[31] Embracing 'agile' governance, adapting and reinventing themselves in a fast-changing environment will require close collaboration with both business and citizens.

Covid-19 demanded agile governance, and we have seen governments make rapid and radical decisions, such as committing unprecedented amounts of money to furlough schemes and closing businesses and schools. These actions have highlighted issues such as limited scrutiny and concerns about a loss of freedom. We have also seen how failures to collaborate closely with citizens and the front line have contributed to poor decisions, U-turns and significant heartbreak.

Notable in the UK was the failure, at the beginning of the pandemic, to listen and respond to the basic personal protective equipment (PPE) needs of those in the health and care services.[32] As Adelina Comas-Herrera, a research fellow at the London School of Economics and Political Science, said: 'You had a situation where care homes were forced to bring in people who probably had the virus, they did not have any means of testing, and they did not have the tools to keep people safe. It was a toxic combination.' According to The Lancet, estimated excess deaths in UK care homes between March and April 2020 were roughly 20,000.[33]

Again as seen during the pandemic, businesses will be challenged by increasing innovation and disruption. On the supply side, new technologies will create different ways of serving needs, leading to situations where innovative competitors can oust well-established incumbents. On the demand side, with increasing transparency, consumer engagement and patterns of behaviour are shifting, forcing companies to adapt the way they design, market and deliver products.[34] In the words of Klaus Schwab: 'Business leaders and senior executives need to understand their changing environment, challenge the assumptions of their operating teams, and relentlessly and continuously innovate.'[35]

These changes have been brutally illustrated during the pandemic as the shift to online retail has accelerated, highlighting both the plight of our high street stores and the ingenuity and agility of some of them. My local deli now seamlessly morphs between serving sit-in/take-out food and being a grocery shop and wine store depending on what regulations allow at any given time.

Table 2 on the next page shows how the identity of the top four global companies (by worth) has changed over the last decade.[36] What will this picture look like in 2029?

For citizens, our notions of privacy, control and ownership will change. What will the impact of technology be on our ability to connect? Could it diminish our capacity for compassion and cooperation? I have wondered about this during the pandemic, as I imagine the harrowing moments for all those who have had to say remote final farewells, with none of the rituals of hand holding and stories and

Table 2. Top companies by worth (market capitalization).

APRIL 2019	APRIL 2009
1. Microsoft (US$905 billion)	1. Exxon Mobil (US$357 billion)
2. Apple (US$896 billion)	2. Petro China (US$279 billion)
3. Amazon (US$875 billion)	3. Walmart (US$209 billion)
4. Google (US$818 billion)	4. China Mobile (US$183 billion)

hugs as comfort. And I have noticed the pull, during remote virtual working, to transactional meetings and interactions, and the loss of informal networks and connections.

As we confront the limits, possibilities and dangers of the digital world and human augmentation, our identity will be challenged. We will be forced to redefine our moral and ethical boundaries.[37]

Expanding our understanding of complexity – and our ability to navigate through it – will be critical for all of us.

SAFETY, AND CATASTROPHIC EVENTS

There are many similarities between the evolution of thinking around safety and our understanding of complexity.

For many of us, the word 'safety' is synonymous with overly bureaucratic rules that limit our freedom and our ability to innovate and operate effectively; when we picture a safety professional, we probably see something like a caricature of an overly controlling police officer who gets immense pleasure from discovering errors and failures.

But when you are working in high-hazard industries, you are forced to have a different relationship with safety, because it permeates every decision. In the face of the seemingly irreconcilable goals of maximizing safety, production, quality and profit, safety is engaged with from a 'both/and' rather than an 'either/or' perspective. The question is not do we *either* produce more *or* be safe, it is how do we *both* produce more *and* do it safely? As we'll see in the remaining chapters, there are still many failures in these industries, but there are also many lessons and principles borne from devastating tragedies and loss of life that we would do well to heed.

Old and new views of safety

Turning hindsight into foresight is complex, and views about safety and its management are shifting as we learn about the limits of traditional bureaucratic responses. From this traditional view, human error and failure to comply with rules are typically seen as the cause of accidents. If we can find, punish or remove the 'bad apples', safety will be restored.

But, as we increase our understanding of the complex socio-technical systems and interactions that enable safe outcomes (or do not), new views of safety (table 3) are emerging that see human error not as the cause of an accident, but as symptomatic of deeper issues.

Table 3. Old and new views of safety. (*Source: The Field Guide to Understanding Human Error* by S. Dekker (© 2006). Reproduced by permission of Taylor & Francis Group through PLSclear.)[38]

THE OLD VIEW OF HUMAN ERROR ON WHAT GOES WRONG	THE NEW VIEW OF HUMAN ERROR ON WHAT GOES WRONG
Human error is a cause of trouble	Human error is symptomatic of trouble deeper inside the system
To explain failure, you must seek failures (errors, violations, incompetence, mistakes)	To explain failure, do not try to find where people went wrong
You must find people's inaccurate assessments, wrong decisions, bad judgements	Instead, find how people's assessments and actions made sense at the time, given the circumstances that surrounded them
THE OLD VIEW OF HUMAN ERROR ON HOW TO MAKE IT RIGHT	**THE NEW VIEW OF HUMAN ERROR ON HOW TO MAKE IT RIGHT**
Complex systems are basically safe	Complex systems are not basically safe
Unreliable, erratic humans undermine defences, rules and regulations	Complex systems are trade-offs between multiple irreconcilable goals (e.g. safety and efficiency)
To make systems safer, restrict the human contribution by tighter procedures, automation, supervision	People have to create safety through practice at all levels of an organization

According to Professor Sidney Dekker, author of several seminal texts in the field of safety science, under the old view of safety, there is a tendency to rely on bureaucratic 'rule inflation' to manage and control people.[39] We add rules and procedures in the mistaken belief that this guarantees safer outcomes. Not only does this increasing bureaucracy drive calls for deregulation (more on this in chapter 4) and contribute to the public having a negative relationship with safety, with a plethora of 'health and safety gone mad' jokes (see figure 4),[40] but it is unclear whether increasing the number of rules actually improves safety. Since nobody really knows which rules are actually linked to the final safety outcomes, the system becomes entirely additive.[41]

'You're right; there's a frozen pea on the floor.
I'll cordon off the area, sound the store alarm
and call in the disposal experts.'

Figure 4. The bureaucratization of safety (www.CartoonStock.com).[42]

Over 200 new policies, elements of guidance and rules are added to the European Joint Aviation Regulations annually, and yet global aviation safety has plateaued for years.[43] Similarly, research in Australia has found that more than 600 rules apply to the work of a ward nurse – but ward nurses can, on average, recite fewer than three of those rules. But work gets done, and, for the most part, it gets done without patients getting hurt.[44]

An overly bureaucratic approach can have serious implications, including

- an inability to predict events, as the focus is on compliance not on understanding or looking for signs of weakness;

- numbers games in which figures are fudged to produce the most favourable looking dashboards;
- the limiting of freedom and the hampering of innovation;[45] and
- as old rules and guidance are never cleaned up, regulations sometimes become inapplicable leading to more violations.[46]

A couple of years ago an offshore oil and gas worker shared with me that the instructions for climbing a ladder were ten pages long, whereas the guidance for conducting a highly hazardous activity was two pages long – and was unclear. Another worked divulged how they were being made to attend briefings on new procedures, only to be told, when they had questions, to 'shut up and sign the attendance sheet'. And I have been told many times by frontline workers that they believe that safety rules, rather than being designed to protect them from injury, are intended to protect the company from prosecution.

As high-hazard industries realize the importance of the tacit knowledge, skills and resilience of those at the coalface, and understand the dangers of overly bureaucratic approaches, there is an increased focus on 'decluttering' burdensome regulations, policies and procedures.

Post Grenfell, my concern is that we are going to increase bureaucracy and focus on blind compliance, which will not only fail to guarantee safety but may actually hinder it.

We need to redefine how we think about safety. Rather than viewing it as the absence of an accident – which we can impact and control through creating more and more rules – we should begin to explore, understand and measure what is present that enables safe outcomes. We should be encouraging frontline workers (or residents) to raise concerns and making them integral to decision making. We should be fostering cultures where it is safe to say you've made a mistake or are worried that 'something is not quite right'. We should be striving for clear, accessible regulations and procedures that do not drive blind compliance or create a false sense of security.

We need also to treat low-probability, high-consequence events and risks distinctly.

Catastrophic (low-probability, high-consequence) events

High-hazard industries such as oil and gas have, through tragic loss of life, learned many lessons about preventing so-called 'unexpected' catastrophic events. The starting point is confronting our blindness to these low-probability, high-consequence risks and accepting that just because something is unlikely to happen, it doesn't mean it won't.

Our blindness to catastrophic risk

On 28 January 1986 the space shuttle *Challenger* exploded 73 seconds after take-off, killing all seven of its crew (including Christa McAuliffe, who would have been the first teacher in space). Several of the crew are known to have survived the initial breakup but there was no escape system, and no one could have survived the impact of the crew compartment hitting the ocean at terminal velocity.[47]

The cause of the explosion was the failure of the O-rings in the solid rocket booster. Launching in unseasonably cold weather, the O-rings failed to seal, leading to what is known as 'blow-by', whereby pressurized burning gas was able to reach the outside, leading to the explosion.

Evidence of O-ring erosion had been present since the second launch; the disaster happened on the tenth. Engineers had raised concerns about its safety and recommended not launching, but that was overturned by management.

The Nobel-winning physicist Richard Feynman was involved in the subsequent investigation. He said:

> The argument that the same risk was flown before without failure is often accepted as an argument for the safety of accepting it again. Because of this, obvious weaknesses are accepted again and again, sometimes without a sufficiently serious attempt to remedy them, or to delay a flight because of their continued presence.[48]

Prior to Grenfell, as with the *Challenger* disaster, we knew of the risks of facade fires, just as we knew of the risk of a pandemic.

A pandemic has been in the top risks both globally and within the UK for a number of years. A 2019 National Security and Risk Assessment dealt specifically with the threat of a pandemic and raised issues such as the need to ensure sufficient PPE. Among its warnings were that[49]

- a pandemic would play out in up to 'three waves';
- the potential cost to the UK could be £2.35 trillion;
- even after the end of the pandemic, it is likely that it would take months or even years for health and social care services to recover;
- there would be significant public outrage over any perceived poor handling of the government's preparations and response to the emergency; and
- a pandemic of moderate virulence could lead to 65,600 deaths.

On 27 January 2021 the UK exceeded the tragic milestone of 100,000 Covid-19 related deaths.[50]

Catastrophic events are by nature low probability but come with extremely high consequences, and high-hazard industries think about these types of events and risks distinctly from lower-consequence events, such as slips, trips and falls (personal safety). You cannot mitigate against the catastrophic failure of an aeroplane exploding in mid-air in the same way that you can try to prevent a baggage handler from hurting their back.

This is not to say that the management of personal safety is not important – many people die from such accidents. And yet, by the very nature of its greater frequency, personal safety is much easier to focus on. Most companies and governments measure lagging indicators such as days away from work, or lost time incidents: all metrics that are associated with personal safety. Fewer pay attention to measuring or managing lower-probability, higher-consequence risks that are both harder to identify and more complex to mitigate.

The consequences of this failure can be devastating. Prior to both the Texas City Refinery (fifteen deaths) and Gulf of Mexico Macondo (eleven deaths) explosions, personal safety records had been exemplary. In fact, executives were on board the day of the Macondo explosion to present prizes for performance in personal safety.[51]

Grenfell and the pandemic illustrate how our blindness to catastrophic risk seems to have led us to accept the risk of catastrophic failure, more than likely justified by narratives such as 'it won't happen'.

The nature of catastrophic events and the role of chronic unease[52]

Understanding the nature of low-probability, high-consequence events might help us become more effective at preventing and responding to them.

Rarely the result of a single failure, they are a systemic outcome resulting from the 'lining up' of several latent or pre-existing conditions, triggered by an active failure, such as an ignition source from a small kitchen fire in a tower block.

This is illustrated in the barrier or Swiss cheese model (figure 5).[53] This model illustrates how we put barriers in place to protect us from major accidents. In high-hazard industries, these are often categorized into layers of protection related to the plant or asset, policies and procedures, and people – although the categories can be adjusted to suit any industry or setting.

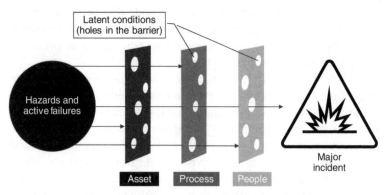

Figure 5. The barrier or Swiss cheese model.[54]

In each of these barriers, there are 'latent conditions', or holes, which are either known or unknown weaknesses. In a catastrophic event, usually triggered by an active failure, these holes line up and a hazard finds its way through all of the barriers, with catastrophic results. While overly linear in its depiction, it is a useful model.

Practising chronic unease – imagining and mitigating against the worst thing that can happen, and planning how you would respond to it – is key to preventing lower-probability events. If I asked anybody the worst thing that could happen in a high-rise residential building, I'd expect 'the building becoming engulfed in fire and escape routes being compromised' to be somewhere near the top of the list. People would say this even without knowledge of events at Grenfell or any technical understanding of risk.

The application of fairly simple methods, such as the major accident bow tie (figure 6),[55] could have helped predict, prevent and respond effectively to events such as Grenfell. Imagine what might have happened if, as part of the preparation for refurbishment, the full supply chain, the key product manufacturers, the residents, the LFB, the other emergency services and the RBKC had sat down and conducted a major accident bow tie exercise collaboratively, to help understand the hazards and the worst possible outcomes related to the refurbishment, and to implement barriers to threats and come up with recovery measures should something go wrong.

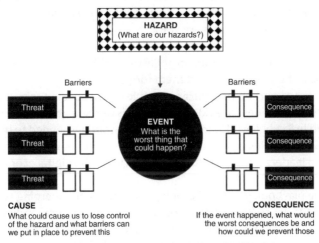

Figure 6. Major accident bow tie.[56]

I have yet to see any evidence that catastrophic risks were viewed distinctly, or that chronic unease was practised in a systematic way at Grenfell. There is evidence that suggests the contrary. Dany Cotton, the LFB commissioner at the time of Grenfell, said during evidence at the inquiry that preparing for Grenfell would be akin to preparing for a 'spaceship landing on the Shard' (a famous triangular-shaped building in London), indicating a lack of understanding of the nature of low-probability, high-consequence risks.[57]

The same can be said of all those involved in the refurbishment, who seem to have been more interested in deferring risk (or perhaps liability) to other parties than in taking collective responsibility for the management of change and ensuring the work was done safely.[58]

There is, unfortunately, an 'awful sameness' to catastrophic events. There is usually a failure to listen, to practise chronic unease or build strong cultures in which the voices of those at the sharp end, such as residents, are heard; and errors and mistakes fail to be viewed as an opportunity for learning. All of these things point to a failure of leadership.

LEADERSHIP

'The new leadership playbook for the digital age' was published in the *MIT Sloan Management Review* in 2020.[59] Based on a survey of nearly 4,500 global leaders, executive interviews and focus group discussions, the findings were stark.[60]

- Just 12% of respondents strongly agreed that their leaders had the right mindsets to lead them forward.
- Only 40% agreed that their companies were building robust leadership pipelines to tackle the demands of the digital economy.
- While 82% believed leaders in the new economy needed to be digitally savvy, less than 10% strongly agreed that their organizations had leaders with the right skills to thrive in the digital economy.

The playbook identified eroding, enduring and emerging leadership behaviours (table 4[61]). It found that 'some cultural and behavioural leadership norms that worked well in the past are no longer effective', and that many organizations are holding onto leadership behaviours – such as command and control – that might have worked in the past but 'now stymie the talents of employees throughout their organizations'. Debjana Ghosh, the president of NASSCOM (an India-based software and service company), is quoted as saying:

> The idea of top-down leadership is a thing of the past, or should be anyway. It's not what people are looking for. Leadership needs to be democratized. Decision-making has to be more distributed so that every person feels it is his or her responsibility to lead, because that is what will lead to speed, which is so important for business success today.[62]

Table 4. Eroding, enduring and emerging leadership behaviours. (*Source*: MIT Sloan Management Review/Massachusetts Institute of Technology. All rights reserved. Distributed by Tribune Content Agency. © 2020.)

ERODING	ENDURING	EMERGING
Asks for permission	Creates a clear vision	Is purpose-driven
Has no-exception protocols	Focuses on performances	Nurtures passion
Reinforces command and control	Maintains a profit orientation	Makes data-driven decisions
Manages top-down	Is customer-centric	Demonstrates authenticity
Avoids transparency	Leads by example	Demonstrates empathy
Micromanages	Demonstrates ethics and integrity	Employs an inclusive approach
Creates rigid long-term plans	Takes risks	Shows humility
Takes a one-size-fits-all approach	Leads change	Works across boundaries

While the review focused on organizations, its relevance certainly stretches to the political landscape. When we look globally at the response of political leaders to the pandemic, there are few examples of the emerging leadership behaviours and many examples of the eroding ones.

Navigating the gap between the traditional bureaucratic approaches and the emerging leadership styles highlights the tensions between the traditional and emerging worlds, and this often leads to a sense of inertia, with many organizations remaining slow, siloed, densely hierarchical and excessively focused on short-term returns.[63] Some of the tensions that exist are listed below.

- *Old power values* versus *new power values*.[64] According to authors Henry Timms and Jeremy Heimans, old power values formal governance, competitive behaviours, maintaining confidentiality and 'secrecy', holding onto specialisms and expert-driven approaches. New power values informal governance, collaboration, radical transparency and more transient affiliations, with expertise coming from non-traditional sources.
- *Bureaucratic* versus *organic* forms.[65] According to organization development consultant Andrew Day, bureaucratic forms are

characterized by hierarchical control, established rules and behaviours, divisions of labour and standardization of tasks. Leadership (or more accurately management) is authoritarian and hierarchical. Motivation is carrot and stick. Organic forms are characterized by flat structures, flexible roles, cross-disciplinary project teams. Leadership is negotiated and fluid, and authority is based on competence and personal authority rather than role. Members self-organize, and shared values are important. Organic forms are innovative, flexible and adaptive, and they struggle with standardization.

- There is compelling evidence that our *traditional 'carrot and stick'* views of motivation are counterproductive as we discover the role of *purpose and values* as motivators.[66] Research by the author Daniel Pink reveals that what motivates people is a desire for *autonomy* (self-direction), *mastery* (a simultaneously frustrating and alluring desire to infinitely improve) and *purpose* (a cause that is greater and more enduring than themselves). Where this is not available in paid work, it drives highly skilled, technically proficient people to give their discretionary time to do meaningful work such as contributing to Wikipedia or Linux (an open-source operating system[67]) or campaigning for change: witness the rise of effective global grass roots movements on issues such as climate change and inequality.

These tensions and leadership styles are best viewed as spectra, not dichotomies, and the art of leadership is agilely adopting approaches that are appropriate in a given context – because, in reality, traditional top-down bureaucratic approaches are sometimes appropriate.

As I have learned to operate in this complex world, both in relation to Grenfell and also in my consulting work, I've found two models both practical and helpful: Ronald Heifetz's work on adaptive leadership and Dave Snowden's Cynefin framework.

Adaptive leadership: understanding the limits of our expertise[68]

According to Heifetz, 'the most common cause of failure in leadership is produced by treating adaptive challenges as if they were technical problems'.[69]

Technical problems describe situations where both the problem and solution are known, and it is therefore appropriate that competent technical experts be accountable for solving them. Adaptive challenges differ in that either the solution or both the problem and the solution are unknown. Adaptive solutions are discovered through our collective wisdom rather than traditional expertise, and they demand both learning and new ways of thinking. In the words of Edgar Schein, author and former professor at the MIT Sloan School of Management:

> In an increasingly complex, interdependent and culturally diverse world, we cannot hope to understand and work with people ... if we do not know how to ask questions and build relationships that are based on mutual respect and the recognition that others know things that we may need to know in order to get the job done.[70]

An emerging school of post-normal scientists suggest that when dealing with highly uncertain and/or 'high-stakes' decisions, the democratization of expertise is called for. According to Oxford University's Jerome Ravetz, one of the developers of the field of post-normal science, we need to go beyond traditional assumptions and approaches to science and policymaking and use new methods such as peer communities and citizens' forums that embrace different ways of knowing (such as narratives and collective sense-making): 'The previous belief that scientists should and could provide certain, objective factual information for decision-makers is now being increasingly recognised as simplistic and immature' (see chapter 4).[71]

Many of the problems we are dealing with post-Grenfell are not technical, but we are treating them as such. For example, how do we make our current housing stock safe? What is the solution to residents having voice and agency over making buildings safe? While there are technical elements to these challenges – such as processes by which residents can raise concerns, and technical solutions for the replacement of cladding – the challenges are adaptive. Do we really understand why so many homes are unsafe? Or why residents voices are not being heard? How can we fairly fund the remediation of historic building safety issues?

We need to engage with these questions – to harness our collective wisdom and discover new ways of thinking. This will require authentic enquiry, to be as interested in the question as the answer, to be willing to sit with uncertainty and not knowing. We need to move beyond traditional notions of expertise and top-down bureaucratic solutions and learn to listen to one another.

We see a similar approach with Covid-19, where governments implement traditional top-down policies to lockdowns or opening schools or managing the use of PPE that are unworkable to those at the sharp end.

As much as I am critical of political leaders for adopting traditional, technical, expert-driven, top-down approaches to adaptive challenges, there is also an imperative for us as citizens to understand that there is not always an easy answer. We need to be willing to embrace uncertainty and experimentation.

The Cynefin framework: decision making and leadership[72]

I find the Cynefin framework (figure 7[73]) useful as a decision-making tool, to determine when more innovative solutions and experimentation are appropriate, depending on how closely coupled cause and effect are. That is, are outcomes predictable or not? Developed by welsh researcher and consultant Dave Snowden, the model distinguishes four contexts, each of which requires a different response.

Simple contexts
Simple contexts are characterized by stability and clear, easily discernible, cause-and-effect relationships. This is the domain of *best practice.* Examples include well-defined processes such as processing loan payments. Directive leadership approaches are appropriate, but micromanagement can lead to blind compliance and a failure to identify looming dangers. Oversimplifying, failing to see shifts in context, and complacency can drive you off the 'cliff' into chaos.

For example, when regulations were tightened and blindly complied with and enforced with complete disregard for the people of the Windrush Generation.[74] This resulted in people who had lived and paid taxes in the UK for decades – and in some cases were born

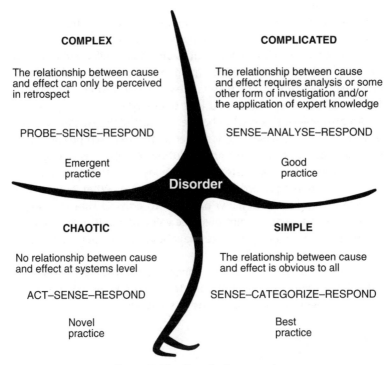

Figure 7. The Cynefin framework.

here – being unfairly deported and detained, or losing their jobs and homes, if they could not produce the right paperwork.

Complicated contexts
Complicated contexts are the domain of expertise and *good practice*. Cause and effect are coupled, and solutions require understanding the issue and exploring a number of valid alternatives before selecting one. For example, when designing a new feature for a phone, there will be a number of equally valid options. There is a trade-off between spending time making decisions and finding the right option.

Experts can also fail to explore more innovative approaches, relying on what they know, or can suffer from 'analysis paralysis' and not make any decision at all. Leaders should make sure that the views of non-experts are considered to guard against these problems.

Complex contexts

Complex contexts are the domain of experimentation and *emergent practice*. Most situations in organizations and society are complex because any major change introduces unpredictability and flux. You can only understand why things happen in retrospect and you cannot guarantee repeatable results. Leaders need to create 'safe to fail' experiments and allow solutions to emerge.

An example of this is what happened during the Apollo 13 space mission, where astronauts encountered an unknown problem and experimented until they found a solution. A danger is falling back into command-and-control leadership styles. We need to understand that trying to impose order on complexity fails. What is needed is to take a step back and allow patterns to emerge that can reveal innovative and creative solutions. The value of traditional expertise is limited, and involving diverse stakeholders and perspectives to create solutions is critical.

Remediating historic safety concerns, for example, could be aided by creating an innovation fund to experiment and find creative and less expensive and time-intensive solutions.

Chaotic contexts

Chaotic contexts are typically the area of crisis management, where directive authoritarian top-down approaches and communication is appropriate. There is no time to reflect; leaders need to act swiftly to restore some stability and alter course as needed. Communication of the most direct top-down or broadcast kind is imperative, as there is simply no time to ask for input.

At the time of the September 11 attacks in New York, the city's mayor, Rudy Giuliani, demonstrated this top-down leadership approach effectively in the immediate aftermath of the crisis. He was widely criticised, though, for maintaining this same approach in the longer term. A danger for leaders following a crisis is to fail to understand a shift in the context and adapt their leadership style to match it. Leaders who are successful in chaotic contexts can develop an overinflated self-image, which effectively ends up making leading harder for them, as they are surrounded by a circle of admiring (or perhaps fearful) supporters who cut them off from accurate information.

Adaptive challenges and the Cynefin framework are two examples of models that can help leaders navigate an increasingly complex and disruptive world. They are offered not as *the* solutions but as models that have been useful in my analysis of Grenfell and systemic change.

REFLECTIONS AND ANALYSIS: THE METHODOLOGY

My intent in this chapter was to create a shared language and make transparent the lenses – complexity, safety and leadership – that I have used to explore why our failure to learn makes sense. These form threads through the remaining chapters and have informed the methodology for the analysis. This has required stepping back, observing and articulating the messy kaleidoscope and the conditions holding our inability to learn in place.

The analysis is inquiry based (figure 8). Ultimately, it tries to understand why our failure to learn makes sense.

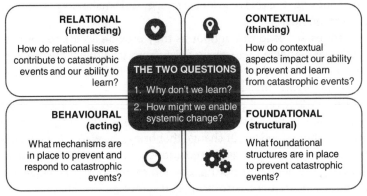

RELATIONAL (interacting)
How do relational issues contribute to catastrophic events and our ability to learn?

CONTEXTUAL (thinking)
How do contextual aspects impact our ability to prevent and learn from catastrophic events?

THE TWO QUESTIONS
1. Why don't we learn?
2. How might we enable systemic change?

BEHAVIOURAL (acting)
What mechanisms are in place to prevent and respond to catastrophic events?

FOUNDATIONAL (structural)
What foundational structures are in place to prevent catastrophic events?

Figure 8. Why does our failure to learn make sense?

Chapter 4 asks what foundational structures are in place to prevent catastrophic events, and chapter 5 considers what mechanisms are in place to prevent and respond to catastrophic events. Chapter 6 looks at how relational issues contribute to catastrophic events and our ability to learn, before we move on to explore how contextual elements impact our ability to prevent and learn from catastrophic events in chapter 7.

The analysis is not concerned with individual failings: it considers systemic issues. In each case, I ask what myths we hold onto, articulate key issues and challenges, and consider what lessons Grenfell offers. I conclude each chapter by 'making the water visible' by answering the following questions.

- Why don't we learn? I propose the key factor holding conditions in place and inhibiting systemic change. Rather than working to shift these factors, which are all complex and entrenched, my view is that considering them as 'givens' and working to enable change despite them will be more effective.
- How might we enable systemic change? Here I offer what I consider the key opportunity to disrupt the status quo.

Chapter 8, the concluding chapter, begins by drawing the analysis from previous chapters together to create a picture of why our failure to prevent and respond to catastrophic events makes sense. I go on to consider the role of grief in change, and I make suggestions for key stakeholders.

Stories are used throughout as they provide access to complex worlds and enable us to move away from traditional bureaucratic cause–effect thinking. They also engage our hearts, rather than just appealing to our intellect.

I have discovered post Grenfell that change is as much about unlocking the best parts of human nature – creativity, empathy, stewardship[75] – and about change that brings forward our heart and soul as it is about changing regulations. It is as much about understanding the need for grieving as a natural response to change as it is about procurement, resourcing and safety.[76]

My wish is not that people agree with my analysis but that it sparks thinking and conversations that will perhaps begin to shift the conditions holding our inability to learn in place.

Chapter 4

Foundational elements: 'of bricke or stone'

It appears to us that there has been a blind spot among many of those concerned with this type of construction. ... They fell victim ... to the belief that if a building complied with the existing building regulations and Codes of Practice it must be deemed to be safe. Experience has shown otherwise.

Griffiths Report into the collapse of flats at Ronan Point, 1968[1]

One could occasionally detect in the evidence of senior officers a reluctance to believe that a building could ever fail to comply with Building Regulations.

Grenfell Tower Inquiry, Phase 1 Report, 2019[2]

On 16 May 1968, at around 5.45 a.m., Ivy Lodge went into her kitchen in corner flat 90 on the eighteenth floor of Ronan Point and lit a match to ignite the gas stove and make a cup of tea.[3] The match sparked a gas explosion that blew out the load-bearing walls that supported the four flats above, leading to the collapse of the entire corner of the building, killing four and injuring seventeen. Ivy survived despite being thrown across the room (and so did her stove, which she later took to her new home).

Ronan Point, a twenty-two-storey block in East London, was constructed using an innovative methodology called large panel system (LPS) building, driven by a political commitment to build large numbers of houses. The explosion happened two months after the block opened.

As with Grenfell, this disaster revealed systemic issues in the housing sector: thousands of blocks were built using this flawed construction method, and there were issues with poor workmanship, including cavities being filled with newspaper rather than concrete, compromising compartmentation. When the building was eventually demolished in 1986, largely because of concerns about fire safety, cracks were found in the concrete. Some believed that high winds could have led the building to collapse.[4] The inquiry into Ronan Point found that those involved in this type of construction 'fell victim ... to the belief that if a building complied with the existing building regulations and Codes of Practice it must be deemed to be safe'. As the inquiry concluded, 'experience has shown otherwise'.

In the aftermath, regulations were altered for new-builds, and some measures, such as a ban on gas and the strengthening of structures, were put in place for existing buildings. Despite calls for councils to check for LPS construction and reinforce as necessary, this was not done exhaustively and was not centrally tracked.

While many buildings were demolished, it is estimated that, fifty years after Ronan Point, there are still more than 200 high-rise LPS buildings.[5] In the wake of Grenfell, these received renewed interest, with reports that several local authorities no longer held records on the building work of their LPS blocks and didn't know if recommended repairs had been undertaken.[6] Some blocks had not been structurally strengthened and still had gas supplies. Others needed to be evacuated as their structural safety could not be guaranteed.[7]

Ronan Point points to the complexities of regulations.

While regulations are one of the key foundational elements in place to prevent catastrophic events, it is a myth that they guarantee safe outcomes. After exploring this, I consider key challenges with regulations and legislation in the UK, including the role of political agendas and lobbying. 'Lessons from Grenfell' questions how so many buildings ended up with dangerous cladding, and 'Making the water visible' considers two questions: why don't we learn, and how might we enable systemic change? I conclude that known weaknesses in governance and accountability mechanisms help maintain the status quo, and that developing our capacity to deal with ambiguity and complexity could enable systemic change.

THE MYTH THAT REGULATIONS GUARANTEE SAFE OUTCOMES

Not only is an increasingly complex world revealing new risks, it is also highlighting regulatory vulnerabilities. While regulations are important and regulatory reform in the wake of catastrophes is appropriate, it is a myth that regulations guarantee safe outcomes. Regulations did not prevent the Ronan Point building collapse; regulations did not prevent the Grenfell Tower fire. Regulations didn't prevent the Great Fire of London either.

Lessons from history: the Great Fire of London (1666)[8,9,10]

In 1666 the Great Fire of London destroyed a quarter of the city. The event has many resonances with modern disasters, from ignoring known issues with building materials and regulations to failures in accountability and leadership. The fire spread horizontally, burning for four days. Official accounts have it that only six people died, but many believe the toll was much higher.

Before the fire
As early as 1559 there had been warnings that London would be destroyed by a fire. In 1605, King James I said that all new houses in London were to be made from brick or stone. Uptake was slow and it appears that many ignored the order.[11] In 1665, King Charles II warned the Lord Mayor of the danger of a fire due to the narrow streets and overhanging wooden houses.

The fire

2 *September*
At 1 a.m. a fire broke out in a baker's house in Pudding Lane. The baker and his family escaped; a maid who didn't want to climb over the rooftops died.

By 3 a.m. the fire had grown so large it could be seen a quarter of a mile away. Residents tried unsuccessfully to douse the fire. The Lord Mayor was woken and told the news but took no action.

By 5 a.m. the Lord Mayor was advised to destroy houses in the fire's path to stop it spreading. He ignored the advice as he didn't want to have to pay for rebuilding the houses, and by 6 a.m. more than 300 houses had been destroyed.

By 10 p.m. the fire had spread half a mile east and north. King Charles ordered the Lord Mayor to pull down houses in the fire's path.

3 September
The fire kept spreading due to hot, dry, windy conditions. King Charles put his brother James in charge of fighting the fire as the Lord Mayor appeared to have left the city.

4 September
By 12 p.m. King Charles had joined a line of people passing buckets of water to pour on the flames.

A large firebreak had been created by James to the north of the city, containing the fire, but, at 4 p.m. the flames leapt across the break.

At 5 p.m. the roof of St Paul's Cathedral caught fire, probably due to wooden scaffolding that had been erected for building works. Molten lead from the roof ran down the streets. By 7 p.m. St Paul's had been completely destroyed.

5 September
By 7 a.m. the wind had changed, blowing the fire towards the Tower of London. Chains of people passed buckets in an attempt to put out the fire and protect the tower.

By 12 p.m. a number of houses near the tower had been pulled down, stopping the spread.

At 4 p.m. the wind dropped and the spread of the fire halted.

6 September
The fire was extinguished. In all, eighty-seven churches and 13,200 houses were destroyed. Around 100,000 people lost their homes.

After the fire[12]
People set up camp in open spaces outside the city. For most, this was temporary; some, though, stayed there for eight years. The king set up a fundraising scheme to help the penniless: it raised about £2.4 million (in today's money). The Lord Mayor allegedly embezzled

large sums from the fund. Throughout 1667, people cleared rubble and surveyed the affected areas. By the end of the year, only 150 new houses had been built. It took fifty years to rebuild the burned areas. There were many disputes between tenants and landlords about who would pay.

Robert Hubert, a watchmaker's son, confessed to starting the fire by throwing a fireball through a window. It is believed he was mentally ill and did not understand the severity of what he was saying. He was found guilty at a trial and executed.

Regulations[13]
The Act for the Rebuilding of the City of London of February 1667 stated that 'all the outsides of all Buildings in and about the said Citty be henceforth made of Bricke or Stone'. The act required

- all houses to be in brick or stone; no wooden eaves were allowed; roofs were pushed back behind brick parapets;
- wooden window frames were reduced; later, they were recessed behind brick so that only a narrow edge of the wooden frame was exposed to possible fire; and
- party walls between houses had to be thick enough to withstand two hours of fire, giving neighbours a chance of rescuing people and extinguishing the flames before they could spread.

Ten years later, in 1676, a terrible fire claimed around twenty lives and 600 houses in Southwark, south of the Thames. The lessons learned during the Great Fire had had little effect. The area was still made up of old timber-framed buildings and narrow streets.

Regulatory vulnerabilities

Regulations will not, on their own, prevent the next catastrophe.

Regulations are, by nature, reactive. They don't have the ability to foresee, or the agility to respond to, unpredicted events. Safety (or lack of it) is an emergent outcome of a complex system; regulations are one important input to that system, but they do not guarantee safe outcomes.

The relationship between regulations and safety is not linear or predictable, as we have seen during Covid-19, where the changing of regulations has not always led to the desired changes in behaviour. And blind compliance can increase risk as we fail to search for weaknesses or think about the – often-unintended – consequences of actions (see chapter 3).

These limitations are ageless, as we have seen in the Great Fire of London, but as the world is both increasingly complex and connected, the nature of risk is changing, and problems are emerging in unexpected ways, further revealing regulatory vulnerabilities.

The changing nature of risk

'Post-normal science' is an emerging field that considers novel approaches to the use of science in complex situations (such as those during the Covid-19 pandemic) where facts are uncertain, values are in dispute, the stakes are high and decisions are urgent.[14] It argues for the need to go beyond traditional assumptions that science is both certain and value free, and calls for the inclusion of different ways of 'knowing', involving the active participation of extended communities in creating solutions to problems.

Post-normal scientists have developed a menagerie of high-impact futures, or potentialities, that expand beyond Taleb's famous 'black swan' events[15] (unknown unknowns), i.e. outlier/surprising events that can have either positive or negative consequences, such as the spread of the internet or major terrorist attacks such as 9/11. The term is often used as a catch-all phrase for any low-probability, high-consequence event, but there are further nuances that are useful to understand if one adds black jellyfish and black elephants to the menagerie.[16]

Black jellyfish (unknown knowns) are catalytic events in which small things escalate rapidly – in essence, an 'unthought' future. Here, conditions that people mistakenly think they 'know' or understand emerge in unexpected or 'unknown' ways and overwhelm, in the way that a bloom of jellyfish might. In 2013 one of three reactors in Sweden's Oskarshamn nuclear power plant, which provided nearly 10% of the country's energy, was unexpectedly shut down as tonnes of jellyfish clogged its intake pipes. Jellyfish are prone to proliferate in unexpected places, triggered by small shifts in conditions, such as temperature changes or the prevalence of predators.[17]

In the context of Grenfell, the creation of the EWS1 process to assess the safety of the external wall system of high-rise buildings has 'bloomed' and overtaken the market in unexpected ways. Intended to promote safety and understand risk in high-rise blocks, the 'unknown' and shifting conditions around risk appetite among insurers and mortgage lenders post-Grenfell has led to an unthought future in which lenders are unwilling to give mortgages without the certificate on blocks of any height. Additionally, difficulties in obtaining indemnity insurance have contributed to a shortage of qualified experts able to issue the certificate. This has left up to 3.6 million people facing waits of up to a decade to sell their flat or get a new mortgage (see chapter 2).[18]

Black Elephants (Known Unknowns) are used to describe high impact events that are widely predicted but have low public urgency so are ignored, in essence a combination of the 'elephant in the room' and a 'black swan event'. For example, climate change, cyber-attacks and, of course, a global pandemic.

David Spiegelhalter, professor of risk at Cambridge University, has pointed out that the National Risk Register, which is 'given no publicity at all', not only recognized the risk of a pandemic but gave it the highest possible rating for impact: 5. Threats such as terror attacks, cyberattacks on infrastructure and widespread flooding were all rated as less impactful.[19]

In 2015 Bill Gates gave a Ted Talk on the dangers of a pandemic,[20] and in March 2019 the director general of the World Health Organization, Dr Tedros Adhanom Ghebreyesus, said:

> The on-going risk of a new influenza virus transmitting from animals to humans and potentially causing a pandemic is real. The question is not if we will have another pandemic, but when. We must be vigilant and prepared – the cost of a major influenza outbreak will far outweigh the price of prevention.[21]

Ghebreyesus's statement both reveals the known risks of a global pandemic and points to an assumption that this would be an influenza virus rather than a coronavirus. These are warnings and assumptions that many governments and organizations must now be regretting they failed to heed.

While many class Grenfell as an unexpected event – a black swan – it is more accurately described as a black elephant. As we saw in chapter 2, the risks of cladding fires were known, and there is evidence that the number of facade fires globally is increasing (see figure 9).

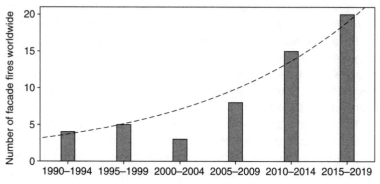

Figure 9. The number of large facade fires worldwide.[22]

And yet, supporting the post-normal scientists' argument for the need to accept different ways of knowing, it was not the experts that predicted such a fire, but rather the residents from the Grenfell Action Group who, in a frighteningly prescient November 2016 blog post titled 'Playing with fire', said:

> It is our conviction that a serious fire in a tower block or similar high density residential property is the most likely reason that those who wield power at the KCTMO will be found out and brought to justice![23]

We will return to this in chapter 6.

Regulatory complexities and vulnerabilities
The changing nature of risk and the nuances over how to predict and respond to it continue to reveal regulatory complexities and vulnerabilities. In the words of a 2021 Foresight Review:

> Regulatory systems are facing challenges that can be vastly different from what they are designed for or used to dealing with. High levels of uncertainty, the scale and degree of interconnections within and across systems, the pace of decision

making, and conflicting societal values can all combine to bring complexity, chaos and contradiction. Under these conditions, traditional methods of regulating may lose relevance and can become dangerous if misapplied.[24]

We are seeing a proliferation of disruptive factors that are exposing regulatory vulnerabilities (see figure 10).[25]

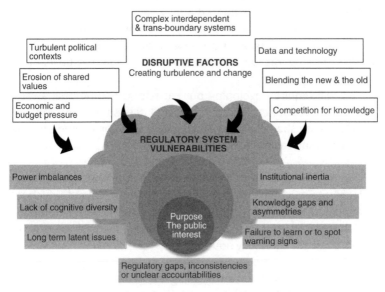

Figure 10. Disruptive future trends mapped onto regulatory system vulnerabilities.[26]

Globally, we are grappling with how to regulate effectively in a highly connected, complex, disruptive world. How will we regulate cyber and biotech? How can we effectively regulate for climate change? How can we regulate social media and fake news?

It is perhaps understandable that the purpose of regulation to 'serve the public interest' sometimes gets lost in the midst of these factors.

Politicians need to manage inherent tensions: between national politics and global challenges, between local accountability and system perspectives, between reactive responses and forward-thinking solutions, between siloed actors and collaborative approaches, between the regulator as enforcer and the regulator as catalyst, and between prescriptive rules and principles or outcome-focused approaches.[27]

While decisions like banning flammable materials or remediating unsafe buildings or deciding which countries should be included in a free travel corridor during a pandemic may appear simple, they are played out in this terrain of competing tensions.

The Foresight Review quoted above calls for the adoption of a spectrum of regulatory approaches depending on the level of uncertainty and social cohesion. It proposes that 'regulation depends on context. What works well for one type of problem may be inappropriate for another.'[28]

This will require developing our capacity for contextual awareness, collaboration, experimentation and diverse thinking. We will need to create space to think strategically and consider innovative approaches such as the following.[29]

- Taking a *whole of system view*. This forms the basis of the 'regulatory stewardship' principles adopted in New Zealand, which set expectations for regulators to adopt a collaborative approach that relies on bringing different regulatory functions together to work across regulatory boundaries.
- Adopting *strength-based approaches* that encourage more learning from good practice, introducing mechanisms to share insights by all actors in the regulatory system. Ethical business regulation, for example, focuses on the cultures and processes that lead to good outcomes, and encourages 'doing the right thing' to enable a learning, ethical culture based on shared values. Ethical business regulation includes a recommendation that different penalties should be applied to those businesses that aim to do the right thing, compared to those who fail to implement ethical business practice.

It is a myth that regulations guarantee safe outcomes, and in an increasingly complex world that requires managing complex inherent tensions, traditional legislative approaches may not be the best solution. And anyway, even these traditional approaches and systems are not without their challenges.

KEY ISSUES AND CHALLENGES

I will now move to consider how regulations work in the UK. After discussing primary and secondary legislation, and those relevant to Grenfell, I will look at the role of lobbying and the deregulation and environmental agendas.

Legislation and regulation in the UK

The intent of regulation is to protect and benefit people, businesses and the environment and to support economic growth. Regulations are primarily used to address market failures but they can also be used to promote issues such as innovation.[30]

To enact regulations, the first step is the passing of primary legislation by Parliament.[31] This process involves numerous stages and readings. Some bills are published in draft form, for consultation or pre-legislative scrutiny prior to being presented to Parliament.[32] Regulations are a type of secondary legislation.[33] Their purpose is to 'enact' the primary legislation. Concerns have been raised about the lack of scrutiny required when passing secondary legislation, e.g. in dealing with issues such as Brexit[34] or Covid-19[35].

There are many ways of approaching issues related to regulation. On the one hand, there are government-driven techniques such as prescriptive command and control regulation, and there is economic regulation and enforced self-regulation. At the other end of the spectrum, there are market-driven approaches, such as voluntary self-regulation and the provision of information and education.[36] In general, the UK favours regulation based on principles of behaviour, considering rules-based, prescriptive approaches to be a last resort.[37]

Interestingly, the Independent Review of Building Regulations and Fire Safety after Grenfell found that, despite claims that the regulatory system for buildings was outcome- and performance-based, there was in fact a lot of prescription, which was both complex and at times inconsistent. And this regulatory prescription was largely owned by government, with industry waiting to be told what to do or in some cases looking for ways to work around the prescription. The review called for a fundamental shift in ownership: from government to industry.[38]

Legislation and regulations relevant to Grenfell
Prior to Grenfell, the Regulatory Reform (Fire Safety) Order 2005 scrapped the fire certification process, by which fire authorities could bring about improved safety standards.[39] It introduced a self-compliance regime that shifted the responsibility for fire assessing buildings from the fire service to building owners. Building owners could either hire consultants or carry out their own assessments.

In 1985 the Building Act 1984 came into force. It represented a massive deregulation of the industry, introducing 'performance based' regulation and setting the legal status of the 'approved guidance'. The accompanying building regulations were cut from 300 pages to just 25. They no longer contained technical details, instead setting out only functional requirements. Guidance on how to comply with these was laid out in 'approved documents'. The Act also part-privatized building control, allowing private consultants to compete with local authorities to sign off schemes as being compliant with regulations. How this played out at Grenfell is explored later in this chapter.[40]

The Fire and Rescue Services Act 2004 replaced the Fire Services Act 1947.[41] It abolished national standards and saw the service fragment into local services. The Central Fire Brigades Advisory Council was disbanded, and each service was responsible for setting its own policies and attendance targets. As noted in chapter 2, this was not always done well.

The legislative and regulatory changes since Grenfell have included the following.[42]

- Combustible cladding has been banned on new high-rise residential buildings.
- The Fire Safety Bill and the Building Safety Bill have been introduced and are expected to be bought into law in 2021.[43]
- A new Building Safety Regulator has been created, and a new regulator of construction materials has been announced.

It is easy, with hindsight, to judge the regulatory decisions prior to Grenfell as poor, or to criticize the slow pace of regulatory reform since. But these problems are indicative of the inherent challenges with regulations (see chapter 2).

Challenges with regulations
The UK National Audit Office has identified the following as the key future challenges for regulation in the UK.[44]

- *Complex regulatory frameworks and objectives.* Different regulators and regulations don't always align. There is often a reliance on extended delivery chains that depend on organizations that don't necessarily share the same priorities.
- *Responding to significant and fast-paced change.* As the UK exits the European Union, the scale of the regulatory challenge is likely to increase, requiring alterations to regulatory models. To enhance impact and improve efficiency, many regulators are adapting existing approaches. In addition, the industries that are being regulated are constantly changing, incorporating new technologies, products and distribution channels. Regulators need to be flexible in selecting appropriate tools for regulating.
- *Significant operating demands.* There is pressure for regulators to reduce costs while responding to significant change, and it is often difficult to report meaningfully on the impact of their work.

Competing objectives and tensions

Those with political power must navigate complex political agendas and competing objectives when making regulatory decisions, all while others seek to influence these decisions. After looking at the role of lobbying, I explore the deregulatory and energy efficiency agendas that the 2018 Independent Review of Building Regulations and Fire Safety said had prevailed over fire safety.[45]

The role of lobbying
A 2007 Hansard Society report concluded that lobbying is more widespread than is often assumed by both its critics and its supporters, and that lobbying organizations across different sectors occupy an increasingly central role, not only in the development of policy but also in its delivery.[46]

For instance, documents revealed during the Grenfell Tower Inquiry show how Kingspan – the manufacturer of the insulation used on part of the building – hired a PR firm in the wake of the fire to draw up a 'political engagement plan' to persuade MPs, ministers and industry figures that their products were safe.[47] As part of its campaign, Kingspan set out to produce evidence that a non-combustible insulation made by its rival ROCKWOOL would also perform badly in fire tests. A series of emails from 2018 show how senior Kingspan staff discussed setting up tests to make sure the ROCKWOOL product failed. Prior to a test in Dubai, a Kingspan technician wrote: 'I have introduced as many weak features/details as possible to ensure it has the best chance of performing poorly.'

But despite the deliberately induced weaknesses, the ROCK-WOOL test passed. The test that Kingspan conducted that did fail had been carried out on a system using a product called Vitracore G2. As reported by *Inside Housing* journalist Peter Apps, this material had an 'A2' rating, so it could be used in spite of the combustibles ban. But Kingspan was aware it had a much lower fire performance and had been involved in previous test failures, with one internal email saying it would 'go up like [polyethylene]'. This test was carried out in Dubai and failed. Kingspan went on to present the failure to the Commons Select Committee but did not reveal that Vitracore had been picked due to its poor fire performance, or that the ROCKWOOL test had passed. Asked if Kingspan concealed the ROCKWOOL results from the Select Committee because it undermined the case that non-combustible systems can be dangerous, Kingspan's director of technical, marketing and regulatory affairs Adrian Pargeter, during evidence at the inquiry, accepted that the passed test did not support the case they were trying to make but denied that concealing the ROCKWOOL test or the reasons for using Vitracore amounted to misleading the committee.[48*]

The role of lobbying and competing regulatory objectives are intricately entwined. The deregulation and environmental agendas are also important.

---

* In the initial evidence given by Mr Pargeter in December 2020 the inquiry team had thought that the ROCKWOOL test had failed and Pargeter had not corrected this, later saying he forgot under the pressure of cross-examination. Pargeter returned to the stand in March 2021 to answer questions about the Vitracore tests and his previous evidence after it had emerged that the ROCKWOOL test had passed and the failed Vitracore test was used in the report to the Commons Select Committee. A statement on the company's website says: 'Regardless of the fact that the May 2018 test was not shared with the Select Committee, Kingspan also rejects any suggestion that the May 2018 test was "gamed" or "manipulated".' (See 'Kingspan insulation and the Grenfell Tower Inquiry' at https://inquiry.kingspan.com/.)

The deregulation agenda

In comparison with the forty-seven member states of the Organi-sation for Economic Co-operation and Development (OECD), the UK is not, in fact, highly regulated. A 2013 report demonstrated that the UK uses less prescriptive control and command regulation than most, but has more complex regulatory procedures when compared with other countries.[49]

By contrast, a National Audit Office survey in 2016 found that 49% of surveyed businesses agreed that the level of regulation in the UK was an obstacle to business success; this was down from 62% in 2009.[50]

Successive governments have called for, and introduced, various initiatives to encourage deregulation,[51] aiming to reduce the costs to business of compliance, which are estimated at £100 billion per annum.[52] Such initiatives are intended, at least in part, to foster polit-ical support and favour from business.[53]

Regulatory solutions must be seen against this backdrop, includ-ing that previously mentioned Building Act 1984 that reduced build-ing regulations from 300 pages to 25.

The energy efficiency and environmental agenda

The drive to clad buildings was originally driven by an environmental agenda closely linked to the plastics industry.

A 2018 Sky News report revealed concerns about the political lob-bying of the plastics industry, claiming that during their investigation the reporting team was told time and time again that the 'plastics industry was highly litigious and that speaking out about its fire safety was impossible'.[54] A former government scientist, speaking on condition of anonymity about the pressures he faced, revealed that threats to sue him had made him unwell, saying: 'I think perhaps more than anything else other people were silenced – by saying "Oh, you'd better not say anything about that, look what happened to him."'

The Sky report highlighted that the main lobby group for plastic insulation – the Insulation Manufactures Association – went so far as to advertise the fact that they were 'influencing UK and local gov-ernment, specifying authorities, relevant approval and certification bodies', and that they had 'high level involvement in the drafting and regular revision of British and European standards [and] Building

Regulations'. Its members are promised the 'opportunity to influence Government bodies and NGOs' and have 'direct input into relevant British Standards committees'.[55]

The week after the Grenfell fire, a group of six European plastic lobby groups wrote a letter of complaint to the publishers of a peer-reviewed paper by chemistry and fire safety expert Professor Anna Stec on the dangers of toxic smoke from burning plastic. "We request that the article is withdrawn,' it said: "The consequences ... are enormous and could well lead to significant consequential losses."[56]

Lobbying is not limited to the plastics industry, of course. As noted in previous chapters, there have been concerning fires in timber-framed buildings since Grenfell.[57] It is far from clear that timber is safe, particularly during the construction phases, with the National Fire Chiefs Council saying, in 2010: 'Large timber framed buildings under construction pose a significant risk to firefighters, construction workers and members of the public.'[58]

And yet, in June 2020, days before the third anniversary of Grenfell, the *Observer*'s architecture critic Rowan Moore argued that the government should reconsider the post-Grenfell ban on the use of timber despite 'continuing testing and research' being needed to ensure its safety.[59] Reporting on the fact that organizations such as the Architects Climate Action Network and the Royal Institute of British Architects had urged the government to reconsider the ban, he concluded: 'A strange aspect in all of this is that Grenfell Tower was not made of timber. ... It is perverse to ban a blameless material.' That a material was absent on Grenfell has no bearing at all on its safety.

This kind of argument reminds me of the *Challenger* disaster, where the degradation of norms from 'prove safe' to 'prove unsafe' contributed to the deaths of seven astronauts. Commenting on that disaster, Richard Feynman said: 'When it comes to risk, though, we have just proved a long-term version of Murphy's Law – what can go wrong, will go wrong eventually. Just give it time. ... Nature cannot be fooled.'[60]

When safety is one of a number of competing tensions, and when it is managed from siloed ministries and departments, it's difficult to see how you might enable safe outcomes without ensuring safety is pivotal to all decisions that would require 'both/and' versus 'either/or' thinking.

Proving the safety of a product should surely be demanded as a starting point by those being lobbied?

LESSONS FROM GRENFELL: HOW DID SO MANY BUILDINGS END UP WITH DANGEROUS CLADDING?[61]

Let us look at the question of how so many buildings ended up with dangerous cladding. Without wanting to second guess any outcomes of the Grenfell Inquiry, it seems likely that this is down to a lethal combination of

- issues with *product testing* and *classification*;
- a difference in interpretation of the *guidance documents* (Approved Document B);
- changes to *testing regimes*, including allowing *large-scale testing* and *desktop studies*; and
- the *privatization of building control* without ensuring competency, enabling unsafe systems to be signed off as compliant.

Product testing and classification[62]

There are two important classifications in relation to high-rise buildings in the UK: 'class 0' and 'limited combustibility'.

The limited combustibility test subjects materials to two hours in a 750 °C furnace. Neither the ACM cladding nor the PIR insulation used on Grenfell would have passed this test.

The class 0 classification is a national product performance classification. It can be achieved in one of two ways: either the product must be comprised entirely of materials of limited combustibility, or it must meet certain requirements when tested with two small-scale tests. These tests do not measure the combustibility of the core of a composite (or sandwich) material.[63] According to cladding expert Dr Jonathan Evans, these are low-power tests intended to reflect how materials behave in the early stages of a fire; they do not break down composite materials and expose the highly flammable core to the flame. As such, materials that could perform very poorly in a fully developed fire can achieve class 0.[64]

By contrast, in the European testing for class B (which, while not equivalent to class 0, is also accepted for products used in the UK), there is a crucial difference. Class B relies on a 'single burning item' test. The test is still low power and can lead to variable results, but the test samples are mounted representatively with panel joints, and consequently the core of the composite is exposed to the heat source and can leak molten PE, which can then ignite.

The guidance documents (Approved Document B)

One of the functional requirements of the Building Regulations 2010, made under the Building Act 1984 in force at the time of the Grenfell refurbishment, was that the external walls 'adequately resist the spread of fire having regard to the height, use and position of the building'. As we saw in chapter 2, the Grenfell Tower Inquiry ruled that this was not complied with, and that the ACM cladding was a major cause of the fire spread.[65]

Approved Document B (ADB) was the statutory guidance document approved by the Secretary of State for Housing, Communities & Local Government. ADB provides guidance on how to comply with the functional requirements regarding fire safety. While it is not mandatory to use Approved Document guidance, if you are using it and comply with it, there is a tendency to assume that you have complied with the functional requirements, and vice versa.

A 2017 government study found that most of the building industry relied on Approved Document guidance and that ADB was the most used, to the extent that prior to Grenfell, according to Dr Evans, ADB would commonly be referred to as the regulatory requirement, as opposed to a guidance document.[66]

The document was known to be confusing. The Lakanal House inquest coroner found that ADB was a 'most difficult document to read' and recommended it be reviewed (see chapter 5).[67] While it is clear from ADB that the insulation should meet the rating of limited combustibility, there has been much argument since the fire between industry and the Ministry of Housing, Communities & Local Government about what rating was required for the ACM cladding. One of the crucial objectives of the Grenfell Tower Inquiry will be to determine this.

The difference in interpretations appears to be down to two critical paragraphs that will 'likely become the two most litigated paragraphs in history'.[68] Paragraph 12.6 says that the external wall surface (typically interpreted to be the 'cladding') must meet the requirement of 'Diagram 40',[69] which indicates that class 0 (or European class B) is required for buildings over 18 metres in height. Paragraph 12.7 applies to buildings over 18 metres and says that any 'insulation, product, filler material, etc' needed to be of 'limited combustibility'.

The government response since Grenfell has repeatedly stated that paragraph 12.7 applied to the ACM cladding, as the PE core was 'filler'. Four days after the fire, Philip Hammond, the Chancellor of the Exchequer, insisted during a prime-time BBC interview that the cladding used on Grenfell was 'banned'.[70]

However, it is less than clear cut; historically, government ministers and officials are on record as saying something else. In 1999, Housing Minister Nick Raynsford, giving evidence at the Select Committee considering the dangers of cladding, said the requirement was class 0.[71] So did civil servant Brian Martin when he gave evidence at the Lakanal House Inquest in 2013.[72]

Inquiries and courts will eventually reach their conclusions about which standard applied. For the purposes of understanding why so many buildings have flammable cladding, there was at a minimum a difference of interpretation about which standard applied for high-rise buildings.[73]

While giving evidence at the Grenfell Tower Inquiry in 2018, expert witness Dr Barbara Lane said:

> For the avoidance of any doubt, I consider an external surface formed with a composite of polyethylene core to be unable to comply with the functional requirement of B4(1) of the Building Regulations. I am concerned, therefore, about the provisions made in Diagram 40 of the ADB 2013, which is statutory guidance, and advise these are changed as soon as possible.[74]

Testing regimes

In addition to the ACM cladding, the external-wall system at Grenfell also had flammable insulation. Regulations are clear that this should have been of limited combustibility, and it clearly failed to meet this requirement. How did this happen?

There were essentially three routes to showing compliance with ADB.[75]

The linear route
The 'linear route', where all the materials used would individually meet the prescribed standard in diagram 40 (i.e. for buildings over 18 metres in height, class 0 or class B for cladding and 'limited combustibility' for insulation). This route was not used in Grenfell as the insulation was not limited combustibility.

Large-scale tests
These were first introduced into ADB in 2002, are a test method for assessing the fire performance of cladding systems that do not meet diagram 40. They represent an alternative route to compliance.[76] If passed, this route allows manufacturers to prove their products – or combination of products – could be used on high-rise buildings, but, importantly, only in the combination tested.

The manufacturer determined the composition of materials tested. Accredited laboratories conducted the tests and treated the results as commercially confidential; this meant that if a test failed, it was not made public.[77]

We saw in chapter 2 how manufacturers manipulated these tests, e.g. by using undisclosed fire-retardant materials, and how, having passed the tests, they marketed products for use in high-rise buildings without making it absolutely clear this could only be done in the exact combination of materials used in the test.

Full scale test data/desktop studies
The final route to compliance was to use 'full scale test data', which opened the door to 'desktop studies'. This was never officially written into guidance documents, but subtle changes to wording in Approved Document B in 2006, including the words 'using full scale test data', opened the door to the use of desktop studies that relied on test data as opposed to products needing to undergo the test themselves. The Building Control Alliance, which represents building control bodies, formalized this process in 2014.[78] It began by recommending desktop studies be done by accredited laboratories but later changed this to any 'suitably qualified fire specialist'. No qualification or certification was required to call yourself 'suitably qualified'.

The fact that Celotex and Kingspan had passed large-scale tests opened the floodgates to this 'data' being used in desktop studies.

The Grenfell Inquiry has heard evidence that Kingspan used failed test data in twenty-nine desktop studies.[79]

What about Building Control?

Building Control's role is to check that building work meets the Building Regulations. In 1985 this was part-privatized, allowing competition with local authorities. Initially, the National House Building Council (NHBC) was the only private player allowed, but in 1997 this was broadened, leading to a competitive marketplace for approving plans.

In 2016, just after the Grenfell refurbishment was completed, the NHBC listed several common combinations of cladding and insulation that could be signed off without the need for any further tests (essentially bypassing the need even for a desktop study). This included the exact combination used on Grenfell: Celotex RS5000 and 'class 0' ACM cladding.

This guidance was withdrawn after the fire.[80]

The lethal combination of inadequate product testing and classification, different interpretations of regulatory guidance, changes to testing regimes that left them open to secrecy and gaming, and weak building control has led to thousands of buildings in the UK having flammable facades.

THE TWO QUESTIONS: MAKING THE WATER VISIBLE

Why don't we learn? Failures in governance and accountability

As I grew up in South Africa, I had very little knowledge (or interest) in the working of the UK government prior to Grenfell. I watched in anything from amusement to anger as ministers in the Houses of Parliament engaged in acrimonious, elitist, public-school-style debates that felt as far removed as it was possible to be from the kind of collaborative, enquiry-based conversations that I believe are needed to operate effectively in a complex world.

Nearly four years later, while a bit clearer about how things work, I am astounded at the complexity and inaccessibility of governance in the UK, and I consider this a key constraint to our ability to change and to learn from events such as Grenfell.

The complexity of governance structures

The UK is a constitutional monarchy,[81] with an 'unwritten constitution' existing of many individual laws, conventions and interpretations.[82] Its governance is complicated and overlapping. In addition to the two houses of parliament and the executive, and all the central Whitehall ministries, there are more than 300 other agencies and public bodies. In September 2019 there were 419,000 civil servants doing the practical work of government.[83]

More than a million people work for local government in England. This work takes varying forms, and the people involved are responsible for a range of services within a defined area.[84]

Devolved governments in Scotland, Wales and Northern Ireland are responsible for many domestic policy issues (such as health, transport and education) and they have law-making powers in those areas. Covid-19 has exposed the practical implications and difficulties of this complexity, as each devolved government has responded differently, highlighting tensions between central and local governments.

Weaknesses in accountability

There has been a failure to ensure that accountability has kept pace with this increasing complexity of government at all levels, including local and devolved governments.[85] Services are delivered through complex networks of departments, public bodies, private and voluntary sector providers, with inconsistent oversight, inspection, regulation and scrutiny.

You cannot have effective governance without effective accountability. Symptoms of weak accountability include lack of clarity about who is responsible for what, no rewards or consequences for good or bad performance, and a lack of transparency and information.[86] All of these problems are present in the UK according to a 2018 Institute for Government report, which states that 'accountability is about a relationship between those responsible for something, and those who have a role in passing judgement on how well that responsibility has been discharged'.[87]

At its best, accountability should be used proactively to ensure that those in positions of power think hard about decisions and their consequences, and consider the range of decisions available as well as the fairness, appropriateness and proportionality of each possibility. Concepts such as 'exploratory thought'[88] and 'chronic unease'[89] emphasise the importance of understanding multiple viewpoints, ensuring cognitive diversity and considering potential unintended consequences.

However, fundamental gaps in accountability have led to relationships between officials and ministers that 'promote a tradition of secrecy, which results in a lack of clarity about the responsibilities of senior officials and ministers'.[90]

I follow Grenfell extremely closely but I'm still unable to keep abreast of who is involved, who is accountable for what, and what progress has been made. Official reports that I've printed (which is a fraction of what's been produced) take up three large lever arch files. They neatly summarize the steps that individual departments have taken in nicely worded rhetoric that could leave one believing that everything has been brilliantly managed. But this contrasts starkly with the reality of the slow pace of change in making buildings safe – and with the experience of those most impacted.

Much of the work produced is of a very high calibre, and I'm not questioning people's intent. But it's hard to see if anyone is maintaining sufficient oversight. It feels very much as if we have ended up with a complex, siloed response that will, over time, fix some piecemeal technical issues but will fall far short of the kind of coordinated, holistic, systemic approach that is called for.

High turnover of ministers and civil servants

The high turnover of both ministers and civil servants adds to failures of accountability, as new incumbents bring different priorities and visions and struggle to maintain knowledge and expertise.[91]

As of January 2020, three-quarters of ministers had only been in post for six months.[92] The Ministry of Housing, Communities & Local Government lost almost a quarter of its staff in 2017/18. Up to a third of Cabinet Office staff change each year.[93] Within three years of Grenfell there were three different Secretaries of State for Housing, Communities & Local Government and five Ministers for Housing.

Possibly exacerbated by the political turmoil surrounding Brexit, the trend for ministers to remain in positions for shorter and shorter periods is troubling from an accountability perspective, as former chancellor Kenneth Clarke told the Institute for Government:

After six months ... you have got an agenda. You know exactly what you are going to do. The next stage, after two years, you are really on top of it. ... But you realise that the decisions you took after six months were wrong and you have changed your mind. After two years, you are sitting in control now, behind your desk, where you are really going to do this, this, and this. And then the phone rings and the prime minister is having a reshuffle and you move on to the next department and you are back at the beginning, there you are, panicking again.[94]

These weaknesses in governance and accountability – characterized by the complexity of government structures, a lack of clear accountabilities, and high turnover of ministers – maintain the status quo.

How might we enable systemic change? Embracing complexity and ambiguity

Chapter 3 explored how our over reliance on traditional bureaucratic command-and-control responses is ineffective in an increasingly complex world. And we've seen in this chapter how this complexity is revealing regulatory weaknesses and vulnerabilities, speaking to the need for agile and context-dependent regulatory solutions.

As such, developing our capability to operate effectively with increasing complexity is a key opportunity to disrupt the status quo. Doing so will demand embracing ambiguity and adopting agile regulatory solutions.

Embracing ambiguity
During a speech at the Warren Centre in Sydney, Australia in July 2018, Jose Torero, an expert witness for the Grenfell Inquiry, said (edited for ease of reading):[95]

Ambiguity is not a bad thing in that it enables an engineer to make choices. This is what gives you the freedom to innovate and it gives you the opportunity to be able to create leaner solutions. But as ambiguity expands, so does the need for competency, as you start creating ambiguity you need somebody to interpret it in the appropriate way. The more flexible, the more complex. As you introduce new methods of construction, new materials, etc., then the more complex things become and the more ambiguous and the more you are reliant on competence.

What ended up happening in Grenfell was that the engineers that delivered the building, those engineers did not exercise competency adequately. Their competence was not consistent with the complexity of what they were doing. ...

We have created a system that is way too complex for our current definition of competency.

Far from being limited to fire engineers, the same could be said for all those involved in the refurbishment at Grenfell, for the sector more broadly, and for those who regulate it.

And while a lot of (welcome) work has been done to define and improve competencies post-Grenfell, I remain concerned that this will do little more than enable incremental piecemeal change and spurn a lucrative 'training industry' that provides 'tick box' courses to licence organizations and individuals to work on high-rise buildings.

While prescriptive regulations are sometimes appropriate, and the cladding ban in response to Grenfell was arguably needed, this is due to weaknesses in competence rather than because prescriptive regulations are the answer. To succeed in our increasingly complex and disruptive world, we cannot rely solely on prescription – not least because this hinders innovation. We need to think differently and embrace ambiguity and complexity.

Agile regulatory approaches

Regulatory effectiveness could be seen as part of a bounded system, where effectiveness is limited by weaknesses in governance and accountability, by sector risk and regulatory complexity, and ultimately by the sector and regulator's capability to deal with complexity and ambiguity (figure 11).

Our regulatory approaches should take into account these contextual constraints while also addressing weaknesses in them. Doing so will force us to use a range of regulatory approaches appropriate to the context. According to the aforementioned Foresight Review on the future of regulatory systems, responses should fall along a range from 'define and control' to 'navigate and adapt'.[96]

Traditional define and control responses are appropriate when the sector and risk complexity are low. This situation is characterized by high levels of cohesion and shared values in the sector, high levels of predictability and low levels of ambiguity. Governance is strong, there are few political agendas, and accountabilities are clearly defined and fulfilled. Capability is appropriate to the level of ambiguity and complexity. In these situations, more traditional regulatory responses are probably appropriate.

The danger will be complacency, so practising chronic unease and developing the capability to identify new risks would be important.

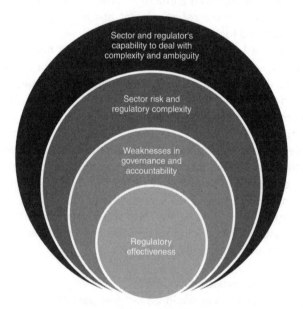

Figure 11. Regulatory effectiveness.

Navigate and adapt strategies are more appropriate when there is a greater degree of unpredictability and volatility, and the sector and risk complexity are high.[97] In this situation, governance is weak, with unclear roles and complex political agendas. There is a high level of ambiguity, and neither the government nor the sector has the sufficient capability to match the level of complexity. A range of approaches – such as tackling systemic risk and the values-based and strength-based solutions mentioned earlier – may be appropriate.

Experimentation (and learning from failures) will be needed, as will agile, multi-stakeholder engagement.

This would require a willingness to confront the fact that issues with extreme levels of uncertainty may be almost unmanageable in practice. As the Foresight Review concludes, 'it may also be that regulation, "as typically understood" is not the answer'.[98]

Adopting agile and innovative approaches would require courage from politicians, civil servants, industry and citizens alike, and by their nature, a willingness to experiment and learn from failure would be involved. This would demand new ways of thinking, engaging all stakeholders and communicating differently.

Post-Grenfell, regulatory responses are not as complex as, for example, regulating biotech, cyber or social media, and a mix of traditional and more agile approaches could be used.

What is clear is that embracing ambiguity and complexity offers an opportunity to disrupt the status quo.

IN SUMMARY

This chapter has looked at what foundational structures are in place to prevent catastrophic events.

I began by exploring the myth that regulations guarantee safe outcomes, and went on to look at legislation and regulation in the UK, showing how regulatory challenges, competing objectives and political agendas drive the role of lobbying to influence regulatory outcomes. 'Lessons from Grenfell' showed how a lethal combination of regulatory guidance, product classification and testing, and building control functions contributed to thousands of buildings having unsafe cladding.

Weaknesses in governance and accountability create the conditions holding our failure to prevent and learn from catastrophic events in place.

Until we begin to deal with these regulatory, governance and accountability vulnerabilities and develop our capability to navigate complexity and the inherent ambiguity this brings, we will become increasingly vulnerable. An over reliance on prescriptive and traditional regulatory approaches will not lead to systemic change. Rather, developing our capability to deal with complexity offers the opportunity to disrupt the status quo.

Chapter 5

Behavioural elements: 'blame fixes nothing'

Any member of the public reading these statements ... would be forced to conclude that everyone involved in the refurbishment of Grenfell Tower did what they were supposed to do and nobody made any serious or causative mistakes.

Richard Millett (QC), lead counsel to the Grenfell Tower Inquiry[1]

I cannot doff my hardhat to a company that blamed me for the deaths of two of my workmates, the burning of five others, the destruction of half a billion dollars of gas plant and wish them well.

An operator blamed for the Esso Longford gas explosion
(cited by Andrew Hopkins in 'Lessons from Longford'[2])

In 1998 there was a catastrophic accident at the Esso Longford gas plant in Australia. Two workers were killed and eight were injured. Gas supplies to the state of Victoria were affected for two weeks. The company blamed some of the operators on duty at the time of the explosion. However, a subsequent Royal Commission cleared the workers of any negligence or wrongdoing and found Esso fully responsible for the accident.

After being cleared, this is what one operator had to say:

While I'm not facing a lifetime of corrective surgery to mitigate disfigurement, I can't work in a place where I once thought I would spend the next 27 years of my life. I cannot doff my hard-hat to a company that blamed me for the deaths of two of my workmates, the burning of five others, the destruction of half a billion dollars of gas plant and wish them well. I cannot respect a company that would gladly have me face the tearful, bewildered stare of a workmate's bereaved family, while the directors of that company seek refuge in the judicial cocoon of their legal advice.[3]

After a catastrophe, our approach can either be past-focused (reactive and searching for who to blame) or future-focused (proactive and searching for what we can learn). Shifting to a proactive approach requires believing in, or at least aspiring to the possibility, that we can prevent catastrophic events, which many accept as simply inevitable. Which approach we adopt impacts the urgency with which we approach the need for change.

This chapter explores the mechanisms we have in place to prevent and respond to catastrophic events (the behavioural aspects).

Firstly, I explore the myth of the perfect error-free world, also known as the bad apple theory. In the 'Key issues and challenges' section I look at the mechanisms for preventing and responding to catastrophes, such as the role of inquests and inquiries. 'Lessons from Grenfell' tells the story of the failure to heed the issues raised by government scrutiny mechanisms in the wake of the Lakanal House inquest. Finally, in 'Making the water visible', I propose that our obsession with blame is the key condition holding the status quo in place, and that ensuring fairly borne consequences after an event offers an opportunity to disrupt the status quo.

THE MYTH OF THE PERFECT ERROR-FREE WORLD: ALSO KNOWN AS THE BAD APPLE THEORY

Alongside the myth that regulations keep us safe (see chapter 4) is the myth of the perfect error-free world. That is, that all buildings comply with all regulations and that all workers follow all procedures, but then, suddenly, a 'bad apple' does something wrong. Perhaps they fudge a test or fail to comply with regulations or procedures – and then we have an accident.

The mythology is that the cause of the accident is human error, and if we simply replace the bad apples, the world will again operate perfectly.

But it's not that simple. Behaviour is context dependent. The Boeing 737 MAX crashes offer an outstanding insight into this world.

Lessons from the air: the Boeing 737 MAX crashes

On 28 October 2018 a Lion Air Boeing 737 MAX landed in Jakarta. During the flight there, its pilots had experienced issues with the plane inexplicably lurching downwards. The captain reported the incident to the airline and the maintenance team then checked for serious equipment failure, finding none.[4]

The next morning, at 6.20 a.m., operating as flight 610, the plane took off on its way to Pangkal Pinang, Indonesia. Soon after take-off the flight crew found themselves struggling to control the plane as automatic anti-stall software, known as MCAS, overrode their instructions and pushed the nose down more than twenty times. The plane crashed into the Java Sea at around 450 miles per hour, killing all 189 people on board.[5]

The problems with the plane can be traced back nearly a decade.

Boeing's 737s and Airbus's A320s are the two main players in the profitable 'narrow-body' passenger jet market.[6] On 1 December 2010 Airbus announced that it had, in secret, developed a more efficient, A320neo jet, which would burn 6% less fuel than the Boeing 737. Airbus sold the plane in record numbers.

In response, Boeing executives decided to launch a new-generation 737 in record time. But the designers couldn't update it too much. By law, a pilot can fly only one type of plane at a time. They can, however, fly different models of planes with similar designs that share a common 'type certificate'.[7] This allows airlines with common-type fleets to make their operations more flexible as they can more easily substitute planes and pilots.

To gain this certificate, the MAX needed to be similar to the three previous generations (launched in 1993, 1980 and 1964). It needed to be cutting edge but also similar enough to the original 1964 design to gain the same type certificate. Failure to achieve this would mean that pilots would need to be retrained, adding significant costs and inhibiting the ability to compete with Airbus.

The new plane also needed to be developed within six years.

Two years into development, Boeing promised it would be 8% more efficient than the A320neo. Five and a half years in, the new model was granted the amended type certification. Announcing that pilots would need only two and a half hours of comput-er-based training to switch to the MAX, Boeing sold a record breaking $200 billion worth of aircraft before the first prototype took to the skies.[8]

MCAS, the system that failed during the Lion Air crash, was designed to ensure the MAX kept its common type certificate. The MAX engines were more efficient but they were also bigger and heavier, so Boeing placed them further forward and slightly higher on the wing. This created an aerodynamics problem, causing the MAX to handle differently from previous versions when it was climbing steeply. Concerned this might jeopardize the rating, Boeing designed a software solution rather than a physical one. MCAS compensated by activating the plane's trim system in modest increments until it detected the plane had returned to normal. During the fatal accident this system kept overriding the pilots and pushing the plane's nose down.

Pilots were not told about MCAS until after the Lion Air crash. Commenting on the Boeing crashes, Captain Laura Einsteler, a pilot with thirty years' experience, said: 'We need to have the understanding and knowledge of how everything works in a jet, so that we can command the jet to do what we need it to do, not just be along for the ride.'[9]

While the Federal Aviation Authority (FAA) is accountable for safety, it delegates much of the relevant certification process to manufacturers, saying it would need $1.8 billion of taxpayers' money every year to bring all certification in house.[10] During the MAX's certification, FAA managers pressured teams to delegate as much as possible back to Boeing.[11]

MCAS was not included in the FAA information that listed the ways in which the new plane differed from other models; it didn't (as required) have any redundancies in place should the system fail, and the version installed allowed for 2.5 degrees of movement, where the original design approved only 0.6 degrees.[12]

Less than five months after the first crash, on 10 March 2019, 157 people were killed when an Ethiopian Airways Boeing 737 MAX flight from Addis Ababa to Nairobi crashed within minutes of takeoff.[13] The plane struck the ground with so much force that there were no identifiable remains. Instead of their loved-ones' bodies, families received bags of soil from the surrounding fields.[14]

These crashes wiped nearly a tenth – around $25 billion – off Boeing's stock market capitalization.[15] 737 MAXs were grounded globally. Boeing estimates the cost of the crashes to be $19 billion, and the company posted annual losses of $636 million in 2019.[16] Dennis Muilenburg was removed as chairman in October 2019 and fired as CEO two months later, albeit having received $60 million in pension benefits and stocks.[17]

The final House Committee Report into the crash, released in September 2020, offers clear indications that either Boeing or the unit tasked with overseeing the certification process on behalf of the FAA could have caught flaws during the design stage, but they both failed to act on concerns raised about MCAS.

According to the report, Boeing employees were driven in part by what investigators concluded was pressure to get the new planes to customers quickly and without requiring their pilots to undergo extensive retraining – a goal symbolized by 'countdown clocks' on the wall of a conference room.[18] The report concluded:

> [The two crashes] were the horrific culmination of a series of faulty technical assumptions by Boeing's engineers, a lack of transparency on the part of Boeing's management, and grossly insufficient oversight by the FAA. ... The facts laid out in this report document a disturbing pattern of technical miscalculations and troubling management misjudgements made by Boeing. ... It also illuminates numerous oversight lapses and accountability gaps by the FAA that played a significant role in the 737 MAX crashes.[19]

Human error and the context-dependent nature of action

Our instinctive response when something goes wrong is to find someone to blame. Identify who 'messed up' and remove those bad apples so that we can return to our 'perfect world'.

While it is easy (and emotionally satisfying) to blame individuals, doing so fails to reveal deeper issues. Behaviour is context dependent. The actions of those working on the 737 MAX that led to the catastrophic failures, must be viewed in the context of the schedule pressure and a 'culture of concealment that the most senior executives and officials were accountable for creating'.[20]

James Reason has written extensively on human error and unsafe acts, his interest having originally been piqued by the

Chernobyl nuclear disaster in April 1986, which was largely due to human actions. His categorization of unsafe acts (see figure 12) provides a useful framework for shifting away from simplistic blame narratives.

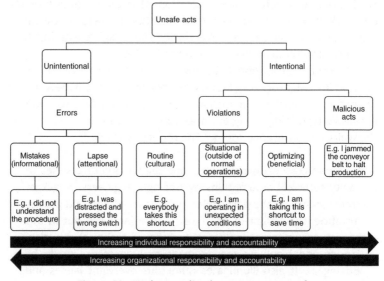

Figure 12. Understanding human error: unsafe acts, responsibility and accountability.[21]

According to Reason's model, there are three types of 'unsafe acts':[22]

- errors where there is neither the intent to deviate from procedure nor to cause harm;
- violations where there is the intent to deviate but there is not an intent to cause harm; and
- malicious acts, where actions are taken with the intent to harm.

Mistakes and lapses are normal and to be expected, and those in positions of power in organizations and institutions must ensure their systems are sufficiently resilient to allow for them. You cannot argue that unsafe acts are an individual's responsibility without ensuring that the necessary conditions for minimizing errors were in place (e.g. design, training, competence, assurance, culture and leadership). Common error traps include time pressure, poor design (e.g. when you cannot distinguish easily between different parts of machinery), fatigue, stress and burdensome workloads. You cannot justifiably blame someone for making a mistake that leads to an accident when they have been forced to work overtime for ten days straight and are fatigued.

Violations are not always the responsibility of an individual either. Routine violations are cultural – the way everyone does things – and accountability for this rests with those in positions of power. Common violation-provoking conditions include poorly written and unclear procedures, lack of competency, poor supervision, lack of inspections, and a tolerance of violations when they serve organizational goals, such as production or schedule. If a violation leads to an accident, you cannot justifiably blame the individual for the violation if, in fact, it is how people normally conduct work, and the violation has repeatedly been overlooked by supervisors and managers.

At the other extreme, responsibility for malicious acts or intentionally setting out to cause harm likely rests more with the individual. That said, to reveal systemic issues you still need to understand the context in which malicious acts were taken. I recall a story about a site in a remote desert location with very limited access to communication. A number of fires had been intentionally started in the camp. The culprits were never found but, interestingly, after requests by workers to provide them with the means of speaking with their families were heeded, the fires stopped.

Overlaying accountability on the model in this way helps us move away from looking at individual blame, revealing deeper organizational issues. A blame narrative considers who is at fault, is highly personal and assumes that removing the individual bad apple(s) will solve the problems. However, simply replacing one person with another operating in the same context is likely to lead to little change or learning.

An accountability narrative instead considers what practices and structures (e.g. competency, inspection and assurance mechanisms) were/are in place and how these were/are (or were/are not) fulfilled. When practised reactively and focused on blame avoidance, accountability ends up promoting defensiveness. When practised proactively, it has the opportunity to promote prevention and learning.[23]

We all make errors, and relying on a lack of them to keep people safe is simply irresponsible.

Developing resilience

Author and safety guru Todd Conklin maintains that error is not really very interesting. As he says:

> Every failure that happens has human error. But every success that happens has human error. Error is really not very interesting. It's a part of the operational fabric that always exists. When a failure happens because of human error, the error is not the problem. It's the lack of tolerance in the system that's the problem. We can expect the error to happen, and we should build systems that are tolerant enough to be able to manage that kind of variability.[24]

From a resilience-engineering perspective, 'things that go right and things that go wrong happen in basically the same way'.[25] A system is resilient when it 'can sustain required operations under both expected and unexpected conditions by adjusting its' functioning prior to, during or following events (changes, disturbances, and opportunities)'.[26]

Rather than perpetuating the myth that accidents are caused by 'human error' and that removing bad apples will restore the perfect error-free world, we would do well to focus on developing resilience. Author and academic Eric Hollnagel has written extensively on resilience engineering and its application. He identifies four interdependent resilient potentials.[27]

- The potential to *respond*. Being able to respond to changes, disturbances and opportunities by activating prepared actions or adjusting current ways of operating.
- The potential to *monitor*. Monitoring a system's own performance as well as what happens in the surrounding environment; knowing what to look for; and being able to monitor that which is seriously affecting, or could seriously affect, the system's performance in the near term.

- The potential to *learn*. Being able to learn from experience, knowing what has happened, and learning the right lesson from the right experience.
- The potential to *anticipate*. Being able to anticipate developments further into the future, knowing what to expect, such as possible disruptions, novel demands or constraints, new opportunities, or changing operating conditions.

When these potentials are lacking, there is increased risk of being unable to respond well to disruptions. Key to developing these potentials is an organizational ability to welcome bad news.

Challenging good news and embracing bad news

While recently working with a large company (one with more than 35,000 employees), I spent a lot of time listening to people at all organizational levels.

The senior executives wanted to understand what was really going on but kept getting fed good news stories and sanitized reports.

Middle management, despite being told there was no pressure to present good news stories, did just that, afraid that their careers would be in jeopardy if they laid bare the real challenges they were facing. Their job was to solve these problems, and they assumed that despite what the executives said, they would not be happy if they knew how messy things really were.

Those on the frontline had given up on the truth. They were expert in telling those up the chain exactly what they wanted to hear, and then getting on with navigating the gap between work as planned and work as done as best they could. They knew that if something went wrong, they would likely be blamed and punished – or worse still, injured or killed.

I do not think this is unique.

When we become interested in building resilience, then rather than trying to stamp out any deviance and drive blind compliance or remove those who deviated, instead we become interested in the difference between work as planned and work as done – in the gap between planned and actual outcomes. Failure to do this drives responsibility for risk unfairly down the chain.

Those on the frontline are continually navigating the gap between work as planned and work as done, and for the most part things function well, often with better-than-expected outcomes. But unless there are opportunities for these workers to openly and without fear tell people about the deviances – unless there is a culture that embraces this – those on the frontline have to navigate the gap without a holistic picture of risk, all while pretending to those up the line that they are, of course, following all the rules and that everything is going according to plan. Knowing, from experience, that telling the truth is a flawed strategy.

Senior executives, boards and regulators can fall into the trap of wanting to hear only good news. Of not welcoming stories of deviance and non-compliance. This needs to be actively resisted and guarded against. Good news reports should be rigorously examined and questioned. Bad news should be welcomed. We need to learn to 'question the good news and embrace the bad'.[28]

KEY ISSUES AND CHALLENGES

Let us consider the proactive and reactive mechanisms that are available to help prevent and respond to catastrophic events.

Proactive mechanisms

Mechanisms for preventing unwanted outcomes are available to governments, regulators and supply chains.

Governments
The practice of accountability is a cornerstone of how government is intended to work, and the primary role of Members of Parliament (MPs) is to hold government to account by debating, questioning and voting on issues, supposedly representing the views of their constituents.

However, as a 2018 Institute for Government report states:

A tradition of secrecy pervades Whitehall. This makes it difficult to understand who is responsible for ... decisions, and the evidence on which they are based. Ultimately, this enables ministers to promise more than their department can realistically achieve, and the civil service to escape responsibility for the advice that it provides.[29]

Given the political nature of parliament, accountability and scrutiny can be compromised by political agendas and priorities. For example, MPs are mostly expected to vote in accordance with their party whips' instructions (whips are senior members of a political party tasked with organizing backbench MPs). And there is a pull to scrutinize reactively and emphasize blame as the political elements of accountability come into play.[30]

Other barriers to practising accountability proactively include

- the complexity of government and overlapping accountabilities;[31]
- a lack of scrutiny over the services offered by local authorities and councils;[32]
- weak accountability oversight of the civil service and a failure to develop the specialist capabilities needed to deliver on government objectives;[33] and
- a lack of resources and time for Select Committees to provide the necessary scrutiny.[34]

Scrutiny is a key aspect of holding government to account, and Select Committees[35] are one of the primary mechanisms for doing so. They check and report on areas ranging from the work of government departments to economic affairs. Each government department has its own Select Committee, and others such as the Public Accounts Committee and the Environmental Audit Committee cross departmental boundaries. The committees set lines of inquiry, gather evidence and publish their reports and recommendations. The government is usually required to respond to these recommendations within sixty days.

Prior to Grenfell, concerns about the risk of cladding were raised through numerous government scrutiny mechanisms.

For example, in 1987, thirty years before Grenfell, the Department for the Environment warned that:

A risk of increased vertical fire spread has been identified during the laboratory testing of overcladding systems incorporating combustible insulants. ... Where the cladding is sheet aluminium, laboratory tests have shown that a fire within the cavity can melt the aluminium and burn through to the surface several storeys above the fire. These emergent flames could re-enter the block via windows. Fires of such severity are rare. ... However, it is advised that both existing and proposed overcladding systems should be examined to determine if modifications are required as a precaution against fire spread.[36]

Then, in 1999, in response to the Garnock Court fire in Scotland, a Select Committee investigation into the dangers of cladding heard the following evidence from Glyn Evans, representing the Fire Brigades Union:

The main risk [posed by cladding with regard to fire safety] is the problem of vertical envelopment of a building in fire. ... If a fire occurs within a building it leaves the building through a window opening in an external wall. ... If the cladding cannot resist the spread of flame across the surface, then it will vertically envelop the building. ... If you get multi-storey buildings, you will get fire spread up the outside if the cladding will permit it.[37]

The Select Committee nevertheless concluded that:

The evidence we have received during this inquiry does not suggest that the majority of the external cladding systems currently in use in the UK poses a serious threat to life or property in the event of fire.[38]

Adding that 'the responsible attitude taken by the major cladding manufacturers towards minimising the risks of excessive fire spread has been impressed upon us throughout this inquiry'.

Concerns were raised about testing though:

The evidence we have received strongly suggests that the small-scale tests which are currently used to determine the fire safety of external cladding systems are not fully effective in evaluating their performance in a 'live' fire situation. As a more appropriate test for external cladding systems now exists, we see no reason why it should not be used.[39]

Scotland did change its guidance following this, requiring external-wall cladding on high-rise buildings to be constructed of non-combustible products. [40] England did not.

I had expected when researching this book to find failures in preventative scrutiny by government, and while there are certainly weaknesses driven by political agendas, Select Committees and other departments such as the National Audit Office produce outstanding reports scrutinizing government and civil service behaviour. The issue is perhaps not with the scrutiny mechanisms themselves, then, but with the failure of successive governments to respond to them.

We shall return to this later in 'Lessons from Grenfell'.

Regulators

The list of missed opportunities by regulators to prevent future failures is long. One notable and expensive example is the 2007–8 financial crisis: there were plenty of indicators, backed up by critics' warnings, that something odd was going on.[41]

And this phenomenon is certainly not limited to the UK. In 2015 it was revealed that Volkswagen had installed 'defeat device' software to manipulate emissions levels under test conditions. But rather than being a 'scandal' without warning, there had been many previous allegations that emissions when vehicles were being driven on normal roads with regular drivers bore little resemblance to emissions during formal tests. These allegations had never previously been thoroughly investigated, though. This failure, along with the fact that manufacturers were able to choose their testing company, is a good example of regulatory failure – in this case in the EU and the US.[42]

These cases raise one of the fundamental dilemmas with regulation: should it be practised proactively (ex ante) or after the fact (ex post)? Should the focus be on prohibiting undesirable behaviours or on punishing people when things go wrong?

Martin Stanley, a retired senior civil servant and the former chief executive of the UK's Competition Commission, says that there are essentially two views about what drives the right behaviours. One is that we are naturally law abiding and will comply with reasonable regulations. The other is that we will only comply through fear of getting caught. That is, either decency or the risk of punishment is needed to keep people on the straight and narrow.

From a risk-of-punishment perspective, while executives may suffer reputational damage and be forced to resign in the aftermath of disasters, they are seldom found guilty in civil or criminal investigations and they usually leave with a healthy bank balance (as we saw in the Boeing case earlier).

Additionally, there is little evidence that even apparently eye-watering fines – such as the £20 million one given to Thames Water for pumping 1.9 billion litres of untreated sewage into the Thames[43] or the £129 million levied on Tesco for overstating its profits by £250 million[44] – are effective. Some people also argue that they result in shareholders suffering unfairly.

Stanley concludes:

> Fines and other *ex post* regulatory penalties have relatively little deterrent effect on those who are not naturally inclined to comply in the first place. It is vital, then, that important regulations are backed up by effective quality management – and strong inspection and enforcement regimes.[45]

Examples of proactive regulatory tools include providing guidance, performance moderation and education.[46]

In the wake of Grenfell and following the Independent Review of Building Regulations and Fire Safety led by Dame Judith Hackitt, a new building regulator is currently being established under the Health and Safety Executive. It will

> oversee the safe design, construction and occupation of high-risk buildings so that residents are safe and feel safe. It will be independent and give expert advice to local regulators, landlords and building owners, the construction and building design industry, and to residents.[47]

It has the potential to enable more rigorous proactive regulatory oversight.

The named duty holders during occupation, under the new Building Safety Bill, will be required to submit a safety case to the regulator showing that risks are being managed 'so far as reasonably practical'.[48] While safety cases have been shown to work well in high-hazard industries – notably being introduced after the Piper

Alpha explosion – it remains to be seen how effective they will be in ensuring building safety. There have been criticisms that the approach will prove overburdensome and costly, both to regulate and to implement.

The new regulators' impact will, at least in part, depend on the competency and quality of the regulators themselves. It would be encouraging to see the use of more innovative methods, such as strength-based approaches (see chapter 4) that encourage learning from things that go right.

Organizations and the supply chain

While it is important that accountability (and legal responsibility) for risk be clearly defined and managed, risk is not a 'static' phenomenon. People need to work collectively across supply chains to understand, mitigate and respond to hazards and risks. This is particularly important when making changes (such as refurbishing a tower block), and it is normally done through 'control of work' and 'management of change' processes.

In chapter 3 the notion of practising chronic unease (imagining and proactively mitigating against the worst thing that could happen) and techniques for understanding and mitigating hazards and risks, such as the Swiss cheese and bow tie models, were introduced. For such techniques to be useful, you need to create an environment across the supply chain where hazard identification and risk mitigation are collectively owned. This requires strong leadership and a willingness to move beyond purely commercial or contractual concerns.

At the very least, clients and project managers need to understand how, given their positions of power, their behaviour can impact decisions. They need to work to ensure 'bad news' is welcomed and shared rather than hidden.

Returning to the 1986 *Challenger* disaster, the issues with the O-rings (which failed to seal, leading to the explosion) had been known about by NASA since the second launch and were deemed an 'acceptable risk'. Engineers from Morton Thiokol (the manufacturer of the O-rings, whose contract was up for renewal) had raised concerns prior to the fateful launch and initially recommended that NASA did not proceed with the launch.[49] According to Morton Thiokol engineer Roger Boisjoly,[50] during a conference call to discuss this recommendation not to launch, NASA's George Hardy said, 'I am appalled'. The shuttle programme manager Lawrence Mulloy didn't hide his disdain either, saying: 'My God. ... When do you want me to launch – next April?' After this meeting, Morton Thiokol reversed its recommendation.

Based on his observations, discussions and assessments, retired Navy test pilot and NASA astronaut Jim Wetherbee created a list of ten common conditions that existed in various organizations before they experienced major disaster or minor accidents. Five are related to the technical aspects of socio-technical systems and five to the social aspects (see table 5).[51] Good leaders can apply these to turn hindsight into foresight, using the presence and severity of the conditions as indicators to help determine if their organizations are drifting towards disaster.[52]

Table 5. Ten adverse conditions present before any accident.[53]

TECHNICAL, SYSTEMS AND MANAGERIAL	SOCIAL, HUMAN AND LEADERSHIP
Emphasized organizational results rather than the quality of individual activities	Leaders didn't fulfil the transformational purpose of leadership
Stopped searching for vulnerabilities – didn't think a disaster would occur	Leaders didn't create accountability (nor commitment) before the incident
Didn't create or use an effective assurance process	Leaders didn't sufficiently listen to, engage with or care for their people
Allowed violation of rules, policies and procedures	Some leaders and operators placed self-interests above the organization
Some leaders and operators were not sufficiently competent	Leaders and operators didn't possess error wisdom

Each of these is now explored in more detail, starting with the technical, systems and managerial conditions.[54]

Emphasized organizational results rather than the quality of individual activities. Individuals and groups don't produce results, they conduct activities. All these in-the-moment activities – integrated over time – produce results. High-quality activities, when added together, result in high-quality results.

In organizations drifting towards disaster, executives and senior-level managers emphasized results and didn't mention or pay attention to the quality of activities. And without guidance, motivation or an incentive to conduct high-quality activities, the mid-level managers, frontline supervisors and workers began to compromise the quality of activities to achieve results more expeditiously to satisfy executives and senior managers.

Common phrases that were heard were 'get it done', 'work harder' and 'schedule and cost pressure'. Bosses often used sports analogies in speeches: competition was emphasized (e.g. 'beating our competitors'). Discussions about quality of activities, cooperation, working together and learning to work smarter were absent.

Stopped searching for vulnerabilities – didn't think a disaster would occur. Managers usually thought the organization was performing well just before the disaster occurred and were unaware of performance issues. Worse, they had simply stopped searching for these performance issues or weaknesses in their organizations.

In major accidents, investigators commonly described specific failures that were neither anticipated nor identified. But the failure was not only that managers failed to identify the specific weakness or system breakdown, they had stopped searching for any weaknesses or vulnerabilities in, for example, components, policies, processes, competence, relationships or communication.

Following the *Columbia* space shuttle disaster, one respected manager explained to Jim how it happened by saying, candidly: 'we just forgot how dangerous spaceflight really is'.

Didn't create or use an effective assurance process. Prior to accidents, managers did not understand how to create an effective process of assurance, nor did they understand the value of assurance. An effective assurance process was not in place or used.

No single organization can conduct all the operations necessary to accomplish complicated objectives. Many organizations and groups must contribute to the mission simultaneously. Executives – making strategic decisions – must be able to predict future progress towards goals with multiple organizations involved. No single person is capable of understanding how well each entity is performing, and to succeed – and prevent disasters – executives must rely on an effective assurance process to help predict the performance of each entity.

In operational organizations, providing assurance means a person is given confidence about future performance by another person (or group), based on observations or assessments of past and current performance. The assurance team can give executives confidence that the entity assessed will either continue to deliver the desired performance in the future or will not, and should be qualified with derived and estimated uncertainties.

Before major accidents, managers did not know how well or how poorly supporting organizations were performing; they did not create or use an effective assurance process. Without this, executives erroneously had confidence that organizations would continue to perform well.

Allowed violation of rules, policies and procedures. **After accidents,** investigators usually determined that some organizational rules, policies and procedures were violated before the event.

Often, the workforce unofficially reported that some managers knew of these violations prior to an accident. In some cases, according to the workforce, managers condoned violations in an effort to entice greater production or faster results.

Workers were willing to take excessive risks to satisfy their managers.

Some leaders and operators were not sufficiently competent. **Jim** observed inadequate and misjudged competence in some executives, managers, supervisors and operators before major accidents. From inflated self-assessments, their confidence was erroneously high and unjustified, and most leaders were unwilling to admit they didn't have all the answers.

Deficiencies in knowledge, skills or attitudes at any level in the organization can result in a failure to prevent accidents. Qualified assessors should have been assigned to test the knowledge, assess the skills and evaluate the attitudes of all people involved. Employees should be able to demonstrate skill through practical application of knowledge in real or simulated hazardous environments.

And executives and managers in the operating chain of command should have been responsible for evaluating the knowledge, skills and attitudes of their people.

Now let's move on to the social, human and leadership conditions.[55]

Leaders didn't fulfil the transformational purpose of leadership. **Before** accidents, most leaders understood the purpose of leadership only in a transactional sense. They understood their role was to, for example, develop a strategy, provide guidance, issue directives, create schedules and procure supplies, and handle other one-way transactions.

The operating workforce was already creating value and advancing the mission, in addition to facing the hazards every day on the frontline of operations. The workforce would probably have continued to do their jobs with or without transactional guidance from leaders.

It was the rare leader who understood the transformational purpose of leadership, the essence of which is 'enabling, motivating, and inspiring a group of people to perform better individually and accomplish more collectively with higher quality, in service of a mission or pursuit of a goal, than they would have without the leader's influence'.

Leaders didn't create accountability (nor commitment) before the incident. **The** concept of accountability was not well understood. A manifestation of accountability was often executed after an incident, where the managers held a person or group to account by applying adverse consequences such as blame, letters of discipline, reassignment or termination.

Jim almost never saw accountability being created before an incident.

The root of the word accountability is to give an account, or to provide justification to someone. The two-person (at a minimum) process of exercising accountability should be accomplished on a routine basis in a supportive way. The managing supervisor should require the subordinate manager, team leader or operative to regularly provide an account and answer questions such as: What did you and your team accomplish last week? What did you and your team learn? What issues have you uncovered? What is your schedule and predicted performance in the near future? What obstacles do you foresee? What resources do you need? How can I support you?

Prior to accidents, Jim saw accountability exercised extensively after incidents bur rarely exercised before an incident.

Leaders didn't sufficiently listen to, engage with or care for their people. Large organizations tended to forget that people – not machines or systems – were doing the work. Managers should have helped the people who were trying to use the systems, but they tended to focus on improving the systems.

Often, frontline workers understood the fragile, volatile and uncertain state of operations in complex and dangerous endeavours. Major accidents might have been predicted and averted if the managers had engaged in a better way with their people. What is more, performance improvements that managers were pushing for might have been realized, as performance goes up when leaders tap into the collective energy of people who feel supported while working together.

Before accidents, executive and managers often pushed people beyond their individual limits and didn't really listen to their workforce.

After the *Columbia* disaster, one senior executive defended the excessive pressure he was exerting on the workforce to accelerate the schedule by telling Jim: 'if we back off on the schedule they will relax'. Jim's opinion is that the executive had no idea how hard people were already working, as they put their hearts and souls into the mission to launch people into space.

Some leaders and operators placed self-interest above the organization. Organizations and groups that performed poorly generally had individuals who displayed little or no sense of duty to the mission and were more concerned with the politics of the organization than with supporting the mission or their teams. Rather than being motivated by executing their responsibilities in a high-quality way, some people were motivated by getting promoted, receiving bonuses and how they appeared to bosses.

Because of self-interest, some managers and operators were reluctant to admit they didn't have all the answers, leading to misplaced confidence, poor decisions and damaging actions.

Leaders and operators didn't possess error wisdom. Managers and operators in organizations headed for disaster rarely understood patterns of errors or biases in decision making in themselves or their teams. They rarely dedicated time or effort to analysing errors and decision making. Errors were viewed as a sign of individual weakness rather than as possible indicators of systemic deficiencies in the organization.

All humans make mistakes and high-performance teams understand this and embrace learning from mistakes. In hazardous activities, the best organizations have acquired error wisdom and developed techniques and systems to eliminate or reduce the consequences of errors.

Based on the evidence heard to date, all of the conditions discussed above were present at Grenfell. From emphasizing organizational results rather than the quality of individual activities; to not creating effective assurance mechanisms; to a failure to listen to, engage with or care for people. Yet these warnings were either not recognized or not heeded.

Listening to the supply chain give evidence at the Grenfell Inquiry has been disheartening. While the high-hazard industries with which I work are far from perfect, supply chains do look for ways to work collaboratively to both understand and mitigate risks. We cannot expect there to be significant change without addressing how to create collaborative supply chains. This needs to start with procurement and selection, and a willingness to move away from such low margins on jobs. We have to understand the pressures and tensions that contracting terms place on people and what behaviours they drive.

Let us now turn to the mechanisms used after a catastrophe.

Reactive mechanisms[56]

Table 6, adapted from a 2017 Institute for Government report titled 'How public inquiries can lead to change', illustrates some key options available to the government for formally investigating an event.[57] There are many challenges with these mechanisms.

Except in the case of an inquest, whether or not these investigations are called for is at the discretion of ministers, as is the appointment of chairs and panels, and the setting of terms of reference. This obviously calls into question their independence. For example, despite calls to do so, at the time of writing the prime minister Boris Johnson had yet to establish a Public Inquiry into the response to

Table 6. Some key formal investigations available to government.

	STATUTORY INQUIRY	NON-STATUTORY INQUIRY	INQUEST	INDEPENDENT PANEL
Established	By minister … when events cause particular public concern		By a coroner whenever a death occurs under specific circumstances	By a minister
Examples	Grenfell	Morecambe Bay Hospital	Lakanal House	Hillsborough
Terms of reference	Set by minister		No specific Terms of Reference	Set by minister
Public or Private	Public to greatest extent possible	Presumed public but may sit partially or wholly in private	Public with option that some evidence can be heard in private	Public
Led	Chair with option of panel		Coroner	Chair-led panel (usually 4–12)
Duration	1–6 years		Less than a year	1–3 years
Can compel testimony and production of documents under criminal sanction	Y	N	Y	N
Can take testimony under oath	Y	N	Y	N
Public access to documents	Duty to ensure this	No duty to ensure this	Duty to disclose relevant documents	Usually disclosed
Maxwellization (core participants see and respond to findings prior to publication)	Must take place	Generally expected	No Maxwellization process	
'Core participants' status available	Available for individuals, organizations and institutions with a specific interest; provides special rights		Not available (note: under the coroner's rules, inquests do have an 'interested persons' designation, which confers certain rights including that of questioning witnesses*)	
Recommendations	Usually required by terms of reference		Required by statute in Prevention of Future Deaths Report	Sometimes required

* Coroners and Justice Act 2009 (www.legislation.gov.uk/ukpga/2009/25/part/1/chapter/7/crossheading/interpretation).

Covid-19. That the prime minister will determine if there will be an inquiry and then select its chair and set its terms of reference – all for an inquiry that will inevitably investigate and pass judgement on his own government's response to the pandemic – is problematic.

These public investigations are complex, costly and rarely satisfy everybody. Concurrent criminal investigations and court proceedings complicate matters and can extend timelines for corrective actions and prosecutions. A 2017 Institute for Government report estimated that £638.9 million had been spent on sixty-eight public inquiries since 1990.[58] Between August 2017 and March 2019, the Grenfell Inquiry cost £40.2 million; this was prior to the Phase 1 report being published or the beginning of Phase 2 hearings.[59]

Notably, there is no process for ensuring that recommendations are either implemented or effective. Ministers are free to either accept or reject recommendations, and even once accepted there is no process for following up on progress. According to the Institute for Government: 'Of the 68 inquiries that have taken place since 1990, only six have received a full follow-up by a Select Committee to ensure that government has acted.'[60]

A 2020 report by JUSTICE, an all-party law reform and human rights organization, raised various issues with the current system, including the following.[61]

- The political nature of the decision to call for a Public Inquiry.
- The discrepancy between the rights afforded to victims in the judicial systems and the lesser rights granted to the bereaved and survivors in inquests and inquiries. This, on top of a lack of coordination between agencies, leads to those most impacted needing to share their traumatic experiences on numerous occasions with different bodies.
- Institutional defensiveness, which can impede the effectiveness of inquiries and inquests and damage public trust. The report recommends establishing a statutory duty of candour, requiring participants to 'lay their cards on the table', thus directing any inquiry to key issues early in the process, reducing time and costs.
- Regarding the implementation of recommendations, the report calls for external oversight, saying: 'Quite apart from those instances where Government has indicated that recommendations will be implemented, there is no routine procedure for

Ministers to explain why they have rejected inquiry recommendations. After initial investigations, several rounds of written and oral evidence, analysis and a final report, there is little to prevent inquiry recommendations vanishing into the ether where the political will to implement is lacking.'[62]

In essence, our reactive mechanisms for investigating and preventing catastrophic events are set up at the whim of the sitting government, they are costly and lengthy, they are burdensome to the bereaved and to survivors, and there is no mechanism for ensuring their recommendations are either implemented or effective.

They are also conducted in silos, with no formal cross-inquiry oversight. By default, this drives piecemeal versus systemic change and does not enable holistic views that point to common themes across inquiries, such as the failure to listen to those at the frontline. The JUSTICE report recommended that an independent body should lead oversight and monitoring of the implementation of recommendations.[63]

I have sat in the Grenfell Inquiry and witnessed the courage and pain of firefighters, the survivors and the bereaved as they have given evidence. I have met with the inquiry team during open forums and I know they want to ensure we get to the truth and learn.

And yet, until government takes heed of the calls from reports such as those by JUSTICE and the Institute for Government to ensure that the implementation of recommendations is not reliant on political will, we perhaps need to own up to the fact that there is no political will to learn, or to prevent the next catastrophe. This is heartbreakingly illustrated in the next section.

LESSONS FROM GRENFELL: LAKANAL HOUSE AND THE FAILURE OF ACCOUNTABILITY MECHANISMS

As mentioned earlier, the failure by government to proactively prevent catastrophes is not a failure of scrutiny but rather a failure by those accountable to respond appropriately to the issues being raised. This is well illustrated by the failure of ministers to respond to known issues regarding Approved Document B, which came to light in an investigation by *Inside Housing* journalist Peter Apps.[64]

This all goes back to the 2009 Lakanal House Fire (discussed in chapter 2), which killed six people when fire burst through a window and lit the combustible cladding outside. Judge Frances Kirkham conducted a jury-led inquest, following which, on 28 March 2013, she wrote to the Department for Communities & Local Government, which was responsible for housing regulations and was led by Eric Pickles, the Secretary of State for Housing, Communities & Local Government from 2010 to 2015.*

The letter (officially referred to as a Prevention of Future Deaths Report) included the following recommendations regarding Approved Document B (the guidance relating to fire safety).[65]

Building Regulations and Approved Document B

The introduction to AD B states that it is '... intended to provide guidance for some of the more common building situations.' However, AD B is a most difficult document to use. ...

It is recommended that your Department review AD B to ensure that it

- Provides clear guidance in relation to Regulation B4 of the Building Regulations, with particular regard to the spread of fire over the external envelope of the building and the circumstances in which attention should be paid to whether proposed work might reduce existing fire protection.
- Is expressed in words and adopts a format which are intelligible to the wide range of people and bodies engaged in construction, maintenance and refurbishment of buildings, and not just to professionals who may already have a depth of knowledge of building regulations and building control matters
- Provides guidance which is of assistance to those involved in maintenance or refurbishment of older housing stock, and not only those engaged in design and construction of new buildings.

---

* During a 2018 Cabinet reshuffle, the Department for Communities & Local Government was renamed the Ministry of Housing, Communities & Local Government.

139

The following is an extract from Mr Pickles's response of 20 May.[66]

> Finally, in relation to Building Regulations, I have noted your concerns about the difficulties that some of those involved in the Inquests had with the interpretation of Approved Document B. I can assure you that my Department is committed to a programme of simplification. However, the design of the fire protection in buildings is a complex subject and should remain, to some extent, in the realm of professionals.
>
> We have commissioned research which will feed into a future review of this part of the Building Regulations. We expect this work to form the basis of a formal review leading to the publication of a new edition of the Approved Document in 2016/17. The revision would be drafted in accordance with a new 'style guide' for Approved Documents, aimed at ensuring the guidance is capable of being more easily understood, and that the need to cross-reference is reduced.

This new edition was not issued prior to Grenfell.

It is easy with hindsight to judge these as bad decisions, of course, but this was not the only opportunity the government had to respond to the issues surrounding Approved Document B.

The Fire Safety and Rescue All-Party Parliamentary Group (an informal cross-party body chaired by the MP Sir David Amess) had written to ministers no fewer than twenty-one times prior to the Grenfell Tower fire calling for actions to be taken to implement the findings of the Lakanal House review.[67]

For example, regarding the building regulations, the group wrote to the minister suggesting that issues with the fire resistance of materials on outside walls could be dealt with by simple amendments rather than having to wait for the official 2016–17 review of Approved Document B. On 9 September 2015 the minister accountable for building regulations, Stephen Williams, responded. His letter said:

> I have neither seen nor heard anything that would suggest consideration of these specific potential changes is urgent and I'm not willing to disrupt the work of my department by asking that these matters be bought forward.[68]

Sir David responded, saying that he was 'at a loss to understand how you had concluded that the credible and independent evidence which had life safety implications was not considered urgent'. He went on to add:

> As a consequence, the group wishes to point out to you that should a major fire tragedy with loss of life occur between now and 2017 in, for example, a residential care facility or a purpose-built block of flats, where the matters raised here were found to be contributory to the outcome, then the group would be bound to bring this to others' attention.

The group never received a response to this letter.[69] Picking it up again in 2015 with Williams's successor, James Wharton. With Wharton, at one stage citing the government's desire to 'reduce the burden of red tape' for his refusal to act.[70]

A lengthy series of correspondence followed, right up to the time of the Grenfell Tower fire, between the Fire Safety and Rescue Group and government ministers, with the MPs frequently requesting meetings and action. Their pleas were rejected or ignored.

Gavin Barwell, who was housing minister in 2016 and 2017, received seven letters, with the last landing twenty-six days before the fire at Grenfell Tower. Mr Barwell sent just three short replies during this period and became so bad at replying that the group resorted to sending their letters by recorded delivery.[71] Barwell lost his seat in the snap general election on 8 June 2017 and was appointed by Theresa May, the prime minister, to be her Chief of Staff.

A week after the elections, a fridge caught fire in a flat in Grenfell Tower.

It is anticipated that these failings will be explored in Phase 2 of the Grenfell Inquiry.[72]

Let us now turn to our two questions.

THE TWO QUESTIONS: MAKING THE WATER VISIBLE

Our obsession with blame is, I would argue, the primary condition holding our inability to learn in place. Ensuring the fair distribution of consequences after a catastrophe has the ability to disrupt the status quo.

Why don't we learn? Our obsession with blame

Our obsession with finding someone to blame after a catastrophe and the preoccupation of politicians with blame avoidance combine perniciously when it comes to learning and building resilience. After three and a half years of observing our response to Grenfell and watching the UK go through Brexit and Covid-19, I am increasingly of the view that learning is impossible and that developing resilient systems is therefore extremely challenging.

Earlier in this chapter I spoke of the importance of welcoming bad news and challenging good news, and of speaking freely about where work deviates from plan. This requires an ability to say, 'I made a mistake', 'I did something outside of procedure', 'I never follow that procedure, I don't think it works'. I don't believe our political system, obsessed as it is with blame avoidance, creates a context in which one can easily say 'I messed up' or raise concerns about current work practices without fear of reprisal.

Politicians and blame avoidance
Political scientist Christopher Hood says that in political contexts: 'We are dealing with a type of risk that seems curiously unmentionable. ... Namely the risk of blame.' Putting 'blame risk' under the spotlight he identifies three key blame avoidance strategies.[73]

- *Presentational strategies,* or 'spin your way out of trouble'.
- *Agency strategies,* or 'find a scapegoat'.
- *Policy strategies,* or 'don't make contestable judgements that create losers'. In other words, take the cautious route that won't upset anyone or anything.

In this context, the lack of any significant progress in dealing with known issues such as failures in governance and accountability (see chapter 4) or the effectiveness of inquests and inquiries (that were explored earlier in this chapter) perhaps begin to make sense.

As Hood says:

Complex partnerships and subcontracting arrangements may or may not deliver better public services on the ground than simpler, more easily understandable organisational arrangements.

But what they can do is spread the blame when things go wrong. Rigid rules may or may not make for a safer society than the application of common sense. But what they can do is help to protect those applying the rules from blame for using discretion that turns out to be wrong. Crooked and ambiguous accountability trails may not serve democracy or good governance. But they can protect the political and administrative class from blame after failure.[74]

I have wondered whether implementing 'blame risk assessments' for politicians would help. While I believe it would be an interesting idea to explore, there is no incentive for politicians to change, and as long as 'crooked and ambiguous accountabilities' save politicians from being blamed after failure, I am under no illusion about the likelihood they would even consider looking at these assessments.

From the perspective of learning and systemic change, the necessity for blame avoidance in our political system is a key condition holding in place the status quo, as is our obsession with blaming others when something goes wrong.

Blaming others when something goes wrong
As explored earlier in this chapter, blaming individuals fixes nothing and diverts us from uncovering systemic issues or understanding where accountability lies. Navigating the world of human error is complex, and the obsession with blaming individuals that is rife among politicians, the media and society in general is a fundamental condition that holds the status quo in place and stops us learning.

Unfortunately, this issue tends to lead to those at the sharp end carrying the blame while senior executives and successive governments who are accountable for creating the 'context for action' bear little consequences.

How might we enable systemic change?
Fairly borne consequences

One of the strongest levers for cultural and systemic change is where consequences, or the fear of consequences, for catastrophic failures lie. The proactive approach to preventing catastrophes in high-hazard industries is driven as much by an understanding of these consequences of failure as by a moral obligation. For organizations, the fear of reputational damage (as in the NASA example discussed earlier), financial losses and declines in share prices (see the Boeing discussion above), and ultimately the fear of losing their licenses to operate, are powerful drivers of learning, innovation and change. We would do well to pay more attention to using consequences as a driver of change, and to look at expanding the scope beyond judicial consequences.

While legal justice is important both as a deterrent to poor practices and as some solace for those impacted, it is often fraught with challenges and long delays, and in many cases prosecutions are unsuccessful: see, for example, the case of murdered teenager Stephen Lawrence that was discussed in chapter 3. The murder took place in 1993, and after years of tireless campaigning by Stephen's family, two of the five suspects – David Norris and Gary Dobson – were eventually found guilty of murder in 2012. The road to justice involved two Public Inquiries and a failed private prosecution.[75]

In no way am I arguing that legal justice is not important or that it should not be pursued with those individuals and organizations found accountable for contributing to catastrophic events. However, due to its limitations, relying on judicial consequences alone is too narrow a focus for driving systemic change.

Likewise, firing and replacing individuals has limited systemic impact. Although such actions might be appropriate for malicious acts, behaviour is context dependent as we've seen in this chapter, and removing individuals from an organization will not guarantee that the culture and context for behaviour changes. Simply putting another individual in the same context is unlikely to lead to meaningful change.

In an ideal world, governments and other institutions would creatively use consequences as a driver of systemic change. Imagine if, in the wake of Grenfell, the industry (designers and developers, constructors and housing associations) and government had come together and voluntarily agreed to a series of levies and taxes that would pay for remediation while not putting the survival of companies at risk. Or a levy on all new developments payable over a ten- or twenty-year period. Maybe a licence fee or a one-off tax could be introduced that would be required from anyone wishing to participate in temporary mitigation measures (such as waking watch) or remediation of existing buildings (which will cost in excess of £15 billion, and therefore earn revenue for those involved in the remediation and raise tax revenue for the government).

As with many other catastrophes, we are seeing unfairly borne consequences after Grenfell, with those leaseholders caught up in the cladding scandal (see chapter 2) facing life-changing bills for historic fire safety issues while the 'polluter pays' principle seems to have been forgotten.

This was eloquently captured in a January 2021 *Sunday Times* article, which stated that:

> Those who created this problem – the builders and their suppliers, some of whom have shown a blatant disregard for public safety – should be made to pay for it. The blameless leaseholders should not. The government has to use its muscle, and not be influenced by whether some of these businesses are Tory [government] donors.[76]

Perhaps due to blame avoidance, history tells us that it is often left to those most impacted to campaign for fairly borne consequences. Whether it is the Lawrence family or the Hillsborough bereaved (see chapter 7) or those caught up in the cladding scandal, it seems that, for now at least, external pressure on government is required. The impact and the importance of these campaigns for change and fairly borne consequences should not be underestimated.

IN SUMMARY

This chapter has sought to explore the actions we take to prevent and respond to catastrophic events.

I began by exploring the myth of the perfect error-free world, arguing that rather than relying on the lack of human error to keep us safe, we need to build resilient systems. Doing so would require a willingness to embrace bad news.

I went on to look at proactive and reactive mechanisms for preventing and responding to disaster, considering the proactive mechanisms of government scrutiny, regulators and the supply chain. The effectiveness of inquiries and inquests as the primary reactive mechanisms is limited, particularly because of the lack of any accountability structure to scrutinize the implementation or effectiveness of recommendations.

The 'Lessons from Grenfell' section discussed how known issues with Approved Document B were raised through official mechanisms over a number of years prior to the fire, but they were ignored or were not adequately responded to. This reveals that rather than being a failure of proactive scrutiny, there is a failure for the accountable ministers to respond appropriately to issues raised through scrutiny mechanisms.

I then argued that our obsession with finding someone to blame combined with politicians' obsession with blame avoidance has created a condition holding the status quo in place, and that campaigning for and ensuring that consequences are fairly borne after a catastrophe provides an opportunity to disrupt the status quo.

The foundational and behavioural elements of systemic change are the ones given the most attention, but the impact of relational elements is equally impactful, if not more so. We go on to discuss this in the next chapter.

Chapter 6

Relational elements: 'I thought I will make happy both of them'

In safe cultures, there is equality of life and equality of voice. All life matters and matters equally, and all voices count. The job of those with power is to ensure the voices of those with less power are both heard and count.

Gill Kernick, BBC Radio 4's *Today Programme*, 14 December 2017

... wise and articulate, situated voices are flourishing, so the question is not so much about allowing voices to be expressed, but about ensuring their legitimacy and power. ...Participation is nothing without power.

Dr Flora Cornish, 'The importance of people's voices', 2020[1]

On Saturday 5 October 2019, thirty-one candles were lit at St Helen's Church, North Kensington – one for each of the victims killed in the 1999 Ladbroke Grove rail crash. In the same church, nearly four months earlier, on 14 June, the second anniversary of the Grenfell Tower Fire, seventy-two candles were lit to honour those that had died.[2]

That is not the only connection between the disasters. In both cases, individuals had raised concerns that were not heeded.

Michael Hodder, the train driver who died in the Ladbroke Grove crash, passed a red signal and collided with another train. The subsequent inquiry revealed that, since 1993, train crews had warned about the 'inadequate sighting of certain signals', including SN109, the one missed by Mr Hodder. In the preceding six years, seven train drivers had failed to see the red light and stop. No action had been taken.

Alison Forster, the train operator's director of operations and safety, had raised the issue with Railtrack repeatedly. In August 1998 she wrote to Railtrack's production manager about SN109, asking 'as a matter of urgency what he intended to do about this high-risk issue'. She never received a full response.[3]

The term 'soft skills' is often used to lump together less tangible 'non-technical' skills such as listening, leadership, emotional intelligence and problem solving. They are often referred to with disdain, as if they are somehow of lesser importance than technical skills. This chapter explores how these non-technical issues impact our ability to prevent and respond to catastrophic events.

We begin by looking at the myth that relational issues aren't that important through the lens of the *Costa Concordia* disaster. Then, in 'Key issues and challenges', we investigate how relational issues hinder effective regulations and consider both the challenges and importance of speaking truth to power and public policy consultations. 'Lessons from Grenfell' looks at the narratives we use to silence, before 'Making the water visible' concludes that our unwillingness to rebalance power holds the status quo in place and that embracing diverse, tacit and distributed knowledge offers an opportunity to disrupt it.

THE MYTH THAT THE 'SOFTER' RELATIONAL ISSUES AREN'T THAT IMPORTANT

This myth is a key contributor to our inability to prevent catastrophic events.

Lessons from the sea[4]

At 9.45 p.m. on 13 June 2012 the cruise liner the *Costa Concordia* capsized. Thirty-five people lost their lives. At the request of the ship's maître d'hôtel (its manager), the captain, Francesco Schettino, had diverted from the normal course to sail past the island of Giglio, where the ship ran aground.

Wanting to understand what had motivated the decision, Nippin Anand, a former master mariner and human factors and safety specialist, interviewed Schettino. Anand says that with the benefit of hindsight it is easy to judge the captain's decisions as stupid, but this fails to take account of the conflicting pressures and tensions that professionals at the sharp end face.

Anand paints a picture of an industry that – like many others – says safety is its top priority while actions taken at board level portray a different picture: one that says that financial risks dominate and dictate choices.

As in many organizations, there is a divide between 'revenue-earning' and 'resource-exhausting' units in cruise ships. Revenue-earning units often end up having more power and influence. The hotel department on a cruise ship is 'the supreme', with the role of taking care of guests being seen as the core revenue earner for the business and its main source of profits.

A week before the accident, when the captain had first been asked to sail past Giglio by the maître d'hôtel, he had refused, citing bad weather. When reminded of the request, he felt pressure to do so, saying he felt the need to deviate because 'fleet wide [there] was … a sort of mentality to reward the hotel managers on board by paying attention to them'. Trying to balance the tensions between safety and paying attention to the hotel manager, Captain Schettino made a decision to change route and pass the island.

In this context the decision to sail close to the island was a very human one. As Schettino said:

> The maître was asking me to perform the manoeuvre, so I said OK. … It was kind of reward for this man was good and also there was a former captain at Giglio so I thought I will make happy both of them.[5]

Sustainable change: an integral perspective

Consider.

A House of Commons Transport Committee report on driving while using a mobile phone reported that 'a driver using a phone – hand-held, or hands free – is four times more likely to be involved in a collision'. One expert contributor, Dr Helman, explained that 'being at the UK legal limit for alcohol blood levels is the same amount of distraction, if not slightly less, than having a hands free call'.[6]

And yet a 2018 RAC survey found that 25% of drivers admit to making calls on their mobile phone while driving, with 16% saying they used their phone for texting, emailing or posting on social media. Both of those percentages represent increases since 2017.

I have seen companies implement 'no-mobile' policies with little success. Many organizations implement big brother methods of controlling and checking compliance, while those stuck in cars all day – with no other means of communicating and with looming pressures and deadlines – create ingenious workarounds, like taking calls on their personal mobiles instead of their work ones, insisting this complies with the letter, if not the intent, of policies. Many senior executives turn a blind eye to these violations perhaps because they promote business outcomes. And drivers continue to be exposed to the risks associated with talking on mobiles while driving.

So what does work in changing behaviour?

There is a very short video I have used in workshops that alters behaviour immediately. It is the story of Jacy Good, whose life was shattered by a driver on their phone. In the video, Jacy shares her personal testimony of losing both of her parents and nearly losing her life in the accident.[7] The video is less than four minutes long, and I have seen it create more sustained behaviour change than any government policy or organizational edict.

The four-quadrant 'integral model' in figure 13 helps elucidate this. On the left is the interior, subjective side, which is accessible through conversation, and in particular through listening. On the right is the exterior, objective side, which is accessed through observation. The top two quadrants represent the individual; the lower two quadrants represent groups.

We tend to focus change efforts on the exterior (objective) side. We want to change a behaviour, or develop a competence, so we write a policy or a procedure or develop some training. And when it fails to produce the change we want, we implement audit and assurance mechanisms to 'catch people' when they break the rules.

We end up in a vicious circle, with some attempting to alter behaviour by issuing policies and guidance and then checking and auditing these behaviours, while others at the sharp end work hard to avoid getting caught for not complying. The lack of compliance is often driven by the fact that the rules are ill conceived, so getting the job done requires deviating from them.

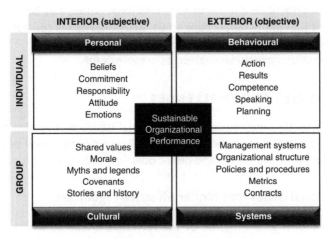

Figure 13. The integral model.[8]

Critically, despite a lot of effort and work, little changes, and what does change is fragile and dependent on careful monitoring and control. Research in Australia has revealed that one in eleven people works in compliance: that is, of every eleven people in work, one is observing the work of the other ten.[9] There must surely be more efficient, sustainable and enjoyable ways to impact behaviour?

The interior (subjective) side of the integral model provides a different way of accessing sustainable change. When people believe that they shouldn't talk on mobiles while driving because doing so puts them at great risk of dying, and thereby of hurting those that they love, they do not do it. They also speak up and stop others from doing so, and they raise concerns about organizational barriers to effective 'no mobile' policies. When there is a shared value across a supply chain to ensure refurbishments are done safely, there will be a natural pull for collaboration and understanding risk collectively, no matter what contracts say or what processes are in place.

The success of regulations such as the smoking ban or the law relating to drink driving is arguably due to their integral nature: a combination of policies, enforcement and building shared, embodied values and beliefs at both a personal level and a cultural one. This is what leads to sustainable change.

Subscribing to the myth that relational issues and 'soft skills' are not that important is dangerous. Relational issues can have dire consequences.

Let us explore these challenges in more detail.

KEY ISSUES AND CHALLENGES

In this section we consider the relational issues that hinder effective regulations and look at the challenges and importance of both speaking truth to power and public policy consultations.

Relational issues that hinder effective regulation

We will now look at some of the relational elements that impact effectiveness, both with regulators and with the institutions that are being regulated.

Regulators[10]
Regulators are often large and complex, and unaware of the problems that arise from their size and their established ways of doing things. They tend to focus on the object being regulated rather than question their own effectiveness, and they typically devote little time to considering the regulated organizations' likely responses to regulatory pressure. In a Bennett Institute Policy Brief titled 'Getting regulation right', Martin Stanley says that a regulator's effectiveness is, to a large extent, determined by the strength of its chief executive and how demanding its board is.

The role of regulators is not straightforward. For example, because they are under intense political and public pressure, regulators may not be keen for their industry to take the risks associated with innovation. There is also an 'urge to meddle', and the scope of regulation can be extended as politicians load regulators with confusing extra objectives.[11] Two key challenges regarding catastrophic events are the principal–agent problem and regulatory capture.

The principal–agent problem describes the strong tendency for people to align their goals and behaviours with their own interests and those of the people around them, rather than with those of the more senior 'principals' they are agents for.

The principal–agent problem can lead to what is called regulatory capture, where regulators who are meant to be the agents for citizens (the principals) enter into implicit understandings with entities they are meant to supervise. These relationships are often described as 'sensible, pragmatic or light touch'.

According to Stanley, evidence of regulatory capture includes

- regulators giving notice of inspection visits,
- frequent staff interchange between the regulator and industry,
- a reluctance of either party to be critical of one another, and
- increasingly introverted consultation processes.

The Boeing 737 MAX example we looked at in chapter 5 provides a perfect example of regulatory capture between Boeing and the regulator the Federal Aviation Authority (FAA). As a US House Committee report said: 'Boeing failed in its design and development of the MAX, and the FAA failed in its oversight of Boeing and its certification of the aircraft.'[12] The committee found that a series of failures in the plane's design combined with regulatory capture had 'compromised the process of gaining safety certification'.[13]

The regulator was found guilty of inherent conflicts of interest and grossly insufficient oversight, with the report concluding that the FAA was in effect in Boeing's pockets and that its management had overruled its own technical and safety experts 'at the behest of Boeing'.[14]

We do not yet have all the evidence with which to assess how these issues played out at Grenfell, but many of the same individuals and organizations who were accountable for creating the conditions inside of which Grenfell happened are now working to enable change. For example, the Independent Expert Advisory Panel established in the wake of the fire (see chapter 2) is chaired by Sir Ken Knight, former London Fire Commissioner and former Government Chief Fire and Rescue Adviser.[15] As reported by *The Times*, Knight had previously been a director of Warrington Certification and had signed dozens of certificates for manufacturers who paid for products to be tested for fire.[16] Knight has defended his position, saying he had approved the process rather than specific products and had resigned this position prior to accepting a place on the advisory panel.

We have also seen internal promotions for the appointments of the new commissioner of the LFB[17] and the new Building Safety Regulator.[18] In no way am I questioning anyone's integrity or qualifications, here; rather, I am concerned at the lack of bold appointments representing new and diverse ways of thinking, which is often best done through external appointment. I worry about the pressure those now in charge will experience to protect their organizations' reputations and justify past decisions.

While I am not in a position to pass judgement on this, I would argue that more diversity is needed in the post-Grenfell response, but culturally that is not welcomed.

Organizations and institutions

These kinds of relational issues don't just impact the regulator and their relationship with the institutions being regulated, they also impact operations within organizations themselves.[19]

The principal–agent problem described above is just as relevant in organizations, and it can lead to situations where executives find it difficult to ensure that middle managers or supervisors work to the corporate agenda. Principal–agent theory predicts that organizations become steadily more bureaucratic as they age, and in an attempt to control this, there is a tendency to reduce the scope for personal discretion, which in turn reduces the tolerance for initiative and innovation and the ability to cope with problems that don't appear in the rulebook. This is one of the factors that underlies the growth of a box-ticking culture.[20]

For regulators it can be hard to obtain reliable information from organizations, and there is often resistance to the introduction of tedious protocols aimed at improving safety or quality. Here's an example from 2018, when railway accident inspectors reported that:

> Members of the team told us that [their supervisor] neither fully briefed them on safety arrangement, nor checked their track safety qualifications. Nevertheless, they all signed ... to acknowledge they'd received the briefing.[21]

As previously mentioned, on numerous occasions I have heard from frontline workers about how they have been forced to attend 'policy briefings' but discouraged from asking any questions and then forced to sign attendance sheets. This has understandably left them with the view that safeguarding legal liability is the prime concern of management, rather than a concern for their own safety.

The concepts of herd behaviour, groupthink and cognitive dissonance help us understand why known problems and issues are allowed to perpetuate over time, and why moving beyond the status quo is so challenging.

Herd behaviour is when groups 'run together', following one another to remain part of 'the pack'. Groupthink is when people blindly accept wrong answers because it is socially painful to disagree. Cognitive dissonance refers to the stress we encounter when faced with seemingly opposing and incompatible views. Rather than explore things further, which can involve painful and challenging conversations and actions, we try to rationalize them and justify the dissonance rather than 'rock the boat'.

We witnessed all of these phenomena during the financial crisis. We saw the government and the financial sector hold onto a rosy view of the virtues of light-touch regulation despite many perceptive commentators warning of a forthcoming catastrophe.[22] Perhaps these behaviours explain why warnings both before and after Grenfell were not and are not being heeded.

In Joseph Conrad's novel *Typhoon*, Captain MacWhirr chose to sail straight through a devastating storm because he knew that his employers would criticize him for delaying their cargo if he sought to sail around it. The MacWhirr Syndrome describes situations in which modern executives mimic him, preferring to take uncertain and dangerous risks rather than face criticism from their boards and shareholders. For example, a number of senior financiers who understood they were running their companies into serious trouble before the 2008 financial crisis felt they would face unacceptable criticism if they followed a less risky course.[23]

'Diffuse responsibility' – where problems are widely known within an organization or an industry but no one feels responsible for raising or solving them – is another issue. For example, at the BP Texas City Refinery explosion, which killed fifteen people, problems were readily apparent to many managers and workers alike but, partly because of pressure to save money, no one felt it was their responsibility to do anything about them.[24]

This is starkly illustrated in the supply chain testimony at Grenfell, where everyone seems to have relied on everyone else to ensure regulatory compliance and safety.[25]

The case for change
As Stanley says: 'Tragic cases of regulatory failure, such as the Grenfell Tower fire ... have in common a failure to comply with existing regulation. These ... indicate that the current approach to regulation is deeply flawed.' He argues that there is a case for a cultural transformation to shift the approach to regulation. Measures might include[26]

- allocating greater prestige to the regulatory profession;
- increasing public debate about the complexities of regulating;
- incentivizing organizations to act with integrity, as opposed to systems that punish misconduct after an event; and
- designing regulations to include more active involvement with citizens.

Our response to catastrophes, if it is to be effective, ought to include consideration of the relational impacts on the effectiveness of regulation. For example, in speaking truth to power.

Speaking truth to power

Whether it is being done by a senior civil servant or a frontline worker, speaking truth to power is intricately linked with preventing catastrophic outcomes. There is an inherent risk in raising difficult views, whether it be pointing out an issue with a railway signal or challenging government policy due to new evidence. Speaking up may not be welcomed, and it could lead to detrimental outcomes, including being fired.

A recent research survey by Hult International Business School[27] found that

- 8% of those questioned knew something that could harm their company but had not spoken up;
- 17% of junior employees thought they would be punished if they spoke up about a risk in their organization; and

- the fear of being perceived negatively and upsetting or embarrassing others are the strongest reasons for remaining silent.

The researchers came to the following conclusions.

- There is a hierarchy to speaking up. The more senior the survey responder, the more they believe (often wrongly) that those junior to them are speaking up. The more senior you are, the more likely you are to speak up.
- Speaking up is *still* gendered. Fear tends to stop females more than males from doing so, and females report being more guarded than males.
- We believe, or pretend to believe, that social bias doesn't exist, which makes it unlikely that we can begin to counter its negative impact.
- Of those surveyed, 90% thought race and gender 'never' or 'rarely' impact listening. Research suggests this is very unlikely. Not a single executive board member surveyed thought that they 'usually' or 'always' have social biases regarding race or gender that affect the way they listen. In the words of the report's authors: 'This persistent blindness of unconscious bias stops dialogue in its tracks because if we refuse to acknowledge it is present then we are unlikely to be prepared to examine our own bias with a view to learning and mitigating negative consequences.'[28]

Interestingly, the government recently scrapped unconscious bias training and urged other public bodies to do the same. The reason they gave was that there was no evidence that the training led to any change in attitude. One MP reportedly said: 'I would really rather gouge my eyes out with a blunt stick than sit through that Marxist, snake oil crap.'[29] It is possible that the training itself was poor, and I am never a proponent of training as the answer to attitudinal shifts. What is troubling, though, is that rather than sparking conversations about how to better create attitudinal shifts, the notion of unconscious bias itself seems to have been dismissed. Writing in *The Times* recently, Lee Rowley, the deputy chairman of the Conservative Party, said that unconscious bias is a medieval fatalism that takes the laudable principle of fighting discrimination and twists it into a weapon.[30]

Does this point to a (perhaps unconscious) unwillingness among politicians to understand the impact of biases on people's ability to raise their voices and be heard? (We will return to this topic in chapter 7.)

While it is critical to speak truth to power in any organization, it has a unique place in UK politics.[31] Civil servants are expected to serve all governments, of whatever party, and they are not permitted to demonstrate any political allegiance. Civil servants have no constitutional power but act as servants to the Crown – which in effect means they serve the government of the day. The obligation to speak truth to power is embodied in the Civil Service Code and is critical to the service's effective operation. But there are worrying signs that senior civil servants are finding it problematic to speak truth to power. Ministers are increasingly publicly criticizing senior civil servants, and a number of senior figures have seemingly been pushed out of their jobs.[32]

As Tracie Jolliff, the director of inclusion at the NHS Leadership Academy, says, speaking truth to power is only one part of a very important equation. The other part is the examination of how power responds to truth.[33]

While whistle-blowing schemes and legislation are important, from a cultural perspective, I am far more interested in creating environments within organizations whereby whistle blowing is not needed, where speaking truth to power is natural and practised without fear, and where the concerns raised are taken seriously and responded to appropriately. This is critical to tapping the tacit knowledge of the frontline, which will in turn help to prevent catastrophic events.

One mechanism for ensuring different perspectives are included in policymaking and for giving the public the opportunity to speak truth to power is public consultations. Let us now explore their effectiveness.

Public policy consultations

Prior to Grenfell, I had never participated in any government consultation, which are supposedly an important way of including broader views in policy development. Having now participated in a number of them related to Grenfell and building safety, the process concerns me. My personal experience is that they are 'tick box exercises' and that they fail to tap the tacit knowledge and distributed intelligence of stakeholders. Rather than gathering views from which to create policy, they seem designed to allow narrow commentary on already formulated views, favouring corporate or institutional responses over individual views.

A particularly ironic consultation was that conducted into the development of policy based on the Hackitt Review 'Building a safer future'. A key proposal was about giving residents a stronger voice in the system and ensuring their concerns are never ignored. And yet the Ministry of Housing, Communities & Local Government consultation document ran to a not-very-accessible 192 pages, with responses required within eight weeks. There was almost no chance that those residents around the country, and those in high-rises in particular, who are most impacted by the bill, would, with their busy lives, be able to provide any meaningful coordinated input by the consultation's deadline.[34]

Perhaps the government would do well to practise its own consultation principles, which include the following.[35]

- Consultations should be concise and avoid lengthy documents.
- They should have a purpose and not ask questions on which there is already a final view.
- They are only part of a process of engagement.
- They should take account of the groups being consulted and consult stakeholders in a way that suits them.
- They should facilitate scrutiny.

If the intention was to give residents a stronger voice and ensure their concerns are never ignored, surely it would have been appropriate to use more innovative consultation methods, such as citizens' assemblies or training and paying local residents to run consultation sessions and summarize responses to feed into the process?[36]

Ensuring that the voices of residents (and other groups) are strongly heard requires careful consideration and a raised awareness of the narratives we use to silence.

LESSONS FROM GRENFELL: THE NARRATIVES
WE USE TO SILENCE

There are two particular narratives I have observed post-Grenfell that silence voices and inhibit our ability to learn. Reactions to criticisms of the LFB response to Grenfell indicate how 'hero and villain' narratives displace our ability to learn. As evidence from the Rydon project manager Simon Lawrence illustrates, bestowing labels such as 'rebel residents' is a way of justifying not listening to concerns.

Let us consider each of these topics in more detail.

The rebel residents

Both residents and those involved in the refurbishment had raised concerns prior to the fire. Residents flagged issues such as broken self-closing door mechanisms and the failure to consult them on the selection of cladding and windows, among other things. We know that both were critical to the rapid spread of the fire; the failure of doors to close on the night contributed to rapidly deteriorating conditions that inhibited rescue and escape.

The following extract is from a letter by Grenfell resident Eddie Daffarn:[37]

> Now we hear that residents will, in fact, be given no choice or opportunity to comment on the windows or cladding that we are to receive as they have already been chosen by the RBKC Planning Dept. Residents in Grenfell Tower that I have spoken with believe that we should have been consulted with before the windows and cladding were chosen and it should be the residents that have a say in the type of window and cladding that we receive and not the sole decision of a Town Hall Planning Dept?

Those accountable for the refurbishment raised concerns too. In an internal email, Artelia – who were contracted by the KCTMO to be the coordinator, quantity surveyor and employer's agent on the project – said: 'Despite all our efforts to ensure a smooth landing I have to say I do not think I have ever worked with a contractor [Rydon] operating with this level of nonchalance.'[38] Even Rydon's own project manager, Mr Lawrence, expressed concerns, saying in an internal email: 'At the moment we have a poorly performing site which is mainly (but not totally) caused by poor surveying and cheap incompetent sub-contractors.'[39] In chapter 2 we also saw how KCTMO project manager Claire Williams asked Lawrence for 'clarification on the fire retardance of the new cladding', referencing the Lakanal House fire.[40]

It is easy with the benefit of hindsight to be astonished that these signals were not heeded, but we have seen over and over again that the failure to listen to and tap the available tacit knowledge is all too common.

It is not necessarily the case that those at the sharp end will be able to identify the exact technical issues regarding issues such as fire doors or cladding, but complaints and concerns are an indicator that all is not well, and they warrant further investigation and exploration.

At Grenfell, the complaint regarding a failed door closer presented an opportunity to identify that this was a broader issue. Consulting residents on the cladding and the window design would have presented an opportunity for their fire safety to be scrutinized. And yet, in the face of an already troubled project, rather than tap the knowledge of residents, what emerged was an insight into the narratives used to silence them.

'I think there were several very vocal, dare I say aggressive, residents that, in my opinion, regardless of what work was being carried out or not, they still would have had reason for complaint,' Simon Lawrence said during evidence to the GTI.[41] Labelling the group 'rebel residents', he used the word 'aggressive' three times and 'vocal' nine times.[42] We heard that Lawrence had been 'tipped off' by the building manager at the KCTMO that 'there were several vocal residents … one of which could be extremely vocal and was quite well known by the TMO'.[43] When pressed, he revealed this to be Eddie Daffarn.

This begins to build a picture of the rebel resident narratives that were used to silence. Rather than questioning the validity of the narratives we use to silence at Grenfell, or in any other context, we should instead be actively seeking and interrogating any narratives that might – intentionally or otherwise – silence voices.

If only this had happened at Grenfell. Here is a 2016 extract from a blog run by 'rebel residents' Eddie Daffarn and Francis O'Connor:[44]

Kensington & Chelsea Tenant Management Organisation (KCMTO) Playing with Fire

20 November 2016

It is a truly terrifying thought but the Grenfell Action Group firmly believe that only a catastrophic event will expose the ineptitude and incompetence of our landlord, the KCTMO, and bring an end to the dangerous living conditions and neglect of health and safety legislation that they inflict upon their tenants and leaseholders. ...

Unfortunately, the Grenfell Action Group have reached the conclusion that only an incident that results in serious loss of life of KCTMO residents will allow the external scrutiny to occur that will shine a light on the practices that characterise the malign governance of this non-functioning organisation. ...

It is our conviction that a serious fire in a tower block or similar high density residential property is the most likely reason that those who wield power at the KCTMO will be found out and brought to justice! ...

We have blogged many times on the subject of fire safety at Grenfell Tower and we believe that these investigations will form a crucial part of a damning catalogue of evidence showing the poor safety record of the KCTMO should a fire affect any other of their properties and cause the loss of life that we are predicting.

Questioning the unintended consequences of our default narratives is essential for preventing catastrophic events. We all have a role to play in this. And while the rebel resident narrative is, sadly, unsurprising, there is another more subtle one that inhibits our ability to learn.

Heroes and villains

As mentioned in chapter 2, in her oral evidence at the Grenfell Inquiry, LFB Commissioner Dany Cotton said that training for an event such as Grenfell would be akin to 'developing training for a space shuttle landing on the shard'.[45] She added that, even with the benefit of hindsight, there was nothing she would go back and change about the firefighters' response on the night. These insensitive remarks were given as evidence in the Grenfell Phase 1 report that the LFB was an 'institution in danger of not learning the lessons from the Grenfell Tower fire'.[46] Dany Cotton stepped down at the end of 2019, four months earlier than planned.[47]

The criticism of the LFB in the Phase 1 Report (see chapter 2) and the resignation of Dany Cotton were both met with public outcry.[48] We hold onto a narrative that says that 'firefighters are good' and that the 'people who put the cladding on/cut LFB funding/wrote weak regulations/etc.' are bad. This simplistic 'hero and villain' narrative inhibits our ability to learn.

It is true both that the building should never have been covered in cladding that promoted the spread of fire and that the firefighters should never have been put in a position of having to fight it. The bravery and courage of the firefighters on the night is beyond question. But the argument that the LFB should be immune from scrutiny because they did not put the cladding on the building is flawed. Their response to the event should be looked at irrespective of its cause. We should avoid buying into the narrative that because they did not cause the event, they should not be held to account for any failings in their response to it, or that because of their bravery and courage, we should not question their actions in order to learn from them.

The Grenfell Inquiry Phase 1 Report concluded that the LFB had failed to learn the lessons of events such as the earlier Lakanal House fire. The LFB should be held to account for their failure to do so.[49] That accountability should rest with the senior leadership of the organization, not with the firefighters on the ground. Using a subtle hero and villain narrative to justify not questioning the actions of the LFB or failing to hold them to account, however well intentioned, will not lead to systemic change and learning.

THE TWO QUESTIONS: MAKING THE WATER VISIBLE

Our unwillingness to rebalance power in meaningful ways is key to maintaining the status quo. Including diverse voices so that we can unearth the tacit knowledge and distributed wisdom of those closer to the front line offers an opportunity to disrupt the status quo.

Why don't we learn? Our failure to effectively rebalance power

On the six-month anniversary of Grenfell, in an interview for the BBC's *Today Programme*, I said: 'In safe cultures all lives matter and matter equally and all voices count. The job of those with more power is to ensure that the voices of those with less power are heard.'

I would go further than that now. In addition to ensuring that voices are heard, we need to meaningfully rebalance power. This is by nature problematic, as the giving up of power is inherent in rebalancing it. Whether it is residents, Black, Asian and minority ethnic communities, women – the list goes on – history shows that we will give lip service to change without there being any significant shift in power.

For example, while 53.9% of civil service employees are women (and the figure has been above 50% since 2010), only 45% of senior civil servants are women, and women report higher rates of discrimination, harassment and bullying than men.[50] Likewise, while the representation of ethnic minorities in the service, at 12.7%, is in line with the general population (12.6%), only 6.3% of senior civil servants are from ethnic minorities. Discrimination and bullying scores are highest for ethnic minorities.[51]

There is a similar trend within organizations. While significant progress has been made in increasing the number of women on boards, there is still work to do. The 30% Club is a campaign group of business chairpersons and CEOs taking action to increase gender diversity on boards and in senior management teams. It set an ambitious target for 2020: that FTSE 350 company boards and senior management positions should have 30% female membership. By November 2018 the target for board members had been exceeded (31.9%) and women held 28.6% of senior management positions. But of the 900 women now serving on FTSE 350 boards, only 25 (less than 3%) have been appointed to the chair role, and even fewer have become CEOs.[52] A 2017 review found that half of the companies in the FTSE 100 did not have a board member from an ethnic minority, and just 8% of all directors were non-white. What is more, seven companies were responsible for 40% of the few ethnic minority placements there were, and there were just six ethnic minority CEOs or company chairs.[53]

Post Grenfell there is unquestionably an increased focus on 'engaging' with residents. This is also the case with BAME groups, partly as a result of Black Lives Matter and the death of George Floyd. But without actually rebalancing power, however well intentioned, this engagement will not lead to systemic change. We cannot pretend that increased engagement or consultations or complaints mechanisms that others control are analogous to rebalancing power. While these may help people to give voice, as long as the 'voice' is dependent on someone else giving it a forum, there is a power imbalance that needs to be addressed.

Post Grenfell reforms call for residents' voices to be central, but they are not. We saw this in the example of the consultation mentioned earlier: 'Disappointing that there is no resident participation' is probably my most tweeted comment. Without meaningful representation, influence and decision-making power in governance structures – within industry, housing and government – systemic change will not happen.

We need a careful examination of the narratives we use that maintain the status quo and justify the perpetuation of barriers: things like 'previous experience' or 'skills required', which stop people successfully applying for positions that would redress power.

As Dr Cornish so eloquently says:

> Wise and articulate, situated voices are flourishing, so the question is not so much about allowing voices to be expressed, but about ensuring their legitimacy and power. ... Participation is nothing without power.[54]

And it is not the moral argument alone that makes this important. Tapping diverse and distributed tacit knowledge is critical to preventing catastrophic events. Doing so offers an opportunity to disrupt the status quo.

How might we enable systemic change? Tapping diverse and distributed knowledge

Increasingly complex environments demand that we access tacit knowledge and distributed wisdom, and this leaves us with some hope that we will have no choice but to embrace diversity. But it is critical to move beyond moralist arguments and understand why doing so is so important.

I have met with frontline workers around the globe, from Scotland to Siberia, from Malaysia to Mozambique. As soon as they know that I want to understand the workarounds they perform to get the job done and that they won't get into trouble for telling me the truth, wonderful stories of ingenuity and looking out for one another and for their organizations emerge.

A number of years ago I was working in Africa, where hand injuries were a big issue. In response, management had issued workers with high-quality gloves and rolled out a new policy that made it compulsory to wear them at all times. But workers didn't always adhere, and people were still being injured. Incensed, managers were determined to punish anybody who violated the policy. In response, any time a manager entered the site, a highly efficient warning system gave workers sufficient time to put their gloves on before they were spotted. But still hands kept getting injured.

Wanting to understand why workers weren't wearing the gloves, we discovered that, while they were high quality, they were very thick, and some of the work required deft manoeuvring in confined spaces. People couldn't do this with their gloves on, so in order to get the job done they took them off. But the relationship with management wasn't strong, and people were frequently fired for failing to follow procedures, so they hid what they were doing rather than speak up.

The solution was simple: provide an additional thinner pair of gloves that could be used when working in cramped conditions.

What is often missed is that many workarounds are done in the service of production. Frontline workers generally want to get the job done, and for the most part they successfully navigate multiple competing goals (relationships, safety, productivity, quality, schedule). But sometimes things go wrong.

At the sharp end, in the service of organizational goals such as productivity or schedule, workers often take shortcuts that put them at risk personally. And those at the blunt end – happy with the resulting impact on productivity and schedule – turn a blind eye to the shortcuts. At least until something goes wrong. Then they act surprised and blame the workers for not following procedures (see chapter 5).

This relationship – between those at the sharp end and those at the blunt end – is critical. Figure 14 illustrates how the actions of those in the former group are constantly adapting and evolving: to the demands of the situation being managed on the one hand, and by the organizational context in which they are operating on the other. The blunt end of the system, at both the organizational and governmental levels, determines the constraints and resources that people at the sharp end have to operate within. Their decisions create latent conditions, such as weak regulations, inadequate testing of materials, inadequate emergency responses or a culture where you cannot raise concerns. These lie dormant and, when triggered by an active failure (such as a small fire in a flat), can end up with catastrophic consequences.

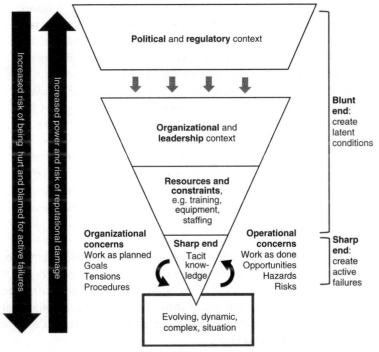

Figure 14. The importance of distributed and tacit knowledge.[55]

Those at the blunt end have more power and higher reputational risk should things go wrong, while those at the sharp end risk being injured or killed and are often blamed and punished when things do go wrong. As the level of complexity increases, without tapping the tacit knowledge and distributed intelligence of those at the sharp end, strategies and policies will at best be less effective and at worst doomed to failure.

The failure of government to listen to and tap the tacit know-ledge and distributed wisdom of those on the Covid-19 frontline has been stark. Instead, an environment of pressure and fear has been created. More than 850 UK healthcare workers are thought to have died of Covid-19 between March and December 2020.[56]

In a *British Medical Journal* opinion piece questioning how this had become acceptable, David Berger, a GP, said:

> Let us speak plainly now, not just about the NHS, but about healthcare systems all over the world. They are top down, 'command and control' bureaucracies, not dissimilar to military organisations. Though they brim over these days with fine words and caring mission statements, we all know they are rigid, unkind bureaucracies, the main purpose of whose management sub-units is less to deliver healthcare, than to take and hold organisa-tional territory. In such authoritarian, often bullying regimes, the pressure to conform need only be explicit occasionally. Fear of censure, and fear of letting others down, will do the rest.
>
> The 'new abnormal' is to believe that it is entirely reasonable for healthcare workers to go to work with the expectation that they will eventually contract a life-threatening illness. Almost everyone, from the public to the healthcare workers themselves, believes this.[57]

A Royal College of Nursing Survey in May 2020 found that 56% of BAME nursing staff felt pressured to work without the correct PPE.[58] A third of respondents had not received training in what standard PPE they should wear, and 41% of those working in care homes felt pressured to care for individuals with possible or confirmed Covid-19 without adequate protection.

Despite the Department of Health saying that no one should be prevented from speaking up, there is evidence of pressure being applied to doctors. One doctor who spoke anonymously (for fear of reprisals) to the BBC's *Newsnight* programme shared how, after posting concerns about PPE shortages online, his bosses 'hauled me up in front of a panel of senior managers – it was very, very intimidating. They kept on feeding me what felt like government type of lines, saying "this hospital has never had PPE shortages" – which I know to be factually untrue.'[59]

There was further outrage when Matt Hancock, the Secretary of State for Health and Social Care, appeared to blame frontline workers for the shortage when he warned staff not to overuse PPE, saying they 'should use the equipment they need in line with guidelines, no more and no less'.[60] On 29 July 2020 a Commons Select Committee report slammed the government's 'slow, inconsistent, and at times negligent approach'.[61]

In contrast to the poor response from those at the blunt end, community responses at the sharp end operated as 'cogs of connection, coordinating volunteering efforts, delivering emergency supplies, supporting isolated groups, and finding creative ways to keep communities together at a time when there is a clinical imperative for them to be physically apart'.[62]

Locality, an organization that supports local communities, argues that:

> The committed and agile way communities have responded to the coronavirus crisis points the way to a new future that's built around community power. But to be truly transformative, policymakers need to catch up with the innovation that's happening locally – and help embed it as the 'new normal' as we emerge from the crisis.[63]

Julian McCrae, the managing director of Engage Britain, an organization focused on tackling the UK's most complicated and divisive challenges, has said that 'for too long, our politics and policy have been remote, designed in Whitehall offices with very little role for those most affected by it'.[64] He argues that what we need is to transfer the energy and innovations of those at the sharp end to national challenges. Rather than seeking bland solutions that everyone can live with, he argues that a 'better method would be to focus on collaboration – where people with different views and experience find a way to build something together, rather than pull each other down'.

More effective decisions will require a blurring of the boundaries between traditional policymakers and policy receivers. We need to move away from the myth that those with power have the answers and towards a more collaborative way of working that draws on the diverse, distributed intelligence and tacit knowledge of those at the sharp end.

IN SUMMARY

This chapter set out to examine how relational elements impact our inability to learn and enable systemic change.

We began by exploring the myth that the softer relational issues aren't that important through the story of the *Costa Concordia* cruise ship disaster.

Some known issues and challenges were then presented. First, by considering the impact of issues such as the principal–agent problem, regulatory capture and groupthink on regulators, institutions and organizations, we looked at how relational issues hinder effective regulations. We then looked at the importance of, and the challenges involved in, policy consultations and speaking truth to power.

'Lessons from Grenfell' explored the narratives we use to silence by considering how hero and villain narratives displace our ability to learn from failures, looking in particular at the LFB's response to the Grenfell Tower fire and at how a 'rebel residents' narratives among the supply chain contributed to a failure to learn from resident concerns.

The 'Making the water visible' section suggested that our unwillingness to meaningfully rebalance power is holding the status quo in place. And we saw that, on the flip side, in an increasingly complex world that is pulling us to include diverse voices and tap the tacit knowledge and distributed intelligence of those closer to the sharp edge, there is an opportunity to disrupt the status quo.

I want to end this chapter with a fairly lengthy extract from veteran broadcaster Jon Snow's 2017 McTaggart Lecture.[65] It beautifully articulates the presence of distributed and tacit knowledge within the Grenfell community, why diversity is so important in accessing it, and the narratives we use to silence. It moved me at the time and moves me now.

As I stood below the smoking remains of Grenfell Tower and I thought about the gulf between us all. ... In that moment I felt both disconnected and frustrated. I felt on the wrong side of the terrible divide that exists in present day society and in which we are all in this hall, major players. We can accuse the political classes for their failures, and we do. But we are guilty of them ourselves. We are too far removed from those who lived their lives in Grenfell. ...

I am still haunted too by my own link with what happened at Grenfell Tower.

On the 20th of April this year [2017], I was involved with Bill Gates in judging a schools' debate, a competition in London. I was there to judge the best floor speech. I had little difficulty in deciding the winner, Firdows Kedir, a remarkably poised hijab-wearing twelve-year-old from West London. She was confident. She used language beautifully. Bill Gates grasped her hand and gave her the award.

On the 19th of June, a mere two months later, reporting from Grenfell, I spotted a picture of Firdows on a 'missing' poster. She and her entire family of five are believed to have been incinerated together on the 22nd floor of Grenfell Tower. Two weeks ago, it was confirmed that remnants of Firdows and her father had indeed been found, in their flat, and that their identities had been confirmed using DNA.

Firdows had been described as 'the most intelligent, wise, eloquent girl'. I was fortunate to witness that first-hand and since then I often think what might she have become ... ?

Like my fellow journalists, I have spent many hours around Grenfell. I've come to know a number of the survivors, and I speak to them regularly by phone or email. So casually written off as nameless migrants, scroungers, illegals, and the rest. Actually, and it should be no shock to us, the tower was full of talent. Not least the wonderful and talented Khadija Saye, who died with her mother, on the verge of a major breakthrough as an artist. Or community leaders like Eddie Daffarn, who survived the inferno, but who wrote that warning blog on October 20th, 2016.

We the media report the lack of diversity in other walks of life, but our own record is nothing like good enough. The Sutton Trust has revealed this year that just under 80% of top editors were educated at private schools or grammar schools. Compare that with the 88% of the British public now in comprehensives.

It's why I want to urge everyone and anyone in this room with the power to do it: give individuals who work with and for you the space to do something, anything, in the wider community we are here to communicate with. It is one fertile route to discovering lives and issues about which we might never learn. ...

I have no desire to find myself at another disaster in another area of social housing that we never knew existed, where people are shouting: 'Why weren't you here before?' ...

I do not dream of the wars and pestilence that I have reported. But when it came to Grenfell Tower, I was haunted. And I still am. I woke every morning possessed by the enormity of it, and of its implications. ...

The flaring walls, the burnt-out husk, the resilience and diversity of the survivors have come together as a wake-up call to the true state of divided Britain.

Chapter 7

Contextual elements: 'the patronising disposition of unaccountable power'

> The patronising disposition of unaccountable power is a cultural condition. … One of its core features is an instinctive prioritisation of the reputation of an organisation over the citizen's right to expect people to be held to account for their actions. … What is needed is a change in attitude, culture, heart and mind.
>
> The Right Reverend James Jones KBE, 2017[1]

> [This has] helped to create a cultural issue across the sector, which can be described as a 'race to the bottom'.
>
> Building a Safer Future, Final Report, May 2018[2]

> There remains a lack of widespread, proactive leadership.
>
> Industry Safety Steering Group, August 2020[3]

Late at night, on 26 April 1986, a team of nuclear workers prepared to conduct a test on Reactor 4 of the Chernobyl nuclear plant.

Part of an otherwise-routine shutdown, the exercise was designed to test a modified safety system to determine how long the reactor's steam turbines would continue to power the coolant pumps following a loss of main electrical power supply. Ironically, conducting it meant that automatic shutdown devices were inhibited and the emergency core cooling system was shut down. A previous attempt to conduct the test had failed. At 1.24 a.m. the reactor was hit by two massive explosions, scattering radioactive material over a large area. It remains the world's worst nuclear disaster.[4]

Two workers died in the initial explosion, and twenty-eight of the firemen and emergency cleaning team that attended the site immediately after the explosion died in the three months that followed, mostly from acute radiation sickness. The official death toll is thirty-one, but a UN report in 2005 estimated that a further 4,000 people might eventually die from radiation exposure.[5] About 200,000 people are believed to have been relocated as a result of the accident.[6]

The Chernobyl disaster led to an understanding of the importance of safety culture in preventing catastrophic events. A report by the International Nuclear Safety Advisory Group concluded:

> The need to create and maintain a 'safety culture' is a precondition for ensuring nuclear power plant safety. The concept of 'safety culture' relates to a very general concept of dedication and personal responsibility of all those involved in any safety related activity at a nuclear power plant. ... [It] even covers the highest spheres of administration, including the legal and governmental ones which, according to the concept, must create a national climate in which attention is paid to nuclear safety on a daily basis.[7]

This statement has relevance far beyond the nuclear sector. We (and I include myself here) bandy about terms like culture without much debate or enquiry about what it means or how we might affect it. For example, Dame Judith Hackitt (author of the 2018 'Independent Review of Building Regulation and Fire Safety') recently said that a key requirement of the proposed legislation would be a 'change of culture', with much more focus on collaboration between the firms working on a project, stating that this needed to start in the boardroom.[8]

And 'rebel resident' Eddie Daffarn said during evidence to the GTI:

> They [the RBKC and KCTMO] didn't treat us with respect or humanity or empathy, and if they had done, we wouldn't be sitting here now. ... But what's really, really important is that the culture of the KCTMO, the lack of scrutiny by RBKC, is I believe a

causative factor of what happened on the night of the fire and what led to the fire.[9]

This chapter considers how contextual elements such as culture and attitudes impact our ability to prevent and learn from catastrophic events. As with relational issues (see chapter 6), this receives insufficient attention.

The *Oxford English Dictionary* describes context as: 'The circumstances that form the setting for an event, statement, or idea, and in terms of which it can be fully understood and assessed.'[10] Contextual issues are difficult to explore as they involve understanding deep-seated and often hidden and unconscious biases, attitudes, values and beliefs. Understanding how these created the context inside of which Grenfell (and other disasters) happened is critical to learning. The importance of context cannot be overestimated.

On a personal level, I grew up white and privileged in South Africa. My family were liberal, and I was taught from a young age that racism was wrong. My mother and grandmother were members of Black Sash, a human rights organization that fought for equality. My dad, a lawyer, was 'silenced' by his company for publishing letters questioning the legality of racism. I worked to bring about change in higher education in a post-apartheid world. I distinctly remember the palpable joy of standing in the long, mixed-race queues to vote in the first free and fair elections in my country in 1994.

But there was another incident that, in retrospect, shaped my worldview significantly.

As is usually the case, my circle of friends and those I worked with held similar beliefs. Our view was that racists were wrong and didn't deserve to be interacted with.

And then, one day, I ended up sitting next to an openly racist white man on a long bus journey. My normal response would have been to say something disparaging, decline to engage and move seats. But the bus was packed, and we were stuck together for six hours. We began talking, and after a while I asked about his racism. As clearly as if it was yesterday, I recall the story he told me. The story of watching his brother being stabbed to death by some black youths. The story of his anger and pain.

For the first time I could understand why someone was racist. Rather than judging and assessing him from some lofty liberal ideal,

I felt deep compassion for him. And while I didn't agree with his views, or condone them, they made sense to me.

That interaction, nearly thirty years ago, taught me the power of context, and that exploring and understanding others' views and perspectives gave access to something very different from judgemental, binary views.

Drawing on the story of the response to the Hillsborough disaster, I begin by exploring the myth that you can enable systemic change without shifting deeply held assumptions and beliefs. I then look at the context we are currently operating in by exploring the web of competing tensions faced by those in power, decision making and bias, the role of media and measurement, and the symbolic significance of actions. 'Lessons from Grenfell' looks at the burning of the Grenfell 'effigy' and how 'othering' inhibits our ability to learn. In the 'two questions' section I propose that a lack of political will and intent is the condition that holds in place our inability to learn, and that collectively exploring our deeply held assumptions is an opportunity to disrupt the status quo.

THE MYTH THAT YOU CAN ENABLE SYSTEMIC CHANGE WITHOUT SHIFTING DEEPLY HELD ASSUMPTIONS AND BELIEFS

Let us explore the impact of context and culture on responding to catastrophic events through the story of those who lost loved ones in the Hillsborough Stadium disaster.

Lessons from the bereaved: the Hillsborough Stadium disaster

On 15 April 1989 a fatal crush at a football match killed 96 people and injured 766. In the aftermath, the police fed the media false stories that hooliganism and drunkenness among Liverpool fans had caused the disaster.

'The patronising disposition of unaccountable power', a 2017 report commissioned by the House of Commons 'to ensure the pain and suffering of the Hillsborough families is not repeated', describes their experience of the police, agencies across the justice system and the media. The report stresses that 'it does not simply describe a historic state of affairs, but instead one that stretches forward to today'.[11]

The report's author, the Right Reverend James Jones, describes a 'patronising disposition' as:

A cultural condition, a mindset which defines how organisations and people within them behave and which can act as an unwritten, even unspoken, connection between individuals in organisations. One of its core features is an instinctive prioritisation of the reputation of an organisation over the citizen's right to expect people to be held to account for their actions. This represents a barrier to real accountability.[12]

Jones goes on to stress that:

As a cultural condition, this mindset is not automatically changed, still less dislodged, by changes in policies and processes. What is needed is a change in attitude, culture, heart and mind.[13]

What happened

Fans had gathered at Hillsborough Stadium, Sheffield Wednesday's football ground. The mood was described as 'boisterous' but jovial. A large crowd built up outside the Leppings Lane turnstiles, and following an urgent request to relieve the pressure, match commander Chief Superintendent David Duckenfield gave an order to open an exit gate.

Two thousand Liverpool fans passed through a tunnel onto already-packed terraces. A severe crush developed in the central pens and people were pulled out in a 'human cascade'.

Ninety-six men, women and children lost their lives. The oldest victim was 67 years old, the youngest was 10.[14]

As the disaster unfolded, Duckenfield told key people that a gate was 'forced' by Liverpool fans. This claim was reinforced in briefings to media sources, and the lie went around the world in TV and radio news bulletins. Newspapers pointed the finger at 'drunk and ticketless' supporters. The Sun printed a now symbolic and infamous front page that alleged that Liverpool fans had 'urinated on police officers' and 'picked the pockets of the dead'.[15] Twenty-three years later, the paper published 'the real truth' and apologized for false reports (figure 15).[16]

Figure 15. *The Sun*'s front page stories about the Hillsborough disaster twenty-three years apart. (*Source: The Sun*/News Licensing. Reprinted with permission.)[17]

The aftermath[18]

A judicial inquiry – 'The Taylor Report' – completed in January 1990 concluded that the failure to close off the tunnel was 'a blunder of the first magnitude' and that match commander David Duckenfield 'failed to take effective control'. Despite this, the initial coroner's inquests completed in 1991 ruled all deaths accidental. Particularly controversial was a decision by the coroner, Dr Stefan Popper, not to accept any evidence from after 3.15 p.m., saying that by then 'the damage was done'. This was strongly disputed by the bereaved, who received no state legal support during the inquests.

Twenty years after the disaster, following continuous lobbying by the families, the Hillsborough Independent Panel was formed in 2009 to review the evidence. Its report, released in 2012, confirmed criticisms against the police, revealed details about the extent of police efforts to shift blame onto fans, and highlighted the errors of the first coroner's inquests. It said that forty-one of those who died might have been saved. The panel's report resulted in the quashing of the previous findings of accidental death and to the creation of new coroner's inquests.

The second coroner's inquests were held between 2014 and 2016. Twenty-seven years after the disaster, these inquests ruled that supporters were unlawfully killed due to gross negligence.[19] The fans had played no part in the deaths, and instead police failures, stadium design faults and a delayed response by the ambulance service were blamed.[20]

In 2017 the Crown Prosecution Service announced that Duckenfield was to be charged with manslaughter by gross negligence. The trial began in 2019 but the jury failed to return a verdict on the manslaughter charge, so prosecutors sought a retrial. In November 2019, after a six-week trial at Preston Crown Court, Duckenfield was found not guilty of the gross negligence manslaughter of Liverpool fans.[21] This serves as further confirmation of the difficulties with 'legal' justice following catastrophes (see chapter 5).[22]

Some quotes from those closely involved are given below. Allowing ourselves to be impacted by the experience of those who were most affected is key to both understanding and shifting context. Rather than judge, or allowing ourselves to be shocked or outraged or defensive, my invitation is to read in order to gain insight into the culture and context that drove these actions. Read with compassion.

In the words of the Hillsborough families[23]

Then that dreadful day [he] went to a football match and never came home. We waited till 12.30 on that day, phoning all day, but no answer. So, we went to Sheffield hoping he was at a hospital. But he was at the gym [where they had taken the bodies]. They [the police] would not let me touch him and said he belongs to us, I shouted at them and said he does not belong to you – Anthony is my son. ... We then made our way to the medical centre. We identified Anthony and still couldn't hold him. They were so stern with us.

Betty Almond, mother of Anthony Kelly

Police officers visited my mum shortly after the disaster. Their behaviour was uncaring, arrogant and insulting – it reduced my mum to tears. They brought my dad's belongings in a bin liner and just tipped them on the floor. They said, 'What was an old man doing going to a game like that?'

Gordon Baron, son of Gerard Baron

I realised for the first time that losing a loved one in any disaster is a very public affair and there is scant regard for the bereaved families. The press and media litter details of disasters to suit themselves without thinking of the consequences.

Dorothy Griffiths, sister of Vincent Fitzsimmons

Police interests were well represented but the families – 43 of them – were represented by only one barrister, which we had to fund ourselves.

A family member

[At the first inquest] they actually read out the names of everybody and the amount of alcohol. They read our 14 year-old son's name out and then said 'nil'. I was horrified. ... It was very hurtful.

Edna Murray, mother of Paul Murray

The [new] inquests started with the family background statements which became known as pen portraits. It was an incredibly difficult process for us but was so important and an excellent idea. Instead of our son being Number 17 we were able to tell the jury about his life. For the first time our son was dealt with as a person rather than just a number.

Barry and Jac Devonside, parents of Christopher Devonside

You can only have reconciliation once you've had truth and accountability.

Trevor Hicks, father of Sarah and Victoria Hicks

Other voices
David Conn, who has written extensively for *The Guardian* on the subject of Hillsborough, wrote the following in a submission to Reverend Jones:

I believe that your report should consider how, after the Taylor report [the initial report] was so conclusive, and the Prime Minister of the day given so severe a warning about the police's inability to 'perceive and admit faults', the police were not held to account at all by the government. ... I have not seen that the government expressed any concern about the conduct and findings of the first inquest, which became the major injustice against which the families had to campaign.[24]

And here are the proponents of a proposed new bill (the Public Authority Accountability Bill, known informally as 'The Hillsborough Law') on why it is needed:

Public authorities and servants should tell the truth and act with candour – the sad fact is that they generally don't. Institutional defensiveness and a culture of denial are endemic amongst public institutions as has been demonstrated not only by the Hillsborough cover up but countless other examples. ... But the police are by no means the only public institution where such a culture prevails.[25]

In advance of the release of the 2012 Hillsborough Independent Panel's report, David Crompton, then the chief constable of South Yorkshire Police, sent an email to senior colleagues:

Can we talk on Mon/Tues about how we use our own website next week. I think we may be missing a trick.

I'm thinking that on Thursday morning at 8am we launch on our own public-facing website a page called something like ...'Hillsborough ... did you know? (I'm trying to think of a non-threatening title.)

We then publish links to CC [Chief Constable] apologies in the past, ... the Peter Wright memo saying we would not criticise the fans etc... etc... We keep it purely factual and always refer to the original source document. We then publicise it on Twitter. In effect, it amounts to the case for the defence. One thing is certain – the Hillsborough Campaign for Justice will be doing their version. ... In fact their version of certain events has become 'the truth' even though it isn't!!

I just have the feeling that the media 'machine' favours the families and not us, so we need to be a bit more innovative in our response to have a fighting chance otherwise we will just be road kill.[26]

On failures to learn

There had been previous incidents of crush. Forty-three years before Hillsborough, thirty-three people died and more than 500 were injured at an FA Cup tie between Bolton Wanderers and Stoke City. The Home Office inquiry that followed criticized the police and ground officials for not realizing the significance of the build-up outside the ground.[27]

And five years prior to Hillsborough, on 18 June 1984, a South Yorkshire Police operation referred to as 'The battle of Orgreave' took place. The operation involved thousands of striking miners. Scenes of police violence including horse charges and officers beating miners dominated television news. Fifty-five miners were arrested and charged with rioting, but the prosecutions fell apart after the trial of the first fifteen in 1985. The court case revealed not the guilt of the accused but the failings of the South Yorkshire Police.

Even after the collapse of the trial, following revelations of what appeared to be police malpractice, the South Yorkshire Police force were not held to account. Nor was there any reform. Four years later, Peter Wright, the chief constable who had overseen the operations at Orgreave, was still in charge, and there still hasn't been an inquiry into Orgreave. According to a 2017 *Guardian* article, 'many of the Hillsborough bereaved believe that the force's inhumane response was bred and given official sanction by the harsh policing of the miners' strike'.[28]

Theresa May, speaking to the Police Federation in 2016 when Home Secretary, said:

> Remember Hillsborough. Let it be a touchstone for everything you do. Never forget those who died in that disaster or the 27 years of hurt endured by their families and loved ones. Let the hostility, the obfuscation and the attempts to blame the fans serve as a reminder of the need for change. Make sure your institutions, whose job it is to protect the public, never again fail to put the public first. And put professionalism and integrity at the heart of every decision, every interaction, and every dealing with the public you have.[29]

The contextual iceberg

I don't believe it is possible to enable systemic change without shifting the context inside of which people are operating. But what does that mean?

While iceberg models are overused, in this instance they are perfect for exploring context, where the hidden underwater aspects are far more ominous and dangerous than the icy peaks above the water's surface. The contextual iceberg in figure 16 illustrates both the visible and the hidden aspects of context in order to provide a framework for understanding the circumstances that form the setting or background inside of which we act and illustrates why simply changing a regulation will not lead to systemic change.

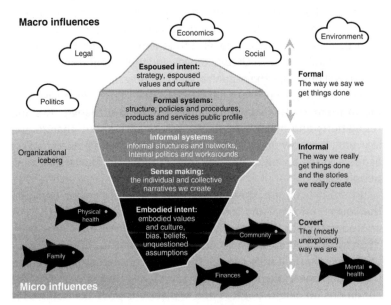

Figure 16. The contextual iceberg.

The iceberg itself represents any organization or institution, in the public sector or the private sector. Above the water line are the espoused intent and formal systems. These constitute what an organization says it values, what it says it does, and how it does it.

Underneath the water are the informal systems. These represent the way things really get done: via informal networks, internal politics and workarounds.

At the bottom of the iceberg is the embodied intent of those within the organization: that is, what is really valued and believed, including unconscious biases, deeply held assumptions, and group norms and culture. This is, for the most part, neither conscious nor articulated – it is simply the way things are here.

Between this layer and the informal systems is a sense-making layer. Humans have a unique ability to create stories and narratives, in order to make meaning and sense of our worlds. Again, this is hidden from the external world and mostly unexamined, consisting of the stories we tell ourselves, and the informal 'water-cooler' conversations we have that are key drivers of change.

Surrounding the iceberg are macro and micro influences. For example, the PESTLE environment (i.e. the political, economic, social, technological, legal and environmental factors) will impact an organization at a macro level, and at a micro level issues such as an individual's personal circumstances and their mental and physical health will influence the organizational iceberg.

When trying to prevent catastrophic events or when responding to them we tend to focus on the visible: we change laws and regulations and make bold public statements about change and learning. But how much attention do we pay to the hidden, covert aspects, or to trying to understand attitudes and beliefs, or how people feel?

In strong cultures there is resonance and alignment between the covert, informal and formal layers of the iceberg, and there is an understanding that openly engaging with and exploring areas of dissonance where these layers are not aligned is critical. Without understanding and shifting both the visible contextual elements and the hidden ones, I do not believe that systemic change – altering the conditions holding the status quo in place – is possible. Doing so is fraught with challenges.

KEY ISSUES AND CHALLENGES

In this section I explore five 'irreconcilable goals' that my observations have told me those in government are facing. These create a web of competing tensions that help to make sense of some seemingly perplexing decisions. I then discuss how an understanding of the role of unconscious bias in shaping context and decisions is critical, as is the role of media and what we measure. Finally, I look at how the symbolic significance of our actions impacts trust.

The web of competing tensions

As we have seen throughout this book, safety (or a lack of it) is created by people (politicians, executives, workers, etc.) who are navigating complex trade-offs between irreconcilable goals.[30] This is particularly important in government given the weaknesses that exist in governance (see chapter 3) and accountability mechanisms (see chapter 4), meaning that good decisions are often reliant on an individual's capacity to navigate these hurdles successfully.

I have observed five 'tensions' that have helped me understand seemingly poor and perplexing decisions. While they are presented as dichotomies below, they are more accurately thought of as a web of competing tensions that create the context inside of which decisions get made. Navigating these tensions well would require shifting from 'either/or' thinking to more complex 'both/and' thinking (see chapter 4).

Importantly, these are collectively created: our role, as citizens, is as important in creating the context as is that of politicians. Ultimately, we determine what is or is not acceptable based on what we demand from politicians and who we vote for.

Siloed versus holistic perspectives

The siloed structure of government and its complex delivery frameworks, involving multiple stakeholders and departments (chapter 4), work against holistic or systemic views or solutions. For example, rather than considering how to tap diverse and distributed knowledge in any complex situation (chapter 6), we instead focus on the siloed and piecemeal issue of ensuring the voices of residents of high-rise buildings are heard. And then we fail to transfer these insights to other contexts, such as listening to frontline NHS staff during the Covid-19 pandemic or leaseholders when it comes to remediating fire safety issues.

The failure to respond to calls for greater scrutiny of recommendations from inquiries, inquests and coroners' Prevention of Future Death Reports (chapter 5) keeps this siloed view in place.

No one is accountable for assessing from a holistic perspective how to best respond to and prevent catastrophic events. And the structure of government does not enable this.

Maintain power and spin versus admitting failure
To learn, you must be able to admit to failures and errors, preferably before anything catastrophic happens (chapter 5). At the heart of politics – whether at an international, national, local, organizational or community level – is the gaining of power and holding onto it. There is an inherent tension when faced with something that could diminish this power. While truth and transparency are laudable, when the potential consequences are a loss of power, it may make more sense to attempt to spin your way out of it, to deceive, or to hope no one will find out, rather than admit your errors.

In an adversarial political context – and with the rise of career politicians, where honour and value-driven leadership seem rare – admitting mistakes and failures would take enormous courage and a willingness to lose both power and the support of those with power.

Blame versus learning
Our failure to respond to and learn from catastrophic events is not new, and it is not simply the failure of one political party or a handful of politicians. Central and local government operate in a context where strategies of blame and blame avoidance (chapter 5) compete with a desire for learning. Faced with a choice between admitting to errors or blaming someone else and avoiding blame oneself, what decision would most politicians take? And what decisions do we reinforce in our responses on social media?

Until blame avoidance is not a primary political strategy, the opportunity for learning will be compromised.

Preventing low-probability events versus limited resources
In a world of limited resources and short-term, siloed thinking, it is easy to justify ignoring lower-probability, high-consequence risks, such as Covid-19 or known issues with external fire spread (chapter 3).

Imagine if, in mid 2019, before anyone had heard of coronavirus, headlines had appeared saying that millions had been wasted on PPE, accusing politicians of overreacting to the threat of a pandemic. Without the experience of going through one, we probably would all have concurred and lamented how bad the decision was.

To be prepared for a low-probability, high-impact event you must be willing to stand accused of overreacting. And given that success means that nothing happens – even if you are successful in, for example, your efforts to limit high-impact disruptions around Y2K – accusations of overreaction may still be posed. Resilience to catastrophic events requires an inbuilt adaptive capacity that is at odds with demands for efficiencies and savings.

Until politicians, key stakeholders, the public and the media are educated about, and supportive of, investment in the mitigation of low-probability events, we will continue to be unprepared. Until we are willing to work collaboratively and invest sufficient resource in understanding, preventing and responding to such events, we must be willing to accept the political, economic, social and human cost of them.

And this may well involve paying more taxes. One of the more amusing interactions in this regard occurred during the World Economic Forum meeting in Davos in 2019. With the rich and powerful gathered before him, the historian Rutger Bregman, participating on a panel about inequality, said he was bewildered that no one was talking about raising taxes on the rich:

> I hear people talking the language of participation, justice, equality and transparency but almost no one raises the real issue of tax avoidance, right? And of the rich just not paying their fair share. ... It feels like I'm at a firefighters conference and no one's allowed to speak about water.[31]

Building resilience to prevent catastrophic events costs money and so does a failure to do so. As the oft-used quote says, 'if you think safety is expensive, try having an accident'. This statement is poignant as we confront the costs of making buildings safe – estimated at £15 billion[32] – and the estimates made in September 2020 that Covid-19 is likely to have cost the UK government £317 billion in increased public borrowing in 2020/21 alone.[33]

Control versus trusting 'sharp-end' voices

Old notions of elitist power, where the few dictate and control the rules for the many, fail to take into account that distributed knowledge and expertise is critical in increasingly complex environments (see chapter 6).

As demonstrated by many of the stories in this book, history tells us that the interplay between those at the top of the power ladder and those at the bottom is critical to both learning from and preventing catastrophic events. Think of the failure to listen to residents' safety concerns in the lead up to Grenfell, or the fact that reports from train drivers about the difficulty of seeing signals were ignored in the lead up to the Ladbroke Grove train crash. Think too about the response to the concerns of frontline health workers about PPE during the Covid-19 crisis.

The tacit knowledge of those at the sharp end is critical to operating effectively in increasingly complex environments. But tapping this knowledge requires people to give up on traditional notions of control, which could be threatening to those in power. This tension played out starkly during Covid-19, where central government attempts at control were met with increasing local resistance: for example, the mayor of Greater Manchester said that a centrally mandated local lockdown would be refused unless the government provided further financial support for those impacted by it.[34]

This network of tensions begins to illustrate the context inside of which decisions such as a failure to prepare for Covid-19 or continued failures to learn from catastrophic events make sense. For me, it creates a compelling (and depressing) case for why politicians might choose to spin, attempt to deceive or make the least controversial decisions, but all of these (in)actions contribute to the persistence of the status quo. As does the role of bias in decision making.

Bias and decision making

Which of the lines below is longer?

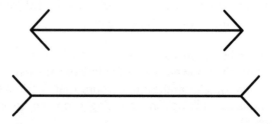

The bottom line, right? Actually, no. You can confirm with a ruler that they are in fact the same length.

The Nobel-winning economist Daniel Kahneman uses this illustration in his book *Thinking, Fast and Slow* to demonstrate system 1 and system 2 thinking.[35] Fast system 1 thinking comes up with the instinctive answer that the bottom line is longer, while the more rational and considered system 2 thinks more slowly about the length and may measure the lines to confirm whether or not they are the same length. I would recommend Kahneman's book to anybody who wants to explore bias and its impact on our decisions.

System 1 operates automatically and quickly, with little or no effort and no sense of voluntary control. Some examples of when we use it include

- driving a car on an empty road,
- understanding simple sentences,
- orienting ourselves to a source of sound and detecting that one object is more distant than another, and
- recognizing that a 'meek and tidy soul with a passion for detail' resembles an occupational stereotype.[36]

On the other hand, system 2 allocates attention to effortful mental activities. It is often associated with the subjective experience of agency, choice and concentration. Some examples of system 2 thinking include

- looking for a woman with white hair,
- checking the validity of a complex argument,
- searching one's memory to identify a surprising sound, and
- monitoring the appropriateness of one's behaviour in a given social context.[37]

Kahneman speaks of the systems as if they were characters in a story. And while most of us, if asked, would describe ourselves as 'system 2 thinkers', this is not the case. The two kinds of thinking fulfil different roles, and every one of us uses both systems. It is in the interaction between them that both efficiencies and dangers lie. System 1 is error prone; system 2 is lazy.

The division of labour between the systems minimizes effort and optimizes performance. This normally works well. System 1 is in control most of the time, mobilizing system 2 only when increased effort is required or if it detects that an error has been made. System 1 efficiently responds to models of familiar situations, usually predicting the short term accurately and deciding on appropriate reactions swiftly. *Usually*.

The problem is that system 1 has biases: systemic errors that it is prone to making.[38] And it cannot be turned off. Kahneman categorizes these flaws into 'heuristics and biases', 'overconfidence' and 'choices', and he details how our decision making can be compromised. Here are some examples.

The law of small numbers (heuristics and biases).[39] We have an exaggerated faith in small samples and pay more attention to the content of messages than to information about their reliability. We end up with a view of the world that is simpler and more coherent than the available data justifies. Statistics produce many observations that beg for causal explanations, but many facts of the world are due to chance. Causal explanations of chance events are inevitably wrong. Jumping to conclusions is safer in our imagination than it is in reality.

Expert intuition: when can we trust it (overconfidence)?[40] When experts are in environments that are regular and where they have sufficient experience, relying on intuition is appropriate. In less regular – or low-validity – environments, system 1 produces quick answers to difficult questions by substitution, creating coherence when there is none. Failing to understand the conditions under which one should rely on one's expertise can lead to overconfidence, from both experts and those that rely on their intuition.

Rare events (choices).[41] When it comes to rare events, our mind is not designed to get things quite right. The probability of rare events will often be overestimated, because of the confirmatory bias of memory. A rare event will be overweighted, especially if it attracts a lot of attention. For example, obsessive concerns, vivid images and explicit reminders contribute to overweighting probabilities. And when there is a lack of attention and hence no overweighting, there will be neglect. And as Kahneman says, 'Given we are likely to be exposed to events no one has experienced yet, this is not good news.'[42] It is likely that, post-Grenfell, due to overweighting caused by significant attention, we are overestimating the probability of another high-rise cladding fire leading to fatalities. Likewise, due to a lack of attention, we may well be ignoring or underestimating an 'unexperienced' event due to issues with product safety that go beyond insulation and cladding, or high-rise buildings.

We are all biased and this impacts our decisions. We saw this in the Boeing and Hillsborough case studies earlier in the book, which demonstrated the dangers of groupthink and herd behaviour. And we looked, too, at how hindsight bias limits our ability to explore why actions make sense.

When we fail to be responsible for our biases, weak decisions are made.

Our biases are sometimes helpful, sometimes dangerous. For example, optimism bias is prevalent, and it can lead to poor decisions, but it is also responsible for bold innovations. What I particularly appreciate about Kahneman's work is that he doesn't advocate for 'removing biases' but rather for being responsible for them. System 1 and system 2 thinking helps us understand how to do that.

This work has influenced me greatly, and in two particular ways.

- I no longer rely on my instincts. I value them greatly and tend to trust them, but I relate to them as a sign to investigate further rather than considering them to be the truth.
- I am obsessive about diversity. I put together consulting teams based on who will bring diverse thinking not on who I like working with. I follow people I disagree with on social media. I read papers I would normally avoid.

When asked for advice about how to avoid ceding important system 2 decisions and calculations to system 1, Kahneman's answer was, 'slow down, sleep on it, and ask your most brutal and least empathetic close friends ... who understand your feeling but are not overly impressed by them'.[43]

I think we often miss the point of diversity. While there are obvious moral arguments for ensuring it, the main thing is that we cannot hope to make good decisions in an increasingly uncertain and complex world without it. Diversity is the most effective antidote to bias that we have. This is why ministers' recommendations to remove unconscious bias training (see chapter 6) – appearing to dismiss the whole notion rather than acknowledging that the training they had procured was ineffective and proposing some other solution to guard against bias and thus ensure good decision making – troubles me.

Media and measurement

As with bias, the roles of the media and of measurement warrant their own books, and while I will not delve into them deeply, they are critical to contributing to and shaping context.

Holding those in power to account is said to be the primary accountability of the traditional media, or the 'fourth estate'. They also have a role in shaping narratives and context, as we saw in the case of Hillsborough. But the media is in crisis. Declining revenues have led to paywalls that restrict access, and political alliances determine readership: for example, *The Times* is mostly ready by Conservative voters, while Labour supporters mainly read *The Guardian*. In addition, the rise of social media and the 'fifth estate' (outlier views published by bloggers, non-mainstream journalists and on social media) means we are increasingly turning to less traditional (and, in many cases, less reliable) news sources.

We have seen throughout this book that diversity is needed if we are to successfully navigate increasing complexity, and the 'internet of things' offers an opportunity for this. The amount of data and information that we have access to is unprecedented. But social media algorithms and how we engage with their platforms mean that we create bubbles of connections. Rather than expand our views, we have used our access to information to create reinforcing loops, narrowing and confirming our existing views and biases rather than challenging them.

In addition to how we engage with the media, how the media reports stories also shapes the broader context.

My experience post-Grenfell has left me concerned that most media focuses on piecemeal news rather than exploring systemic and contextual issues. So, for the most part, the Grenfell Inquiry only makes the news when some particularly controversial evidence is presented. The systemic issues don't get explored, and this reinforces our piecemeal approach to change. (There are exceptions to this, of course, and in the case of Grenfell, the trade magazine

Inside Housing has provided extraordinary and systemic coverage since the fire, as has the BBC Grenfell Inquiry podcast.)

Issues such as the lack of mechanisms for ensuring inquiry and inquest recommendations are appropriately implemented and effective, and our continued failure to tap tacit and distributed knowledge may not be 'news', but from the perspective of holding government to account, these things should surely get more coverage.

The danger with how the media – both the fourth and fifth estates – operates, and how we interact with it, is that it confirms rather than challenge our biases.

A seemingly unrelated topic is measurement. What we pay attention to, measure and control is a key 'culture-embedding mechanism' according to Edgar Schein, former professor at the MIT Sloan School of Management, who has made a notable mark on the field of organizational development.[44]

Regarding safety, we tend to focus on measuring lagging indicators. We concentrate only on the outcome. While that is important, a focus on lagging indicators – especially when linked to performance bonuses – can be dangerous and can unintentionally drive the wrong behaviours. By way of example, I recount the following story about a processing plant.

It was near the end of the year and safety targets were very close to being met. A security guard was suspicious and stopped a contractor truck as it was leaving site. One of the contractors had in fact broken his leg conducting work, but had that been reported, the lagging indicator (the 'lost time injury', or LTI) target would have been missed and bonuses would not have been paid. So rather than treat him on site and report the injury, the contractors were moving him off site. An injury that happened outside the plant did not count, so they planned to report it as having happened elsewhere.

Stories like this are not unusual.

A focus on creating measurement dashboards that combine leading and lagging indicators and on tying rewards to the presence of leading indicators has the potential to alter the context and the culture. What if we were to measure whether frontline workers were being included in critical decisions and whether they felt safe to speak up, or the presence of barriers (such as compliant fire doors) in high rises, or the percentage of items raised in fire risk assessments that have been completed to a high standard.

The world of bias, measurement and the role of the media are intricately entwined with shaping context, as are the actions of those with power.

The resonant dissonant dance

There is often a dissonance between what those in power say, or what we expect of them, and what they actually do. My experience of the last three years has been a constant erosion of my trust, an accumulation of dissonant actions, with the odd resonant one to briefly give hope. There appears to me to be little understanding of – and scant attention paid to – the symbolic significance of actions and their impact on shaping context.

I have come to call this the resonant dissonant dance.

Think of the multiple times that ministers have said that lease-holders should not pay for remediation of unsafe buildings but have then failed to enshrine their words in law – and then subtly changed the narrative from 'should not pay' to 'it should be affordable' (see chapter 2). Or the appointment to the Grenfell Inquiry panel of Benita Mehra, who had links to the manufacturer of the ACM cladding used on Grenfell yet failed to disclose this, leaving it to Grenfell United to discover during their own research?[45] Consider too the appointment of Gavin Barwell to the board of Clarion Housing, the UK's largest housing association, when he ignored letters to change Approved Document B in the run up to Grenfell and is expected to appear at the inquiry.[46]

Irrespective of the qualifications or merits of Barwell or Mehra, or the legitimacy of the decisions to appoint them, there is a symbolism to these actions, and to how they are communicated, that erodes trust.

As the philosopher Onora O'Neill says:

Deception is the real enemy of trust. ... Deceivers mislead intentionally, and it is because their falsehood is deliberate, and because it implies a deliberate intention to undermine, damage or distort others' plans and their capacities to act, that it damages trust and future relationships. ...

Perhaps it is not then surprising that public distrust has grown in the very years in which openness and transparency have been so avidly pursued. Transparency certainly destroys secrecy: but it may not limit the deception and deliberate misinformation that undermine relations of trust. If we want to restore trust, we need to reduce deception and lies rather than secrecy.[47]

A good example of this is the saga of Dominic Cummings's journey to the north of England during the UK's first Covid-19 lockdown. On 22 May 2020 *The Guardian* and *The Daily Mirror* newspapers published details about how Cummings, the British prime minister's most senior aide, had broken lockdown rules by travelling to a family estate with his wife (who had suspected Covid-19) and child. This transgression was the first by someone in public office that was not immediately followed by an apology and/or resignation. Instead, the transgression was justified – including, infamously, a claim that a forty-mile drive to the town of Barnard Castle was so that Cummings could test his eyes.[48]

Research published in *The Lancet* shows that this story had an immediate impact. Analysis of over 200,000 surveys from more than 40,000 individuals in England, Scotland and Wales showed that these events undermined confidence in the government to handle the pandemic. The paper concluded: 'These data show the negative and lasting consequences that political decisions can have for public trust and the risks to behaviours.'[49]

What is often missed when people look at this story is the issue of accountability. As an advisor to the prime minister, Cummings has no accountability to the public. As the Institute for Government's Jill Rutter pointed out in a prescient video more than four months before the saga: 'When [Cummings] causes mayhem, Johnson has to accept responsibility. Cummings has zero authority. Johnson is 100% accountable.'[50]

The experience of deception was therefore multi-layered: it was about the trip itself but also about the lack of consequences or appropriately placed accountability. Amid calls for Cummings's resignation, or at least an apology, the prime minister appeared to place his personal loyalty to his advisor over the will of the people, many of whom were calling for Cummings's resignation.

According to *The Times*, Cummings's instinct was to ignore the story. One source was quoted as saying: 'His attitude was this was a non-story; it's left-wing papers and they can go f*** themselves.

He refused to comment and banned anyone else from commenting.'[51] But research showed that the degree of public interest in the Durham trip was high, surpassing that in Meghan and Harry's royal wedding.[52]

My point is not about passing judgement on the legitimacy of the decisions or the appropriateness of actions. It is about the seeming lack of attention paid to – or understanding of or care about – the symbolic significance of dissonant (and resonant) actions and their impact on trust. In strong cultures, there is an awareness by those with power that trust between all levels of an organization is important, and that the symbolic significance of their actions will either build or destroy this trust.

And as I watch the continued attempts of those in power to deceive and spin, I have begun to view my lack of trust not as a problem but a useful indicator that all is not well. Blindly trusting those in power – which, to an extent at least, I did prior to Grenfell – is not wise, and it contributes to a failure to collectively hold them to account. As so eloquently put by Onora O'Neill in the Reith lectures, it is an issue of trustworthiness rather than trust.[53]

LESSONS FROM GRENFELL: 'OTHERING' AND EFFIGIES

It took a while for the many hurtful statements that appeared on social media after the fire to sink in. I hadn't appreciated the level of racism and ignorance that existed about high-rise buildings – about my neighbours and the place I'd called home. Naively, I had assumed that Grenfell would bring people together, and I was shocked and deeply saddened by the derogatory and inaccurate posts and tweets about 'immigrants' and 'the poor'.

A video of a group of people burning a cardboard effigy of a high-rise with 'Grenfell Tower' written on it and images of people standing at the windows was recorded at a private party in south London on 3 November 2018 (figure 17).[54] It was uploaded to YouTube and sparked outrage. No successful prosecution followed, with the millionaire property developer accused of burning the effigy saying that it was 'just banter' and denying being racist.[55]

I struggle to understand the context surrounding this as I imagine people taking the time to make the model, label it Grenfell tower and laugh and joke as they put it on a bonfire and watched it burn.

Figure 17. The Grenfell effigy.

The notion of 'othering' has helped me make some sense of actions like these – actions that are symbolic of our divided world. 'Outgroup homogeneity bias' refers to the judgements we make about people from other groups. We say: 'We're all different from one another. But them? They are all the same.' The concept of 'othering' is similar to demonstrating this ingroup/outgroup effect, where we see 'other groups' (often defined by arbitrary criteria) as showing less within-group variability.[56] This is true whether we are referring to football supporters or high-rise residents or politicians. I wonder how much we practise 'othering' to avoid having our basic and unconscious assumptions challenged – to keep in place the deep hidden aspects of the context we operate in. I reflect on the story of that bus trip that I shared at the beginning of this chapter, of how I 'othered' racists, and how this stopped me having compassion or meaningful conversations that might, just might, challenge some deeply held assumptions and lead to change.

All of us – politicians, the media, business leaders and citizens – have a role to play in creating contextual shifts. Unless we are willing to explore our biases and challenge our deeply held assumptions, systemic change will not happen.

This leads us to our usual two questions.

MAKING THE WATER VISIBLE: THE TWO QUESTIONS

From one perspective, I feel slightly uncomfortable answering the two questions in relation to context. More research is needed to explore the deeply held unconscious beliefs and values that are displacing our ability to effectively prevent and respond to catastrophic events. And the very lack of this research highlights the issue.

But from what I have observed since Grenfell, I fundamentally think that a lack of political will for real change is a condition holding in place the status quo, and that the creation of safe spaces for enquiry offers an opportunity for disruption.

Why don't we learn? A lack of political intent and will

Sometimes I feel like I've taken the red pill, and I dream of a previous life in which I was blissfully ignorant of the depths of our inability to learn.

A life where I believed that the Grenfell Tower fire, and the associated devastating loss of life, would be a catalyst for meaningful change. A life in which politicians acted with a sense of urgency to make peoples' homes safe. A life where ministers would admit failings and work across party lines to facilitate creative solutions to remediate buildings.

Where stakeholder industries (e.g. developers, construction, insurance and legal firms, and financial institutions) would come together to ensure that those living in unsafe buildings were not burdened with life-ruining financial consequences. Where those responsible for building unsafe buildings were equally responsible for correcting failures.

As I have confronted what meaningful systemic change would take and seen similar issues emerge around our failure to prepare for, or respond effectively to, Covid-19, I have come to believe that the condition holding our inability to learn in place is, at its heart, a lack of political intent and will.

I am not saying people don't care. I think many politicians care deeply. And this is not a party political point either. The failure goes back decades and applies to successive governments, and to the elite and the powerful that lobby and influence government decisions and choices.

So why haven't we dealt with the known failings in governance and accountability? Why haven't we dealt with the known weaknesses in inquiries and inquests?

I suspect many of the issues are simply too complex, and the risks of losing power when making necessary but unpopular decisions to create change are too acute. When considering how to enable systemic change, we should not wait or expect anything more than piecemeal siloed change from those in power in either government or industry.

At the same time, engaging in a different kind of conversation may disrupt things and enable change.

How might we enable systemic change? Create safe spaces to enquire into deeply held assumptions

There is much we can learn from understanding how to effectively change culture. Both cultural and contextual change involve challenging and shifting deeply held assumptions and beliefs.

When we consider the conditions holding our inability to learn in place – the lack of political will or intent, the unwillingness to rebalance power (chapter 6) or deal with weaknesses in governance and accountability (chapter 4), and the obsession with blame (chapter 5) – these don't live in espoused intents or strategies. Quite the opposite. They live under the surface in the contextual iceberg presented earlier – in the unquestioned and hidden embodied intentions: the assumptions, values, beliefs and biases that shape our narratives and actions. Without shifting these things, it is difficult to see how meaningful systemic change is possible.

The role of culture and of these, often unconscious, assumptions is starkly evident in the Hillsborough story. In their submission to Reverend Jones, Pete Weatherby QC and Elkan Abrahamson wrote that 'the families have been appalled at the approach of a range of public authorities even during the recent inquests: two police forces, the ambulance service, the local council – all pointing the finger at each other in order to escape censure'. South Yorkshire's Police and Crime Commissioner, Dr Billings, submitted a written contribution in which he spoke of his thoughts on the cultural change required in South Yorkshire police:

> For me, this was an indication that the force still had a way to go in moving to a place where it was not defensive and was open and transparent; a place which could not be labelled 'the patronising disposition of unaccountable power'. It is one of the challenges facing the new Chief Constable to ensure this cultural shift happens and is maintained.
>
> I would not underestimate this challenge. It is partly about the way many if not most organisations are tempted to react when criticised or found wanting. It is partly about the roles of Parliament, the media and the legal profession in creating an environment in which organisations feel able to admit, and apologise for, mistakes, and then to explore resolution together before positions become polarised and hardened. It is partly about the way each new generation of recruits is unconsciously socialised into an existing culture. In my view, insufficient attention is paid to the mechanism of inculturation by policing as a whole. If anything comes from your review as far as the police service is concerned, I would like to see some acknowledgement of this issue: how do you change a culture?[57]

The challenges of changing culture are critical to our ability to respond effectively to catastrophes. As a 2002 report by the International Energy Agency, titled 'Safety culture in nuclear installations', said:

> The biggest danger in trying to understand culture is to oversimplify it in our minds. It is tempting to say that culture is just 'the way we do things around here', or 'our basic values', or 'our rituals', and so on. These are all manifestations of the culture, but none is the culture at the level that culture matters. A better way to think about culture is to realize that it exists at several 'levels' and that we must endeavour to understand the different levels, but especially the deeper levels.[58]

Let us explore this some more.

Changing culture

According to Edgar Schein, 'Cultures are learned patterns of beliefs, values, assumptions, and behavioural norms that manifest themselves at different levels of observability.'[59] Rather than being static, cultures evolve. They are a shared product of shared learning.

Schein identifies three structural levels to culture: the artefacts of visible structures and process (what we see), espoused values (what we say) and underlying assumptions (unconscious, and the ultimate sources of values and actions). You cannot understand a culture by only looking at its artefacts or espoused beliefs and values, you need to explore and reveal the unconscious and underlying assumptions that are the source of values and actions.

I recall working with a team that was experiencing some quite severe safety challenges, with high-risk errors being made during the installation of a particular product. The managers and trainers kept assuring me that they trained their employees 'to do it correctly', walking me through their nicely laid out training facility and showing me the checklists that proved they covered this during training. They told me they had coaches to support the new recruits when they went into the field. All the usual artefacts and espoused values that are suggestive of a culture committed to supporting and following the correct processes.

And then, when I spent time chatting to the teams that actually did the work, I discovered that as soon as they completed the training, the coaches and supervisors told them to forget what they'd been taught. It was impossible to do the installations within the time allocated, they said, so workers were immediately taught several shortcuts to ensure they got the job done and met productivity targets. This pointed to a culture where workers felt that productivity was valued above following the correct process.

Culture change is difficult. Putting people through training programmes and creating new espoused values that you put on nice posters might help, but unless the unconscious underlying assumptions support whatever content is introduced, they will not be sustainable and they will not enable change. In fact, they may reinforce existing deeply held beliefs if people resist the changes.

Safety culture is often viewed as being distinct from broader organizational culture. In my own experience, focusing on creating a strong safety culture can in fact be an incredibly effective way of enabling broader culture change. In high-hazard industries, at least, changing ways of thinking and operating in the service of everybody being able to go home to their families is a compelling narrative that the majority of people will buy into. I have found Reason's components of safety culture (figure 18) useful both in articulating how complex creating a safe culture is and in pointing to areas of focus. Have we moved the dial on any of these significantly since Grenfell?

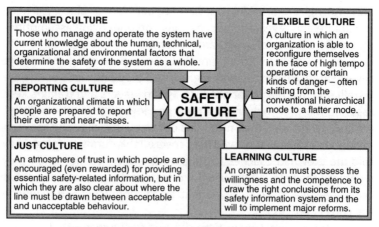

Figure 18. Components of safety culture based
on the work of James Reason.[60]

Culture is a group and social phenomenon through which, over time and with feedback, we learn what is or is not acceptable: 'When members reinforce each other's beliefs and values, they come to be taken for granted.'[61] Shifting cultures requires shifting these group dynamics.

I worry that our approach to 'cultural change' in the wake of Grenfell and other disasters is superficial. I have never seen a culture change come about because a senior executive or official report ordered it to happen or forced people to sit through a 'death by PowerPoint' presentation outlining nicely packaged arguments for change.

I am sceptical of approaches that fail to reveal or address the unconscious underlying assumptions that ultimately drive behaviour. Doing so requires extraordinary leadership by boards and executives, given the need to create a psychologically safe space in which to enquire into these deeply rooted beliefs and, where necessary, shift some of them. Change often entails intentionally creating a level of cognitive dissonance as you expose values and beliefs that are no longer appropriate. This is difficult, and it can have negative consequences if it isn't managed with great care and compassion.

It requires both unlearning and relearning, which can be destabilizing and threatening. I have found enquiry-and-observation-based qualitative approaches to be most effective, so long as the necessary conditions for psychological safety have been created.

I have seen very little of this post-Grenfell. Beyond one-line statements about the need for (and failure to) change culture, I have seen little space created for exploring the deeply held unconscious assumptions and beliefs among those involved in housing. Have we explored the beliefs of developers and architects and construction and building control regarding the role of regulations or their relationship with residents? Do we understand what deep-rooted and unconscious beliefs need to shift to truly have residents at the centre of post-Grenfell reform?

We bandy about terms like culture but we pay insufficient attention to how to change it. Creating psychologically safe spaces to explore difficult issues is critical.

Creating safe spaces
In February 2020 I co-hosted an event with Cambridge University's Bennett Institute for Public Policy that brought together a diverse group to enquire into our failure to learn from catastrophic events. One of the recommendations that participants felt could make a difference was the creation of safe spaces in which diverse groups could 'share and experience learning, and effective practice'.[62]

The creation of such spaces, where deeply held beliefs and unconscious assumptions can be brought to the surface and questioned, is critical if we are serious about systemic change. We need spaces where it is safe for people to share what might be unpopular or politically incorrect views. I find the following questions by Harvard Business School's Amy Edmondson helpful in evaluating how psychologically safe a space is.[63]

- If you make a mistake, will it be held against you?
- Are you able to bring up problems and tough issues?
- Do people in the space sometimes reject others for being different?
- Is it a safe place to take risks?
- Would anyone act in a way that undermines the group's efforts?
- Are unique skills and talents valued and utilized?

If we could learn to create more psychologically safe spaces in which it was possible to discuss our deeply held assumptions and beliefs, it would disrupt the status quo. But this would require bold leadership.

IN SUMMARY

Many contextual elements play out in an invisible, hidden and often unexplored and unconscious world. But the lessons from the Hillsborough bereaved starkly show the dangers of these murky waters and illustrate the myth that you can create systemic change without shifting deeply held assumptions and beliefs.

The 'Key issues' section explored the competing tensions faced by those in power, our biases, and how the media and measurement shape context, while 'The resonant dissonant dance' explored how the symbolic aspects of our behaviour can build or destroy trust. 'Lessons from Grenfell' explored the notion of othering as a way of understanding the context behind seemingly incomprehensible actions, such as the burning of the Grenfell effigy.

I concluded by considering our usual two questions, arguing that a lack of political intent and will is the condition that holds in place our inability to learn from catastrophic events and that the creation of safe spaces for enquiry and discussion about deeply held assumptions and beliefs is an opportunity for creating systemic change.

This chapter completes my analysis of each of the four elements: foundational, behavioural, relational and contextual. In the book's final chapter, 'Of despair and hope', I summarize my findings, present the Grenfell Model for Systemic Change, and offer suggested practical actions for politicians, business leaders, the media and citizens.

Chapter 8

The democratization of change: of despair and hope

If you want to change things then you need to let a thousand flowers bloom; some will thrive, some will not; you can't determine in advance what will work ... you want a wildflower meadow, not a formal garden.

David Snowden, self-destructive tendencies, 2020[1]

Seventy-two people died as a result of what happened. None of them had to die. This could have been prevented and should have not happened. Please make sure there is change.*

Hanan Wahabi, 2018[2]

This final chapter gives tentative answers to the question of why our failure to learn makes sense.

As I sit here writing, more than three and a half years after Grenfell and a year after initially putting down my thoughts for the book, I am filled with both despair and hope. I had not anticipated the depths of the failings of governance and accountability. I had not anticipated how our failure to learn is so entangled in political agendas, weak accountability and maintaining power. I hold little hope for learning or systemic change to be driven by either politicians or organizations. A lack of clear accountability, limited consequences for failure and the pull to maintain the status quo all suggest we need to look elsewhere for hope. And I have found some: in many beautiful, unanticipated and chance encounters.

---

* Hanan survived the fire with her two children. Her brother Abdulaziz El Wahabi, his wife Faouzia and his children Yasin, Nur Huda and Mehdi all died on the twenty-first floor.

In the first of the four main sections of this chapter, 'The messy kaleidoscope', I summarize my analysis and present a picture of why our failure to learn from catastrophic events make sense. The next section, 'Of despair', discusses the areas in which I have little hope for change, exploring how some of our attempts to change in fact do little to shift the status quo. I then share some personal reflections on grief, healing and change. In 'Of hope: the democratization of change', I provide some suggestions for politicians, businesses, think tanks, the media and citizens. The book ends with final concluding remarks.

A reminder: this book is offered in the spirit of enquiry. It paints the picture I see through my own biased lenses.

THE MESSY KALEIDOSCOPE: WHY OUR FAILURE TO LEARN FROM CATASTROPHES MAKES SENSE

On the cusp of the Fourth Industrial Revolution, our failure to learn occurs against a backdrop of increasing complexity and disruption. The merging of the biological, digital and physical worlds has us questioning the very nature of what it is to be human. Top-down approaches by governments are ineffective: agile responses to ongoing disruptions are needed. Power is being redistributed and decentralized, and citizens are more informed, more demanding and more connected. Businesses have to adapt and innovate, and all of us are confronted by the blurring of the boundaries of privacy, control and ownership. Wealth will continue to be unequally distributed as differing skills are demanded, favouring both those who provide relatively unskilled labour in lower-paid jobs and those in higher-paid jobs who have the complex skills needed to lead and manage complexity. This will lead to an increasingly disenfranchized and expanding middle class.

The area of safety is undergoing paradigm shifts as our understanding of complexity expands. Considering low-probability, high-consequence (catastrophic) events and risks distinctly from higher-probability, lower-consequence events (e.g. slips, trips and falls) helps us see their systemic nature, where non-technical issues such as speaking up are as important as well-maintained machinery. Traditional views of safety in which human error is seen as a problem to be controlled and as the cause of accidents are being replaced by new views in which people are seen as the creators of safety.

Likewise, our traditional bureaucratic, linear, command-and-control styles of leadership are becoming obsolete as we learn how to be effective in a highly interconnected world characterized by emergence, unpredictability, adaptability and co-evolution. Ivory tower expertise is being replaced by the need for collaborative ways of working as distributed and tacit knowledge becomes increasingly important.

Systemic change involves shifting the conditions holding the status quo in place as opposed to piecemeal change that changes just one part of a system. Key to systemic change is 'making the water visible': illuminating the messy kaleidoscope of factors that keep things as they are.

My analysis has attempted to reveal this messy kaleidoscope by considering four elements: foundational, behavioural, relational and contextual. In each case, I have explored myths, looked at known issues and challenges, highlighted lessons from Grenfell, and discussed why we don't learn and how we might enable systemic change.

Table 7 summarizes the main points I have covered. These begin to create a compelling picture of why it makes complete sense that we fail to prevent catastrophic events or respond to them effectively – why we fail to learn.

The Grenfell Model for Systemic Change

Prior to Grenfell, I was unaware of the level of regulatory vulnerability and the breadth of weaknesses in governance and accountability that I explored in the foundational structures chapter (chapter 4). I was also unaware that traditional public investigations, such as public inquiries, are fraught with challenges, including that they are called at the discretion of ministers and that there is no accountability mechanism in place to ensure that their recommendations are appropriately implemented or effective (chapter 5). Neither did I fully understand how subtle relational issues (see chapter 6) such as 'hero and villain' and 'rebel resident' narratives silence voices, thereby inhibiting our ability to learn, or how little understood and explored the contextual and cultural elements are (chapter 7).

I had not anticipated the breadth and depth of failures nor how relevant the issues and challenges in Table 7 would be to Covid-19.

Table 7. Why our failure to learn makes sense: the messy kaleidoscope.

	FOUNDATIONAL (STRUCTURAL)	BEHAVIOURAL (ACTING)	RELATIONAL (INTERACTING)	CONTEXTUAL (THINKING)
Characteristics	Foundational, obvious	Operational, obvious	Operational, obscure	Foundational, obscure
Enquiry	What foundational structures are in place to prevent catastrophic events?	What mechanisms are in place to prevent and react to catastrophic events?	How do relational issues contribute to catastrophic events and our ability to learn?	How do contextual aspects impact our ability to prevent and learn from catastrophic events?
Myths	That regulations guarantee safe outcomes	The perfect error-free world	That the 'softer' relational issues aren't that important	That you can enable systemic change without shifting deeply held assumptions and beliefs
Key issues and challenges	Challenges with legislation and regulation in the UK • Complex regulatory frameworks • Responding to fast paced and significant change • Operating demands Competing objectives and tensions Political agendas and the role of lobbying	Preventative mechanisms • Government: challenges include political game playing • Regulators: need to develop stronger proactive approaches • Effective supply chain management: e.g. use of major accident bow ties Reactive mechanisms • Inquests and inquiries, etc. • No mechanism to ensure recommendations implemented or effective	Relational issues with regulators • The principal–agent problem and regulatory capture Relational issues within organizations • The principal–agent problem • The MacWhirr syndrome • Herd behaviour • Groupthink • Cognitive dissonance • Diffuse responsibility Speaking truth to power Public policy consultations	Some contextual issues The web of competing tensions faced by politicians Bias and decision making The role of the media and measurement in shaping context The resonant dissonant dance – not matching words with action Deception and trust
Lessons from Grenfell	How did so many buildings end up with cladding?	The failure of scrutiny mechanisms before Grenfell	The narratives we use to silence	Othering and effigies
THE TWO QUESTIONS				
Why don't we learn? The conditions holding the status quo in place	Failures in governance and accountability	Our obsession with blame and blame avoidance	Our failure to effectively rebalance power	Lack of political intent and will
How could we enable systemic change? Opportunity to disrupt the status quo	Improve our capability to deal with complexity and ambiguity	Ensure fairly borne consequences	Tap diverse and distributed knowledge	Create safe spaces to engage with and challenge deeply held views

I now believe that the framework used in the analysis of Grenfell has broader application. It is offered as the Grenfell Model for Systemic Change (figure 19). It considers the four elements – foundational, behavioural, relational and contextual – and further categorizes them into operating and governing frameworks and obvious and obscure elements.

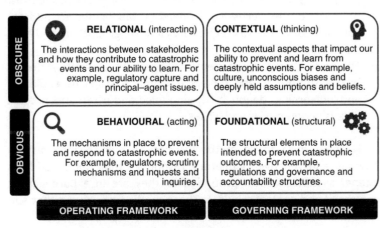

Figure 19. The Grenfell Model for Systemic Change.

My hope is that using this model will help us to look more holistically at catastrophic events, and particularly that we will pay more attention to their obscure and more challenging relational and contextual elements.

As we have seen throughout the book, there are four specific areas that work to hold the status quo in place. Let us now turn our attention to these.

The myths

One way of 'unlearning' or shifting contextual beliefs is to explore myths: the things that we hold to be true. Based on my observations, there are four of these that contribute to our inability to learn.

- The myth that regulations keep us safe (chapter 4) keeps in place simplistic linear thinking and solutions that fail to deal with increasing complexity and ambiguity and the need to build resilient systems.

- The myth of the perfect, error-free world (chapter 5) sees human error and deviation as an anomaly that can be corrected by removing the 'bad apples', thus restoring order.
- The myth that the softer relational issues aren't that important (chapter 6) rationalizes our apparent unwillingness to confront or develop the necessary leadership capabilities to address complex issues such as regulatory capture, groupthink and herd behaviour.
- The myth that you can create change without shifting deeply held assumptions and beliefs (chapter 7) stops us exploring and 'unlearning' deeply held, embodied and often unconscious beliefs, assumptions and biases.

Hanging onto these myths justifies an over-reliance on the obvious and reactive regulatory responses that fail to address deeper systemic issues, grounded as they are in a bureaucratic command-and-control mindset. These myths form a web that surrounds the conditions holding the status quo in place.

The conditions holding the status quo in place

Based on my analysis, there are four conditions that hold the status quo in place – that anchor our inability to learn.

- The first condition is weaknesses in parliamentary governance and accountability (chapter 4), characterized by a lack of clarity over who is responsible, there being no consequences for performance (whether good or bad), and a lack of transparency. This is further complicated by having to keep up with the complexity of change within government and the high turnover of ministers and civil servants.
- There is also our obsession with blame (chapter 5), which plays out on two levels. Politicians practise blame avoidance through strategies such as spin, scapegoating and not doing anything too risky, and all of us are obsessed with blame allocation after an event. Learning requires a willingness to look at actions honestly

and take lessons from mistakes. Blame narratives make this kind of enquiry at best very difficult and at worst impossible.

- Learning from and preventing catastrophic events in increasingly complex environments requires drawing on the available tacit and distributed knowledge and wisdom. Solutions will not be created in ivory towers. We need diverse views and voices to be heard, but failing to rebalance power (chapter 6) means these voices cannot be fully expressed, and their knowledge remains untapped.
- Given the long period over which many of these issues have repeatedly been raised, with no effective resolution, a lack of political intent and will (chapter 7) is the final condition that I believe is holding the status quo in place.

One way of viewing these is as 'givens', where change is either too hard or would disrupt power too much and would be too threatening to undertake. Waiting for the four conditions, listed above, to alter is problematic, as changing them would require extraordinary political will and leadership, which are markedly lacking in our current world. Without a change in political will or intent, there is likely to be little more than snail's pace and piecemeal change in these areas.

I offer the following four ideas that might disrupt the status quo.

The disruptors: opportunities to disrupt the status quo

We often have a negative bias against disruption: we think that somehow it is bad.

But change requires disruption. If a system is operating stably, you need something to disrupt it to allow for change. I find biological metaphors useful. So cells mutate: many of these mutations are ineffective but some stick and enable change. The outcomes can be positive and lead to evolution or negative and lead to, for example, cancer. We don't know what actions will work; we don't know what the tipping point will be.

The method of disruption does not have to be forceful. I have found kindness to be more disruptive than harsh words. There are many people committed to change post-Grenfell. I like to think of us as a tribe of disruptors, each doing what we believe in to enable change. As we expand our capability to manage complex change, we might alter our negative views of disruption and embrace it fully.

There are four areas, in particular, that offer disruptive opportunities.

- Developing our capacity to deal with complexity and ambiguity (chapter 4) would develop our understanding of how to create change and safety in complex contexts.
- Ensuring fairly borne consequences (chapter 5) after catastrophic events would send a strong symbolic message about what is or is not deemed to be acceptable. Consequences are too often borne by the innocent (such as leaseholders post-Grenfell) or the bereaved (such as after Hillsborough) and not by the people accountable for contributing to failures. Consequences could be legal, such as being found liable and paying fines or serving prison sentences, but equally they could be financial or reputational, such as a levy on developers and the construction industry in the aftermath of Grenfell to cover the remediation of historic safety issues.
- Tapping diverse tacit and distributed knowledge (chapter 6) would move us away from the siloed, 'ivory tower expert' solutions that are often ineffective on the ground, as demonstrated so vividly by the responses of many government to Covid-19. With increasing complexity, ivory tower expertise is insufficient, and a failure to tap tacit and distributed knowledge will make us increasingly ineffective.
- Finally, creating safe spaces in which to explore our deeply held values, assumptions and beliefs (chapter 7) would help to enable cultural and systemic change.

Any small action that contributes in any of these areas will move us forward, towards 'goodness'. No one can predict the impact, and I am not advocating for massive macro projects, just simple daily actions that begin to shift these areas.

Making the water visible, the messy kaleidoscope

I set out to make the water visible: to reveal the messy kaleidoscope inside of which our continued failure to learn make sense. Researching and writing this book while continuing to hear new revelations from the Grenfell Inquiry and watching many of the same issues play out in relation to Covid-19 has left me in no doubt that our failure is systemic. That it in fact makes complete sense. At times, it has left me in despair.

OF DESPAIR: THE ROAD TO PERDITION...

Sometimes, when I sit with the picture this book paints, or when I hear another revelation such as that the KCTMO threw away Grenfell evidence, or when I watch the prime minister threaten and fight publicly with Manchester's mayor about whether or not to lock down while hundreds are dying daily, I am filled with despair. Change seems impossible.

The system is perfectly designed to keep doing what it is doing: fail to deal with known issues with regulations and governance; act surprised when something goes wrong; spend enormous amounts of time and effort on inquests and inquiries only to dilute or ignore their recommendations; fail to respond to issues raised via scrutiny mechanisms; implement piecemeal watered-down change; spin the 'we've learned' rhetoric. And repeat.

I sometimes imagine a world where, in the immediate aftermath of Grenfell, the government admitted that it had failed to provide clear guidance over Approved Document B (chapter 4) and then implemented a thorough and rapid risk assessment process that considered the full building risks – not just the cladding – and prioritized remediation based on this holistic view. A world where industry leaders from developers to architects to housing associations to construction contractors to insurers to banks all got together and said: 'We'll make this right. We'll work together to fix this.' For example, by a self-imposed levy that was required in order to participate in remediation work that was used to pay for historic failings, with government acting as insurer of last resort. Where consequences were borne by those who built unsafe buildings not by those who now live in them.

But we do not live in that world, and there are three areas in particular that concern me.

- The government's inability to learn and change.
- The uselessness of divisive positional arguments.
- The ineffectiveness of many well-intentioned forums and activities.

Government's inability to learn and change

A principle I observed after Grenfell was to participate in all the official government responses, in order to give them a chance. I did not want to be someone who simply sat on the sidelines and criticized. And on a positive note, I have found my interactions in public meetings with the Grenfell Inquiry to be valuable. From my initial submission through subsequent meetings, they have been accessible, open to listening to my views, and responsive.

But on a less positive note, I have participated in a number of consultations, and without a change in their format I am unlikely to do so again. As discussed in chapter 6, I do not think they give me a voice. I am expected to 'tick box' pre-formulated plans, and as an individual with no organizational backing or political lobbyist supporting my submission, they have felt like a waste of time.

I have attempted to engage with government and have offered to support and participate in official forums, but I have too often come up against platitudes and closed doors.

As I have watched the responses from all parties to Grenfell and to Covid-19, I am increasingly clear that relying on or expecting systemic change from government would be a mistake. It would take extraordinary political will and leadership for change, and that is sadly lacking.

What is more, I think that we, as citizens, need to own our part in having created this political context. We have accepted it. I am thankfully more educated now about what issues are important.

Positional arguments

I recall hearing a politician on the *Today Programme* saying that he supported the adversarial tone of government because it was how people were held to account. I was astounded at the statement and it has stuck with me.

I would question this. I don't think positional or adversarial approaches are effective: they simply entrench existing views. Positionality brings into existence oppositionality. Good conjures bad; right conjures wrong. After having participated in my share of positional arguments post-Grenfell, I no longer believe them to be effective.

Whether in government, in local communities, or on social media, I believe encouraging enquiry and learning and collaboration and exploration will be more effective.

I have begun to catch myself when I am becoming positional, uninterested in understanding another's view (which has been known to happen). I am learning to step back, take a breath and listen.

But both politicians and the media play a positional game, feeding off simplistic, divisive narratives that do little to promote understanding or enquiry, or to shift assumptions and beliefs. Rather, they are integral to maintaining the status quo.

You do not hold people to account effectively by positional views. You do not create systemic change by arguing.

The road to perdition...

I recall a workshop about housing post-Grenfell. It was interesting, and it was attended by many people I knew. As I sat there I asked myself what change it was likely to cause. I had to confront the fact that we were like-minded people having interesting conversations among ourselves that would amount to little in terms of change.

From a systemic perspective, one view you can take is that actions are either contributing to the status quo or they are disrupting it. There are, I believe, many well-intentioned actions that end up feeding the status quo despite their intent being to contribute to change.

Of particular note, and with great respect, I have been astounded by the amount of very good research and information coming out of think tanks and other academic organizations that has raised issues with governance and accountability and problems with inquiries and inquests, and so on, over and over again. We seem highly skilled at highlighting problems in well-researched and beautiful reports and less skilled at enabling change. These reports get mentioned in the media and I worry that they leave the public with an illusion of change.

I think there is a different role that these organizations could play, particularly with regard to sifting through information and making it accessible in order to help the media and citizens hold government to account. In the absence of a government accountability mechanism for implementing inquiry recommendations, why has no think tank or institution begun publishing the recommendations and tracking progress against them in an accessible manner? When I suggested this to one organization, the idea was met with disdain: that's not our role, the government needs to do that. Well... If the government won't do that, continuing to say that it should will not change anything.

I think we need to question how we assess the effectiveness of well-intended forums and reports. There is much good intent and incredible knowledge, but I'm not clear how much it is leading to change, or how much it unintentionally sustains the status quo by leaving the public with the illusion that something will happen because an important institution has published a new report.

I wonder how we might channel good intentions in a more effective way.

PERSONAL REFLECTIONS: ON GRIEF, HEALING AND CHANGE

> People talk too loosely about closure. They fail to realise that there can be no closure to love, nor should there be for someone you have loved and lost. Furthermore, grief is a journey without a destination. The bereaved travel through a landscape of memories and thoughts of what might have been. It is a journey marked by milestones, some you seek, some you stumble on. For the families and survivors of Hillsborough these milestones have included the search for truth, accountability and justice. But even these are not the end of the road. They are still travelling.
>
> The Right Reverend James Jones KBE[3]

I am concerned about the amount of loss and pain surrounding the pandemic. The loss of loved ones and the absence of grieving rituals, of goodbyes, of squeezed hands, of jobs, of colleagues, of security, of hope.

In this context, I want to share a little of my own experience and thank my employer for encouraging me to share some not particularly positive experiences I've had with them. Experiences that we have worked through and, I believe, both learned from.

Six months after Grenfell I met for the first time with a now good friend who works for the NHS Grenfell Response Team. After a quick coffee and chat, she turned to me and said: 'You are not grieving.'

I looked at her quizzically – I had nothing to grieve about. None of my family died. I needed to carry on fighting for change.

And then I spent a week crying.

I have learned that grief is not hierarchical. It is a journey we all go through in different ways.

I will thankfully never know the grief of the Grenfell bereaved and survivors, and I am unable to imagine that world. But the depth of their grief doesn't invalidate mine.

It was very important, and difficult, for me to understand this. I suspect that my mental health would have deteriorated significantly if I had not had that conversation. At times I still suffer from anxiety and depression, and I am in therapy and probably will be for life. I have learned to manage my mental well-being as if I had a physical ailment. I still spend some days crying and sometimes the grief feels overwhelming. Sometimes I forget that my dad died ten days after Grenfell, and this is all tied up in the tears.

I have learned to live with grief and, I think, I have begun to heal.

But grief is also, I think, inextricably linked with change. There is a temporality to grief: a past and a future of life and a line of grief that somehow connects them. And navigating that line changes you. As American philosopher and author Judith Butler says:

> One mourns when one accepts that by the loss one undergoes one will be changed, possibly forever. Perhaps mourning has to do with agreeing to undergo a transformation (perhaps one should say submitting to a transformation) the full result of which one cannot know in advance.[4]

I don't think I navigated grief well at work. And I don't think my work navigated my grief well with me. I found it isolating. I felt alone and adrift and I didn't know what I needed. So I withdrew from colleagues and, in doing so, I withdrew internal discretionary effort. I poured myself into client work and gave my heart there. My clients were amazing.

I needed someone to ask me how I was and what I needed. I needed them to ask me that not once but over and over and over again. Because how I was and what I needed changed. And often I didn't know. But my experience was that after the first 'asking' it was over, and after some coaching support I had requested, my company's expectation was that I would get back to normal. But there is no normal. There is no going back.

I needed people at work to know I was changed. To rediscover who I was. But instead there was silence. I felt as if people were walking on eggshells around me, and I didn't have the energy or ability to delve into their discomfort as I grappled to cope myself. So I stepped back and found small safe spaces in which to work. It took a new manager and two years to begin to recover from this, and with baby steps we are getting there.

One of the characteristics of a complex world is blurred boundaries, and I think organizations have an important role to play in navigating grief. As we have exceeded 3 million deaths from the pandemic globally, there is a space organizations could step into, to bridge the world that was and the one that wants to emerge. In 2019/20, 17.9 million working days were lost in the UK due to work-related stress, depression or anxiety – up from 12.8 million days in 2018/19 (55% of all absences are due to ill health). Among the reasons cited for taking time off were work pressure, tight deadlines, too much responsibility and a lack of managerial support.[5]

I would encourage executives and leaders in organizations to step into this space.

But now... To hope.

OF HOPE: THE DEMOCRATIZATION OF CHANGE

This book is written inside of the promise I made as I watched the fire: to make sure we learned. To honour that promise, I want to end with hope, and with some suggested actions that will help move in the direction of goodness.

The response to Grenfell has rocked my faith in humanity, but it has also left me with hope. There have been many moments of connection that I cling to and cherish.

In the days after the fire, being stopped in the street by a volunteer – thanking me for my smile. Listening to his story of running into the tower to try and get people out. Hugging and crying and healing.

The countless gentle looks. The kindness in nods and smiles and tears.

My Twitter and LinkedIn communities, who care and love and argue with and cherish one another.

The hugs from firefighters, shared pain in our eyes.

The little notes from clients on anniversaries or 'bad news' days.

And the growing network of people who stand for something new. Something different.

Mostly, it is the Grenfell bereaved and the survivors and the firefighters who give me solace and hope and strength. It is their bravery and courage that spur me on daily.

I think often of the advice that Jim Wetherbee gave me: 'The doors that should be open, won't be. Stop knocking on them, go through the open doors.'

I have learned about change and complexity and the beautiful and surprising twists this takes. And that gives me hope.

I have learned to plant seeds and water them, and then to watch in wonder at what grows and what does not. I have learned to love and appreciate diversity more fully.

I have fallen in love with graffiti (figure 20) and with grime artist Stormzy, after his famous 'Where's the money for Grenfell' BRIT Awards performance in 2018. Stormzy later said of his performance:

> As a young black man coming from the community that I come from, I recognise that I have responsibilities. If I'm going to be on stage for five minutes at the Brit Awards, I have a responsibility. Bearing in mind that not one of us has been on that stage for a very long time, if it's ever happened. If I have five minutes, I've got to use that time wisely.[6]

And this beautiful North Kensington community has my heart forever.

We don't know what will bring change, but small action by small action we can plant seeds.

It is not up to others, it is up to us.

As much as a changing world places different demands on governments and businesses, it has also democratized change.

Think of Greta Thunberg, who in August 2018 sat, alone, outside the Swedish parliament building to protest against climate change. In an incredibly short space of time, she spurned a global youth movement calling for climate change. Or think of the footballer Marcus Rashford, galvanizing support to change government policy on free school meals.

Figure 20. The Trellick graffiti wall tribute to
Grenfell on the second anniversary.

The increasing complexity of the fourth industrial revolution as
well as its disruptive nature give us all an opportunity to contribute
significantly to change. This is, I believe, our duty. Simply complain-
ing about failures of government without doing something about
them will not lead to change. As complexity expert Dave Snowden
says:

> If you want to change things then you need to let a thousand
> flowers bloom; some will thrive, some will not; you can't deter-
> mine in advance what will work. ... You want a wildflower
> meadow, not a formal garden.[7]

Whether it is Grenfell or something else that touches us, if we all
became disruptive seed planters and gardeners – in whatever way
we can – change will happen. I cannot tell you where or when, but I
know that it will.

On their own, words don't change much, so to end this book I ask a final question: what is one thing I wish key stakeholders would do going forward (figure 21)?

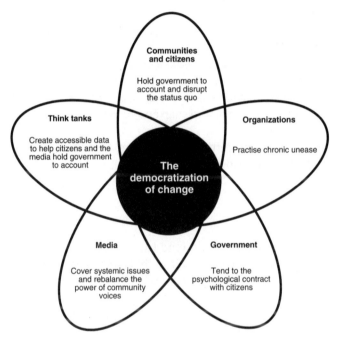

Figure 21. What is one thing key stakeholders can do?

Organizations

In the face of increasingly turbulent times and weak government, businesses have the ability to affect global change. Whether they have the courage and the moral leadership to do so remains to be seen. Shareholders and investors have a critical role to play in this.

On a practical level, I wish that organizations would actively practise chronic unease, imagining and mitigating against the worst thing that could happen. This would help us move towards a focus on low-probability, high-consequence events; be it regarding safety or climate change, doing so would require organizations to become mindful. In their book *Managing the Unexpected*, Karl Weick and Kathleen Sutcliffe suggest the following steps be taken.[8]

- Track small failures: search for indicators that all is not well; be preoccupied with failure.
- Resist oversimplification: the world is nuanced, and you need to understand and create pictures of these subtleties rather than simplify.
- Remain sensitive to operations: remain sensitive to the front line, where work gets done.
- Maintain capabilities for resilience: resilience can be defined as 'the intrinsic ability of an organisation (system) to maintain or regain a dynamically stable state, which allows it to continue operations after a major mishap and/or in the presence of a continuous stress'.
- Take advantage of shifting locations of expertise. Tap distributed knowledge and wisdom.

Governments

I wish the government would tend to their psychological contract with citizens. While radical, I believe that this would alter how they think of their role. Viewing accountability in this way may, admittedly, fly in the face of how career politicians view their job, but it could change how we respond to and learn from tragedies. It would require a fundamental shift in the role of politicians in responding to catastrophic events.

- *Transparency and deception.* Attempts to spin the narrative do little more than inflate already heightened emotions and increase distrust. It might seem counterintuitive, but practising radical transparency and stopping attempts to deceive is what is required.
- *Immediate acceptance of responsibility.* After a catastrophic event there are inherent tensions between the desire of those most impacted to see 'heads roll', the time that formal processes take to reach conclusions, and the need to ensure that systemic failings, rather than individual ones, are identified. A willingness from both politicians and heads of key organizations to accept responsibility – because 'this happened on my watch' rather than because 'it is my fault' – would go some way to easing these tensions.

- *Swift correction.* In the case of Grenfell, failing to make buildings safe promptly is a gross violation of the psychological contract that citizens should be safe in their homes. Failure to correct issues that lead to catastrophes damages trust.
- *Appropriately borne consequences.* This could not be more tragically evidenced than by the consequences of government failings to stock appropriate PPE in preparation for a pandemic being borne by those at the front line of care; or by those leaseholders facing emotional and financial ruin to repair historic building safety issues not of their making. Redressing such imbalances in consequences is key to restoring the psychological contract. This is not a legal argument but a moral one, and consequences can be judicial, financial or reputational, or they could be resignations.
- *Timely and effective learning.* As much as they want some form of justice, those closely impacted by catastrophic events want to prevent similar tragedies. They want to prevent others from experiencing the loss and grief they have endured. Until those in power take learning from previous events seriously, they will fail to restore the psychological contract with citizens.

The media

I wish that the media would focus on the following two things.

- *Systemic issues,* by reporting holistically and not focusing on siloed snippets of disasters. During a conversation with Emily Kasriel, head of Solution Based Journalism at the BBC, she said: 'We are naturally psychologically drawn to be aware of the tigers not the berries – we remember the bad news. But by telling only those stories, we reflect a picture of the world that is not accurate. We only represent conflict, not the stories of how we come together despite our differences.' Showing the full story of agency and communities and revealing systemic issues would shape a different narrative.
- Journalists could play a unique role in *rebalancing power*: not just by giving voice to communities but by giving them editorial power too. By having communities and underrepresented groups shape the story and narrative.

Think tanks (and academic institutions)

I wish this group would make sense of inaccessible and overwhelming amounts of data and present it in ways that facilitate holding government to account. I believe this would help both the media and citizens hold government to account more effectively, which can be difficult amidst the overwhelming maze of data.

Communities and citizens

My wish is that communities continue to hold government to account and disrupt the status quo. For us to see doing so as our responsibility, tiny step by tiny step, and with compassion and uncompromising intent.

This is poignantly captured by Dan Renwick in his poem 'We Walk in Silence',[9] which describes the silent marches held on the fourteenth of each month since Grenfell to remember those that died:

> We walk in silence out of respect.
> We walk in silence because we are mourning.
> We walk in silence because even if we didn't know someone who died directly, someone who lost their world could be standing next to us.
> We walk in silence because words so often offend.
> We walk in silence because to speak is to vent and to vent is to rage.
> We walk in silence because if we spoke, our throats would burn.
> We walk in silence because otherwise our fists would quickly come to talk too.
> We walk in silence because our muted presence should scare those responsible.
> We walk in silence because we cannot say a word that the events of the 14th June don't speak for us.
> We walk in silence because we carry the weight of history and the burden is easier in quiet.
> We walk in silence because it pains those who wish to speak for us.
> We walk in silence because if we even whispered about what justice looks like in totality, the streets would stir with revolt.

We walk in silence because it is stealthy.
We walk in silence because we are waiting to be done right by.
The silence has an end point.
The silence is not there to comfort the powerful, it is to soothe
those living with hell.
The silence speaks for itself.
Respect what it says.
Don't speak over it.

CONCLUSIONS

I wrote this book to try to understand why our inability to learn
made sense. To explore why we don't learn and how we might
enable change.

It is clear to me that without systemic change, without shifting
the conditions that hold our inability to learn in place, we will continue to fail.

There will be piecemeal change and that will help. But we will
not make the changes that are wanted by those most impacted –
those who, beyond their own suffering, want to ensure no one else
endures what they have endured. It might not be another high-rise
fire or another stadium disaster, but there will be some incident
where we failed to listen, where we failed to learn.

If we all developed our capacity to deal with complexity and
ambiguity, ensured fairly borne consequences, tapped diverse and
distributed knowledge, and created safe spaces to explore deeply
held contextual assumptions; *and* if organizations practised chronic
unease, governments tended to the psychological contract with
their citizens, the media covered systemic issues and rebalanced
power, and think tanks created accessible data to help citizens and
the media hold government to account; *and* if communities and citizens disrupted the status quo – then, I believe, we would see change.

The biggest hope for change is us: individually and collectively.

I witness and am moved daily by the Grenfell community, by
the bereaved and the survivors, by the local firefighters, by organizations such as Grenfell United, by their partnership with those
involved in the cladding scandal, by the monthly silent walks that are
so beautiful, so poignant.

Essayist and author Rebecca Solnit has written extensively about the beauty and power of post-disaster communities, most famously in *A Paradise Built in Hell: The Extraordinary Communities that Arise in Disaster*. In this book Solnit explores events such as the 1985 Mexico City earthquake, 9/11 and Hurricane Katrina. She beautifully captures where I too have found hope. I would like to end with her words:

> When all the ordinary divides and patterns are shattered, people step up to become their brothers' keepers, ... and that purposefulness and connectedness bring joy even amidst death, chaos, fear, and loss.[10]

It is in this space that something else becomes possible:

> We are building something immense together that, though invisible and immaterial, is a structure, one we reside within. ... Though there are individual voices and people who got there first, these are collective projects that matter not when one person says something but when a million integrate it into how they see and act in the world. The we who inhabits those structures grows as what was once subversive or transgressive settles in as normal, as people outside the walls wake up one day inside them and forget they were ever anywhere else.
>
> The consequences of these transformations are perhaps most important where they are most subtle. They remake the world, and they do so mostly by the accretion of small gestures and statements and the embracing of new visions of what can be and should be. The unknown becomes known, the outcasts come inside, the strange becomes ordinary. You can see changes to the ideas about whose rights matter and what is reasonable and who should decide, if you sit still enough and gather the evidence of transformations that happen by a million tiny steps before they result in a landmark legal decision or an election or some other shift that puts us in a place we've never been.[11]

Thank you for engaging in this enquiry with me.

Acknowledgements

I am grateful to everyone who has touched my heart since the fire on 14 June 2017. Whether they did so through a smile on the street, via a like on social media or by reaching out in solidarity about the need for change, your acts of kindness have helped me through the darkest times.

I am thankful to have met Martin Stanley and Matthew Price in the aftermath of the fire. I cherish your guidance and friendship. You helped me learn to find and trust my voice.

Alistair and Emma and Abby and Catherine: thank you for helping me heal.

Mike Miller, Andy Banfield and Jeff Williams: thank you for your support at work. And thanks, too, to my clients: your courage, humility and leadership helped maintain my faith in what is possible.

To my friends and family, thank you for putting up with my obsessive writing in any spare time over the last year.

Thank you to my editor, Diane Coyle, and my publishers, Richard Baggaley and Sam Clark, for making this book possible and for taking such meticulous care of it throughout our work together.

To *Inside Housing*'s Pete Apps and the BBC's Kate Lamble: thank you for your tireless quest to reveal what happened that led to those seventy-two deaths, and to make the information widely accessible.

To the Grenfell community – from the bereaved, to the survivors, to the firefighters, to those impacted by the cladding scandal – your grit, resilience, dignity and love keep me going. Hanan, Marcio, Andreia and Milad: no words can ever express how much you have taught me. Thank you.

Finally, I am grateful to be married to Keith, who is my place of solace and peace. You teach me daily what it takes to bring about change.

Endnotes

All URLs correct as of 27 April 2021.

NOTES FOR THE INTRODUCTION

1   Katie Razzall, Nick Menzies and Sara Moralioglu. 2017. The 21st floor. *BBC News*, 28 September 2017 (www.bbc.co.uk/news/resources/idt-sh/Grenfell_21st_floor).

2   Ben Okri. 2018. *Grenfell Tower*. Poem, June, 2017 (https://benokri.co.uk/news/grenfell-tower-2017-poem-ben-okri/).

3   Maritime Executive. 2018. July 6, 1988: the Piper Alpha disaster. Article, 7 May (www.maritime-executive.com/article/july-6-1988-the-piper-alpha-disaster).

4   Emma Norris and Marcus Shepheard. 2017. How public inquiries can lead to change. Report, Institute for Government, December, p. 8 (www.instituteforgovernment.org.uk/sites/default/files/publications/Public%20Inquiries%20%28final%29.pdf).

5   Memorandum by the Fire Brigades Union. 1999. Minutes of evidence to the Environment Sub-Committee of the Environment, Transport and Regional Affairs Committee. ROF 28, 20 July, paragraph 2.2 (https://publications.parliament.uk/pa/cm199899/cmselect/cmenvtra/741/9072002.htm).

6   BBC. 2018. Grenfell Tower: the fires that foretold the tragedy. *BBC News* website, 30 October (www.bbc.co.uk/news/uk-england-45982810).

7   Eddy Daffarn and Francis O'Connor. 2016. KCTMO – playing with fire! Blog, Grenfell Action Group, 20 November (https://grenfellactiongroup.wordpress.com/2016/11/20/kctmo-playing-with-fire/).

8   Ministry of Housing, Communities & Local Government. 2020. Building safety programme: monthly data release for June 2020. Report, issued 16 July (https://assets.publishing.service.gov.uk/government/uploads/system/uploads/attachment_data/file/901051/Building_Safety_Data_Release_June_2020.pdf).

9   National Audit Office. 2020. Investigation into remediating dangerous cladding on high-rise buildings. Report, 19 June, paragraphs 2.5, 2.7 and 2.8 (www.nao.org.uk/wp-content/uploads/2020/06/Investigation-into-remediating-dangerous-cladding-on-high-rise-buildings.pdf).

10 Martina Lees. 2020. Grenfell cladding scandal: Manchester residents clash with government over who pays for remediation works. *The Times*, 14 June (www.thetimes.co.uk/article/grenfell-cladding-scandal-manchester-residents-clash-with-government-over-who-pays-for-remediation-works-9zwzkcn68).

11   Robert Booth. 2020. Social landlords 'face £10bn bill to fix fire safety problems'. *The Guardian*, 2 March (www.theguardian.com/society/2020/mar/02/social-landlords-face-10bn-bill-to-fix-fire-safety-problems).

12   UK Parliament. 2020. Communities and Local Government Select Committee Report: progress of remediation. Report, 12 June, section 1, paragraph 34 (https://publications.parliament.uk/pa/cm5801/cmselect/cmcomloc/172/17205.htm#_idTextAnchor003).

13   Rebecca Solnit. 2016. How to survive a disaster. *Literary Hub*, 15 November (https://lithub.com/rebecca-solnit-how-to-survive-a-disaster).

14   Rebecca Solnit. 2019. Introduction. In *Whose Story is This? Old Conflicts, New Chapters*. London: Haymarket Books.

NOTES FOR CHAPTER 1

1   Barbara Lane. 2018. Grenfell Tower: fire safety investigation. Phase 1 Report, sections 1–4, 12 April, p. 2.46, line 2.18.9.

2   Luke Bisby. 2018. Expert evidence to Grenfell Tower Inquiry (hereafter abbreviated to 'GTI'). Transcript, 21 November, p. 159, lines 2–6.

3   GTI Phase 1 Report, volume 1, chapter 1, paragraph 1.3.

4   Mark Rice-Oxley. 2018. Grenfell: the 72 victims, their lives, loves and losses. *The Guardian*, 14 May (www.theguardian.com/uk-news/2018/may/14/grenfell-the-71-victims-their-lives-loves-and-losses).

5   GTI Phase 1 Report, volume 1, chapter 1, paragraph 1.3.

6   Rice-Oxley (2018). Grenfell: the 72 victims, their lives, loves and losses.

7   GTI Phase 1 Report, chapter 3.

8   Photograph taken by Ian Wright and licensed via Wikimedia Commons under CC BY-SA 2.0 (https://creativecommons.org/licenses/by-sa/2.0). Original image appears at https://commons.wikimedia.org/wiki/File:Grenfell_Tower_from_Latimer_Road_Station_(8202486240).jpg.

9   GTI Phase 1 Report, volume 1, p. 20, paragraph 3.7.

10   BBC. 2019. Grenfell Tower: what happened. *BBC News* website, 29 October (www.bbc.co.uk/news/uk-40301289).

11   GTI Phase 1 Report, volume 1, p. 20, paragraph 3.6.

12   Ibid, volume 1, p. 21, paragraphs 3.9–3.10.

13   Ibid, volume 1, p. 22, paragraph 3.13.

14   Ibid, volume 1, p. 33, paragraph 6.5.

15   Ibid, volume 1, p. 19, paragraph 3.3.

16   Ibid, volume 1, p. 20, paragraph 3.8.

17   GTI, Phase 2, Module 1. Opening statement on behalf of the Royal Borough of Kensington and Chelsea, pp. 23–29.

18   Kensington and Chelsea TMO. About us (www.kctmo.org.uk/main/8/about-us).

19   Royal Borough of Kensington and Chelsea. 2017. Online statement, 27 December (www.rbkc.gov.uk/newsroom/all-council-statements/kensington-and-chelsea-tenant-management-organisation-kctmo).

20   GTI Phase 1 Report, volume 1, p. 25, paragraphs 3.22, 3.23 and 3.24.

21   Ibid, volume 1, p. 26, paragraph 3.28.

22   Ibid, volume 1, p. 33, paragraphs 6.5 and 6.6.

23   Grenfell Tower Regeneration Project. 2012. Design and access statement. Planning Application, October, p. 14.

24   GTI Phase 1 Report, volume 1, p. 13, paragraph 2.16.

25   Ibid, volume 1, p. 34, paragraph 6.10.

26   Ibid, volume 1, pp. 34–40, paragraphs 6.7–6.23.

27   Ibid, volume 1, p. 34, paragraph 6.11.

28   Note: the columns had one layer of insulation and the walls had two layers. In addition to the PIR foam insulation, smaller quantities of phenolic foam insulation were found.

29   Illustration created referencing GTI Phase 1 Report, p. 38, and structure of aluminium composite material created by Phoenix 777 under Creative Commons Share Alike 4.0 International licence: https://commons.wikimedia.org/wiki/File:Aluminium_composite_material.png. Phoenix7777, CC BY-SA 4.0 <https://creativecommons.org/licenses/by-sa/4.0>, via Wikimedia Commons. The placement and language of the labels has been altered. It is distributed under the same license.

30   Bisby (2018). Expert evidence to Grenfell Tower Inquiry (p. 21, lines 17–25).

31   GTI Phase 1 Report, volume 1, p. 35, paragraph 6.12.

32   GTI Phase 1 Report, volume 1, pp. 36–37, paragraph 6.17.

33   Ibid, volume 1, p. 39, paragraph 6.20.

34   Ibid, volume 1, p. 40, paragraphs 6.22–6.23.

35   Bisby (2018). Expert evidence to Grenfell Tower Inquiry (p. 159, lines 2–5).

36   GTI Phase 1 Report, volume 1, pp. 40–46, paragraphs 6.24–6.34.

37   Barbara Lane. 2018. Expert report to GTI, 12 April, Section 11, p. 63, paragraphs 11.18.21–11.18.29.

38   Ibid, sections 1–4, p. 51, paragraph 2.18.12.

39   Ibid, Section 9, p. 38, paragraph 9.7.5.

40   GTI Phase 1 Report, volume 1, p. 47, paragraph 6.35.

41   Ibid, volume 4 chapter 21, pp. 505–516.

42   Ibid, volume 4, chapter 22, pp. 517–539.

43   Ibid, volume 1, chapter 4, pp. 27–29.

44   Jose Torero. 2018. Expert evidence to GTI. Transcript, 20 November, p. 100, lines 18–22, p. 101, lines 2–11.

45   GTI Phase 1 Report, volume 1, p. 12, paragraph 2.12.

46   Ibid, volume 4, chapters 23 and 24, pp. 541–571.

47   Barbara Lane. 2018. Expert evidence to GTI. Transcript, 22 November, p. 84, lines 21–24.

48   Ibid, p. 93, lines 24–25, p. 94, line 1.

49   This section draws heavily on Phase 1 Supplemental Report, Barbara Lane, 5 November 2018, section 2.

50 Barbara Lane. 2018. Expert report to GTI, 12 April, section 19, p. 14, paragraph 19.5.13. Barbara Lane. 2018. Expert evidence to GTI. Transcript, 26 November, p. 9, lines 4–20, p. 21, lines 10–12.

51 Ibid, section 19, p. 33, paragraph 19.7.17.

52 Barbara Lane. 2018. Expert report to GTI, 12 April, sections 1–4, pp. 2–38, paragraph 2.15.27(b).

53 That is, Building Regulations. Specifically 'Approved Document B fire safety volume 2 – buildings other than dwelling houses 2006, incorporating 2013 amendments'. Barbara Lane. 2018. Supplemental Report to the GTI, section 2, p. 64.

54 David Purser. 2018. Expert evidence to the GTI. Transcript, 29 November. And GTI Phase 1 Report, volume 4, chapter 25.

55 David Purser. 2018. GTI Phase 1 Report presentation: 'Exposure of Grenfell occupants to toxic fire products – effects on escape and survival', p. 20.

56 GTI Phase 1 Report, volume 2, p. 176, paragraph 11.30.

57 Meron Mekonnen. 2018. Witness evidence to GTI. Transcript, 9 October, p. 47, lines 1–10.

58 Barbara Lane. 2018. Supplemental report to the GTI, section 20, pp. 20-16 and 20-17.

59 Purser (2018). Expert evidence to the GTI.

60 Ibid, p. 45, lines 17–19.

61 For those wishing for more technical details, all of the Grenfell Tower Inquiry evidence, hearings and expert reports are freely accessible via the Grenfell Tower Inquiry website: www.grenfelltowerinquiry.org.uk.

NOTES FOR CHAPTER 2

1 Barbara Lane. 2018. Expert evidence to GTI. Transcript, 22 November, p. 170, lines 13–15.

2 INQUEST. 2019. Family reflections on Grenfell: no voice left unheard. Report from the Grenfell Family Consultation Day, May, p. 10 (www.inquest.org.uk/Handlers/Download.ashx?IDMF=47e60cf4-cc23-477b-9ca0-c960eb826d24).

3 Sidney Dekker. 2014. The Field Guide to Understanding Human Error, p. 19. Farnham: Ashgate Publishing.

4 Ibid, p. 26.

5 BBC (2018). Grenfell Tower: the fires that foretold the tragedy.

6 Nadia Khomami and Nicola Slawson. 2016. Fire crews extinguish blaze at Shepherd's Bush tower block. The Guardian, 19 August (www.theguardian.com/uk-news/2016/aug/19/fire-crews-tackle-blaze-at-shepherds-bush-tower-block-london).

7 GTI Phase 1 Report, volume 4, p. 588, paragraph 27.13.

8 London Fire Brigade. 2016. Tall building facades. Presentation, 13 July (https://assets.grenfelltowerinquiry.org.uk/documents/LFB%20Powerpoint%20presentation%20on%20Tall%20Building%20Facades%20V2_0%20LFB00003521.pdf).

9   Neil Churchill. 2012. Cigarette caused Tamweel Tower Dubai fire. *Gulf Business News*, 5 December (https://gulfbusiness.com/cigarette-caused-the-tamweel-dubai-fire/).

10 CNN. 2013. Fire put out in 40 storey Chechnya building. *CNN*, 3 April (https://edition.cnn.com/2013/04/03/world/russia-grozny-building-fire/index.html).

11 Martin Chulov, Kareem Shaheen and Ruth McKee. 2016. Massive fire at Dubai skyscraper interrupts new year's eve fireworks. *The Guardian*, 1 January (www.theguardian.com/world/2015/dec/31/dubai-skyscraper-fire-ablaze-new-years-eve-fireworks).

12 GTI Phase 1 Report, volume 4, p. 588, paragraph 27.14.

13 Peter Apps. 2020. Timeline: the three years since Grenfell. *Inside Housing*, 12 June (www.insidehousing.co.uk/insight/timeline-the-three-years-since-grenfell-66551).

14 Fire Brigades Union. 2019. Bolton fire: firefighters condemn 'complete failure' of UK fire safety system. Website article, 16 November (www.fbu.org.uk/news/2019/11/16/bolton-fire-firefighters-condemn-complete-failure-uk-fire-safety-system).

15 Barbara Lane. 2018. Expert evidence to GTI. Transcript, 22 November, p. 170, lines 13–15.

16 GTI Phase 1 Report, volume 4, p. 596, paragraph 28.7.

17 Ibid, volume 1, pp. 53–71, chapter 7.

18 Ibid, volume 1, pp. 55–58, paragraphs 7.13–7.22 and figures 7.1 and 7.2.

19 Ibid, volume 1, pp. 13–14, paragraphs 2.17–2.18.

20 Ibid, volume 4, p. 587, paragraph 27.9.

21 Ibid, volume 4, p. 592, paragraph 27.28.

22 Ibid, volume 4, pp. 592–593, paragraph 27.30.

23 Ibid, volume 4, p. 595, chapter 28.

24 Ibid, volume 4, p. 607, paragraph 28.54.

25 Ibid, volume 4, p. 596, paragraph 28.6.

26 Ibid, volume 4, p. 598, paragraphs 28.11–28.29.

27 Ibid, volume 2, p. 114, paragraph 10.99.

28 Ibid, volume 4, pp. 619–621, paragraphs 28.88–28.97

29 Ibid, volume 4, p. 620, paragraph 28.95.

30 Ibid, volume 4, p. 615, paragraphs 28.80 and 28.81.

31 Ibid, volume 4, chapter 29, pp. 635–687.

32 Ibid, volume 4, p. 650, paragraph 29.54.

33 Ibid, volume 4, p. 645, paragraph 29.39.j.

34 Ibid, volume 4, p. 656, paragraph 29.64.b.

35 Ibid, volume 4, p. 657, paragraph 29.67.

36 Ibid, volume 4, p. 667, paragraph 29.99.a.

37 Harriet Agerholm. 2018. Grenfell Tower Inquiry. *The Independent*, 31 October (www.independent.co.uk/news/uk/home-news/grenfell-tower-fire-inquest-man-trapped-died-told-sister-working-a8611026.html).

38 GTI Phase 1 Report, volume 4, p. 668, paragraph 29.100.a.

39   Ibid, volume 4, p. 668, footnote 196.

40   Ibid, volume 4, p. 635, paragraph 29.1.

41   Ibid, volume 2, p. 108, paragraph 10.79.b, pp. 221–222, paragraph 12.66, p. 286, paragraphs 14.133–135.

42   GTI homepage (www.grenfelltowerinquiry.org.uk/).

43   GTI Phase 2 provisional timetable (https://assets.grenfelltowerinquiry.org.uk/inline-files/Phase%202%20provisional%20timetable_0.pdf).

44   GTI. 2021. Update from the Inquiry. Online article, 28 January (www.grenfelltowerinquiry.org.uk/news/update-inquiry-47).

45   GTI: core participants document (https://assets.grenfelltowerinquiry.org.uk/inline-files/Core-Participants.pdf).

46   GTI. 2018. Update from the Inquiry. Online article, 2 August (www.grenfelltowerinquiry.org.uk/news/update-inquiry-3).

47   GTI Report, part 1, chapter 2 p. 13, paragraph 2.16

48   Ibid, volume 1, chapters 2 and 7, and volume 4, chapter 33: Recommendations, pp. 773–777.

49   GTI Phase 2. 2020. Details of modules, 27 January, pp. 9–16 (https://assets.grenfelltowerinquiry.org.uk/documents/transcript/Transcript%2027%20January%202020.pdf).

50   GTI. 2020. Update on Inquiry. Online article, 24 January (www.grenfelltowerinquiry.org.uk/news/update-inquiry-24).

51   GTI Phase 2 provisional timetable (note 41).

52   GTI. 2020. Ruling on an application. Online article, 6 February (https://assets.grenfelltowerinquiry.org.uk/inline-files/Ruling%20on%20the%20Application%20for%20an%20Undertaking%2006.02.2020.pdf).

53   GTI. 2020. Update from the chairman. Online article, 16 March (www.grenfelltowerinquiry.org.uk/news/update-chairman).

54   GTI. 2021. Temporary suspension of hearings. Online article, 6 January (www.grenfelltowerinquiry.org.uk/news/temporary-suspension-hearings).

55   Robert Booth. 2020. Grenfell Tower Inquiry resumes but distancing rules anger families. *The Guardian*, 6 July (www.theguardian.com/uk-news/2020/jul/06/grenfell-tower-inquiry-resumes-but-distancing-rules-anger-families).

56   GTI Phase 2. 2020. Opening statement by counsel to the Inquiry. Transcript, 27 January, p. 18, lines 21–25 and p. 19, lines 1–2.

57   GTI Phase 2. 2020. Opening Statement on behalf of the Royal Borough of Kensington and Chelsea. Transcript, 27 January, p. 61, lines 18–25 and p. 62, lines 1–20.

58   GTI Phase 2. 2020. Witness evidence from Jon Roper (area sales manager of Celotex). Transcript, 16 November, pp. 198–202.

59   GTI Phase 2. 2018. Written opening submission for module 1 on behalf of Celotex Limited. Report, December, p. 49, paragraph 110 (https://assets.grenfelltowerinquiry.org.uk/CEL00011945_Celotex%20Opening%20Submissions%20Module%201.pdf).

60   GTI Phase 2. 2020. Opening statement by counsel to the Inquiry. Transcript, 27 January, p. 18, lines 9–13.

61 Robert Booth. 2020. Grenfell witnesses threaten to withhold evidence. *The Guardian*, 29 January (www.theguardian.com/uk-news/2020/jan/29/grenfell-inquiry-thrown-into-confusion-over-legal-move-by-witnesses).

62 Peter Apps. 2020. Grenfell Tower: the organisations involved in the refurbishment. *Inside Housing*, 28 January (www.insidehousing.co.uk/insight/insight/grenfell-tower-the-organisations-involved-in-the-refurbishment-64874).

63 GTI Phase 2. 2020. Witness evidence from David Gibson (head of capital investment at KCTMO 2013–6). Transcript, 14 October, p. 40, lines 8–15.

64 GTI Phase 2. 2020. Witness evidence from Mark Anderson (director of assets and regeneration at KCTMO 2011–3). Transcript, 14 October, p. 12, lines 11–15, p. 15, lines 23–25 and p. 16, lines 1–7.

65 GTI Phase 2. 2020. Witness evidence from Andrzej Kuszell (director of Studio E). Transcript, 2 March, p. 20, lines 15–17.

66 GTI Phase 2. 2020. Witness evidence from Bruce Sounes (director of Studio E). Transcript, 3 March, pp. 133–150.

67 GTI Phase 2. 2020. Witness evidence from Stephen Blake (refurbishment director of Rydon). Transcript, 28 July, pp. 162, lines 6–8.

68 Ibid, pp. 181–182.

69 GTI Phase 2. 2020. Witness evidence from Simon Lawrence (project manager for Rydon). Transcript, 28 July, pp. 192–194.

70 Ibid, 21 July, p. 68, lines 9–10.

71 Peter Apps. 2020. Grenfell Tower Inquiry diary week 7. *Inside Housing*, 24 July.

72 GTI Phase 2. 2020. Witness evidence from Simon Lawrence (project manager for Rydon). Transcript, 21 July, p. 160, lines 2–9 and p. 164, lines 1–24. Peter Apps. 2020. KCTMO project manager admits destroying evidence relating to Grenfell refurbishment after fire. *Inside Housing*, 19 October (www.insidehousing.co.uk/news/news/kctmo-project-manager-admits-destroying-evidence-relating-to-grenfell-refurbishment-after-fire-68240).

73 GTI Phase 2. 2020. Witness evidence from Daniel Anketell-Jones (design manager for Harvey Facades). Transcript, 16 September, p. 19, lines 18–19 and p. 20, lines 4–8. Jack Simpson. 2020. Grenfell Tower Inquiry diary week 10: 'As we all know, ACM will be gone rather quickly in a fire!'. *Inside Housing*, 18 September (www.insidehousing.co.uk/insight/insight/grenfell-tower-inquiry-diary-week-10-as-we-all-know-acm-will-be-gone-rather-quickly-in-a-fire-67955).

74 GTI Phase 2. 2020. Witness evidence from Simon Lawrence (project manager for Rydon). Transcript, 22 July, p. 89, lines 23–25 and p. 90, lines 1–3.

75 GTI Phase 2. 2020. Expert evidence from Beryl Menzies. Transcript, 27 October, p. 131, lines 6–8.

76 GTI Phase 2. 2020. Witness evidence from John Hoban (building control inspector for RBKC). Transcript, 29 September, p. 107, lines 4–10.

77 GTI Phase 2. 2020. Witness evidence from John Hoban (building control inspector for RBKC). Transcript, 1 October, p. 217, line 25 and p. 218, lines 1–10.

78 Peter Apps. 2020. The Grenfell Tower Inquiry is uncovering a major corporate scandal. *The Spectator*, 6 December (www.spectator.co.uk/article/the-grenfell-tower-inquiry-is-uncovering-a-major-corporate-scandal).

79 Ibid.

80   Ibid. See also GTI Phase 2. 2020. Opening statement from Adrian Williamson QC, counsel for some of the bereaved, survivors and residents. Transcript, 9 November, p. 5, lines 2–16.

81   Ibid, p. 15, lines 9–11 and p. 16, line 1.

82   GTI Phase 2. 2020. Opening statement from Stephanie Barwise QC, counsel for some of the bereaved, survivors and residents. Transcript, 5 November, p. 38, lines 7–17.

83   Ibid, p. 37, lines 1–19.

84   Robert Booth. 2020. A 'raging inferno' testimony reveals how deadly cladding ended up on Grenfell Tower. The Guardian, 16 December (www.theguardian. com/uk-news/2020/dec/16/a-raging-inferno-testimony-reveals-how-deadly-cladding-ended-up-on-grenfell-tower).

85   Apps (2020). The Grenfell Tower Inquiry is uncovering a major corporate scandal.

86   GTI Phase 2. 2020. Opening statement from Stephanie Barwise QC, counsel for some of the bereaved, survivors and residents. Transcript, 5 November, p. 43, lines 22–25 and p. 44, lines 1–7.

87   GTI Phase 2. 2020. Witness evidence from Jon Roper (area sales manager of Celotex). Transcript, 16 November, p. 95, lines 21–25 and p. 96, line 1.

88   Apps (2020). The Grenfell Tower Inquiry is uncovering a major corporate scandal.

89   INQUEST. 2019. Family reflections on Grenfell: no voice left unheard.

90   Ibid, pp. 10–11.

91   UK Government. 2020. New Grenfell adviser appointed as final Grenfell Taskforce report published. Government news website article, 26 March (www. gov.uk/government/news/new-grenfell-adviser-appointed-as-final-grenfell-taskforce-report-published).

92   Independent Grenfell Recovery Taskforce. 2020. Fifth report. Report, 6 March, p. 1 (https://assets.publishing.service.gov.uk/government/uploads/system/ uploads/attachment_data/file/875500/Independent_Grenfell_Recovery_ Taskforce_fifth_report.pdf).

93   National Audit Office. 2020. Investigation into remediating dangerous cladding on high-rise buildings. Report, 19 June, p. 4 (www.nao.org.uk/wp-content/ uploads/2020/06/Investigation-into-remediating-dangerous-cladding-on-high-rise-buildings.pdf).

94   UK Government. 2021. New regulator established to ensure construction materials are safe. Press release, 19 January (www.gov.uk/government/news/ new-regulator-established-to-ensure-construction-materials-are-safe).

95   Dame Judith Hackitt. 2017. Building a safer future – independent review of building regulations and fire safety interim report. Report, December (https:// assets.publishing.service.gov.uk/government/uploads/system/uploads/ attachment_data/file/668831/Independent_Review_of_Building_Regulations_ and_Fire_Safety_web_accessible.pdf).

96   Ibid, p. 9.

97   Ibid, p. 6.

98   Dame Judith Hackitt. 2018. Building a safer future – final report. Report, May (https://assets.publishing.service.gov.uk/government/uploads/system/uploads/ attachment_data/file/707785/Building_a_Safer_Future_-_web.pdf).

99   Ibid, pp. 12–15.

100 May Bulman and Lizzy Buchan. 2018. Grenfell Tower report that fails to ban combustible cladding is a 'betrayal and a whitewash', says David Lammy. *The Independent*, 17 May (www.independent.co.uk/news/uk/home-news/grenfell-tower-report-cladding-david-lammy-fire-death-dame-judith-hackitt-a8355466.html).

101 BBC. 2018. Grenfell Tower: government will consult on cladding ban. *BBC News* website, 17 May (www.bbc.co.uk/news/uk-44148694).

102 UK Government. 2018. James Brokenshire publishes consultation on banning combustible cladding. Press release, 18 June (www.gov.uk/government/news/james-brokenshire-publishes-consultation-on-banning-combustible-cladding).

103 UK Government. 2018. Government bans combustible materials on high-rise homes. Press release, 29 November (www.gov.uk/government/news/government-bans-combustible-materials-on-high-rise-homes).

104 UK Government. 2020. Fire Safety Bill. News story, 19 March (www.gov.uk/government/news/fire-safety-bill). UK Governement. 2020. Draft Building Safety Bill. Draft bill (www.gov.uk/government/news/explained-the-draft-building-safety-bill).

105 Chris Grainger and Ruth Armstrong. 2020. An overview of the draft Fire Safety Bill. Gately plc website article, 15 September (https://gateleyplc.com/insight/in-depth/draft-fire-safety-bill-overview/).

106 Housing, Communities & Local Government Committee. 2020. Pre-legislative scrutiny of the Building Safety Bill. UK Parliament, 24 November, paragraphs 22–32 (https://publications.parliament.uk/pa/cm5801/cmselect/cmcomloc/466/46603.htm#_idTextAnchor001).

107 Greg Heffer. 2017. Theresa May pledges to rehouse Grenfell Tower victims in three weeks. *Sky News* website, 17 June (https://news.sky.com/story/theresa-may-pledges-to-rehouse-grenfell-tower-fire-victims-in-three-weeks-10917886).

108 Grenfell Support. 2018. Grenfell Tower and Grenfell Walk housing update. Tweet, 13 June (https://twitter.com/Celeste_SPT/status/1277255916954542087).

109 RBKC. 2019. Grenfell Tower and Grenfell Walk housing update. Tweet, 27 June (https://twitter.com/GrenfellUpdates/status/1144253900859596800). (Temporary accommodation includes one in a hotel and one in a serviced apartment.)

110 Ministry of Housing, Communities & Local Government. 2018. Building safety programme: monthly data release for 14 June. Report, 28 June (https://assets.publishing.service.gov.uk/government/uploads/system/uploads/attachment_data/file/901051/Building_Safety_Data_Release_June_2020.pdf).

111 Ministry of Housing, Communities & Local Government. 2018. Building safety programme: monthly data release for 30 June. Report, 16 July (https://assets.publishing.service.gov.uk/government/uploads/system/uploads/attachment_data/file/901051/Building_Safety_Data_Release_June_2020.pdf). (Note that by December 2020, 216 (47%) had completed remediation.) See also Ministry of Housing, Communities & Local Government. 2020. Building Safety Programme: monthly data release for 30 November. Report, 17 December.

112 Ministry of Housing, Communities & Local Government. 2018. Building safety programme: monthly data release for 31 December. Report, 21 January (https:// assets.publishing.service.gov.uk/government/uploads/system/uploads/att achment_data/file/954319/Building_Safety_Data_Release_December_2020.pdf).

113 Matt Hodges-Long. 2020. Twitter thread on prohibitions. Tweets, 16 December (https://twitter.com/MattHodgesLong/status/1339239246981455872).

114 Rupert Jones. 2020. Residents asked to leave London blocks. *The Guardian,* 19 October (www.theguardian.com/society/2020/oct/19/residents-evacuated-london-paragon-site-brentford).

115 UK Parliament. 2020. Progress of remediation. Report Summary, 20 June (https://publications.parliament.uk/pa/cm5801/cmselect/cmcomloc/172/17203. htm#_idTextAnchor000).

116 There were an estimated 1,700 high-risk residential buildings with dangerous non-ACM cladding and 300 with ACM cladding that had not been remediated at the time of the House of Commons report.

117 UK Parliament (2020). Progress of remediation.

118 Ibid, paragraphs 11–12.

119 Ibid, paragraphs 16–17.

120 Ibid, paragraph 34.

121 Martina Lees. 2020. Grenfell cladding scandal: Manchester residents clash with government over who pays for remediation works. *The Times,* 14 June (www. thetimes.co.uk/article/grenfell-cladding-scandal-manchester-residents-clash-with-government-over-who-pays-for-remediation-works-9zwzkcn68).

122 Jack Simpson. 2019. Advice note 14 explained: what is it and why is it stopping the sale of so many properties? *Inside Housing,* 1 November (www.insidehousing. co.uk/insight/insight/advice-note-14-explained-what-is-it-and-why-is-it-stopping-the-sale-of-so-many-properties-63981).

123 Building Societies Association. 2019. Form EWS1: external wall fire review. Report, December (www.rics.org/globalassets/rics-website/ews1-external-wall-fire-review-final-2.pdf).

124 UK Parliament. 2020. Progress of remediation. Report, 20 June, section 2, paragraphs 86–87 (https://publications.parliament.uk/pa/cm5801/cmselect/ cmcomloc/172/17206.htm#_idTextAnchor047).

125 Martina Lees. 2020. Hidden housing scandal: what landlords need to know about cladding, EWS1 forms and more. *The Times.* 20 November (www.thetimes.co.uk/ article/hidden-housing-scandal-what-landlords-need-to-know-about-cladding-ews1-forms-and-more-db5gqvv6c).

126 UK Parliament (2020). Progress of remediation (section 2, paragraphs 86–87).

127 National Audit Office. 2020. Investigation into remediating dangerous cladding on high-rise buildings. Report, 19 June, p. 37, paragraph 2.12 (www.nao.org. uk/wp-content/uploads/2020/06/Investigation-into-remediating-dangerous-cladding-on-high-rise-buildings.pdf).

128 Sebastian O'Kelly. 2020. Greenhalgh to dump 'affordable' cladding bills on leaseholders, which they were promised AGAIN and AGAIN would not happen. *Leasehold Knowledge* website, 21 October (www.leaseholdknowledge.com/ greenhalgh-to-dump-affordable-cladding-bills-on-leaseholders-which-they-were-promised-again-and-again-would-not-happen/).

129   UK Parliament (2020). Progress of remediation (section 2, paragraphs 81–83).

130   Josh Hallliday. 2020. Leaseholders billed up to £115,000 each to remove Grenfell-style cladding. *The Guardian,* 17 July (www.theguardian.com/money/2020/jul/17/leaseholders-billed-up-to-115000-each-to-remove-grenfell-style-cladding).

131   UK Parliament (2020). Progress of remediation (section 2, paragraph 67).

132   Ibid, section 1, paragraphs 75 and 79.

133   Ibid, section 2, paragraphs 92–95.

134   Ibid, section 2, paragraph 92.

135   Ibid.

136   Ibid, section 2, paragraph 95.

137   UK Parliament. 2020. Government to bring an end to unsafe cladding with multi-billion pound intervention. Press release, 10 February (www.gov.uk/government/news/government-to-bring-an-end-to-unsafe-cladding-with-multi-billion-pound-intervention).

138   Martina Lees. 2021. We won't stop campaigning until all buildings are safe and developers pay. *The Sunday Times,* 14 February (www.thetimes.co.uk/article/we-wont-stop-campaigning-until-all-buildings-are-safe-and-developers-pay-up-tnc6opm5h).

139   Richard Willingham. 2019. Flammable cladding to be stripped from buildings under Victorian government plan. *ABC News* website, 16 July (www.abc.net.au/news/2019-07-16/flammable-cladding-removal-fund-victorian-government/11311518).

140   In 2019, Rydon, the design and build contractor in the Grenfell refurbishment, made pretax profits of £16.1 million; Saint-Gobain, owner of subsidiary Celotex, manufacturer of the insulation, reported sales of €42.6 billion; and Arconic, the manufacturer of the cladding used on Grenfell, reported revenues of $14.2 billion. See David Price. 2020. Rydon's £5 million dividend payout revealed. *Construction News,* 16 April (www.constructionnews.co.uk/financial/rydons-5m-dividend-payout-revealed-16-04-2020/); Saint-Gobain in figures. 2019. Saint-Gobain website (www.saint-gobain.com/en/finance/saint-gobain-figures); Fréa Lockley. 2020. Three years on, the Grenfell tragedy epitomizes the UK's brutal inequality, racism and injustice. *The Canary,* 14 June (www.thecanary.co/uk/analysis/2020/06/14/three-years-on-the-grenfell-tragedy-epitomises-the-uks-brutal-inequality-racism and injustice/).

141   Barbara Lane. 2020. Expert evidence to GTI. Transcript, 28 October, p. 120, lines 6–25 and p. 127, line 1.

NOTES FOR CHAPTER 3

1   Richard Feynman. 2019. Tweet, 12 March (https://twitter.com/ProfFeynman/status/1105490809439338496).

2   George Box and Norman Draper. 1987. *Empirical Model-Building and Response Surfaces,* p. 424. Wiley.

3   Gill Kernick. 2017. Interview by Matthew Price. *Today Programme,* BBC Radio 4, 16 June (transcript) (https://grenfellenquirer.blog/2019/06/09/1362/).

4   Marc Waxman. 2011. Changing the system vs. systemic change. Chalkbeat website article, 24 February (https://ny.chalkbeat.org/2011/2/24/21097457/ changing-the-system-vs-systemic-change).

5   'Systemic change' is a website committed to the potential of systemic change in helping education move into the twenty-first century (https://systemicchange. wordpress.com/systemicchange/).

6   John Kania, Mark Kramer and Peter Senge. 2018. The waters of systems change. Paper, FSG, June, p. 3 (www.fsg.org/publications/water_of_systems_change).

7   Robert Booth. 2019. Institutional racism: 20 years since the Stephen Lawrence inquiry. *The Guardian*, 22 February (www.theguardian.com/uk-news/2019/feb/22/ institutional-racism-britain-stephen-lawrence-inquiry-20-years).

8   Alan Travis. 2013. Stephen Lawrence: how his murder changed the legal landscape. *The Guardian*, 22 April (www.theguardian.com/uk/2013/apr/22/ stephen-lawrence-murder-changed-legal-landscape).

9   S. Freeman-Powell. 2019. What has really happened since Macpherson's report. *BBC News* website, 24 February (www.bbc.co.uk/news/uk-47300343).

10 Kania, Kramer and Senge (2018). The waters of systems change, p. 2.

11 Ibid.

12 SiG. 2020. Ecosystems for systems change. Website article, Social Innovation Generation (www.sigeneration.ca/ecosystems-systems-change/).

13 Serena Chan. 2001. Complex adaptive systems. Research Seminar in Engineering Systems, 31 October–6 November (http://web.mit.edu/esd.83/www/notebook/ Complex%20Adaptive%20Systems.pdf).

14 David J. Snowden and Mary E. Boone. 2007. A leader's framework for decision making. *Harvard Business Review*, November (https://hbr.org/2007/11/a-leaders- framework-for-decision-making).

15 Ibid.

16 Chan (2001). Complex adaptive systems.

17 Delara Shakib and Linda Givetash. 2020. Rhodes will fall. *NBC News* website, 18 June (www.nbcnews.com/news/world/rhodes-will-fall-oxford-university- remove-statue-amid-anti-racism-n1231387).

18 Greta Thunberg's Wikipedia entry (https://en.wikipedia.org/wiki/Greta_ Thunberg).

19 Klaus Schwab. 2016. *The Fourth Industrial Revolution*, p. 21. New York: Crown Publishing Group.

20 World Economic Forum. 2015. Deep shift – technology tipping points and societal impact. Survey Report, Global Agenda Council on the Future of Software and Society, September, p. 29 (www3.weforum.org/docs/WEF_GAC15_ Technological_Tipping_Points_report_2015.pdf).

21 Shelley Podolny. 2015. If an algorithm wrote this, how would you even know? *New York Times*, 7 March (www.nytimes.com/2015/03/08/opinion/sunday/if-an- algorithm-wrote-this-how-would-you-even-know.html?_r=0).

22 Sunday Review. 2015. Did a human or a computer write this? *New York Times*, 7 March (www.nytimes.com/interactive/2015/03/08/opinion/sunday/algorithm- human-quiz.html).

23   Schwab (2016). *The Fourth Industrial Revolution*, p. 23.

24   Ibid, p. 3.

25   Klaus Schwab. 2015. The Fourth Industrial Revolution – what it means and how to respond. *Foreign Affairs* website article, 12 December (www.foreignaffairs. com/articles/2015-12-12/fourth-industrial-revolution).

26   Schwab (2016). *The Fourth Industrial Revolution*, p. 3.

27   Alex Gray. 2016. The 10 skills you need to thrive in the Fourth Industrial Revolution. World Economic Forum website article, 19 January (www.weforum. org/agenda/2016/01/the-10-skills-you-need-to-thrive-in-the-fourth-industrial-revolution/).

28   Till Alexander Leopold, Vesselina Ratcheva and Saadia Zahidi. 2016. The future of jobs. Global Challenge Insight Report for the World Economic Forum, January (www3.weforum.org/docs/WEF_Future_of_Jobs.pdf).

29   Schwab (2015). The Fourth Industrial Revolution – what it means and how to respond.

30   Ibid, pp. 5–6.

31   Schwab (2016). *The Fourth Industrial Revolution*, p. 71.

32   Harry Davies. 2020. Advice on protective gear for NHS staff was rejected owing to cost. *The Guardian,* 27 March (www.theguardian.com/world/2020/mar/27/advice-on-protective-gear-for-nhs-staff-was-rejected-owing-to-cost).

33   Talha Burki. 2020. England and Wales see 20,000 excess deaths in care homes. *The Lancet* **395,** 23 May 23 (www.thelancet.com/pdfs/journals/lancet/PIIS0140-6736(20)31199-5.pdf).

34   Schwab (2015). The Fourth Industrial Revolution – what it means and how to respond.

35   Ibid, pp. 4–5.

36   Ranking the world. YouTube video clip (www.youtube.com/watch?v=8WVoJ6 JNLO8). (This video ranks the top ten most valuable publicly traded companies in the world from 1997 to 2019 based on market capitalization. Market capitalization is calculated from the share price of a stock multiplied by the number of outstanding shares. Figures are converted into US dollars (using the rate from the selected day) to allow for comparison.)

37   Schwab (2015). The Fourth Industrial Revolution – what it means and how to respond.

38   Sydney Dekker. 2006. *The Field Guide to Understanding Human Error*, p. xi. Ashgate Publishing (now Taylor & Francis).

39   Sidney Dekker. 2014. The bureaucratization of safety. *Safety Science,* 14 July (www.safetydifferently.com/wp-content/uploads/2014/08/BureaucratizationSafety.pdf).

40   Mike Mosedale. 2010. Cartoon from Cartoonstock website (www.cartoonstock. com/directory/w/work_health_and_safety.asp).

41   René Amalberti. 2001. As cited in Sidney Dekker (2014). The bureaucratization of safety (p. 3, paragraph 2.1).

42   Published by permission. www.CartoonStock.com.

43   Ibid.

44 Dekker (2006). *The Field Guide to Understanding Human Error*, p. 12.

45 Dekker (2014). The bureaucratization of safety.

46 Amalberti (2001). As cited in Dekker (2014). The bureaucratization of safety.

47 The *Challenger* Space Shuttle disaster's Wikipedia article (https://en.wikipedia. org/wiki/Space_Shuttle_Challenger_disaster).

48 Richard Feynman. 1986. Personal observations on the reliability of the Shuttle. Rogers Commission Report on the Space Shuttle Accident, Appendix F (https:// science.ksc.nasa.gov/shuttle/missions/51-l/docs/rogers-commission/Appendix-F. txt).

49 Nick Hopkins. 2020. Revealed: UK ministers were warned last year of risks of coronavirus pandemic. *The Guardian*, 24 April (www.theguardian.com/ world/2020/apr/24/revealed-uk-ministers-were-warned-last-year-of-risks-of-coronavirus-pandemic).

50 BBC. 2021. Covid deaths: 'hard to compute sorrow' of 100,000 milestone – PM. *BBC News* website (www.bbc.co.uk/news/uk-55814751).

51 Andrew Hopkins. 2011. Management walk-arounds: lessons from the Gulf of Mexico oil well blowout. Report, Australian National University, February (http://regnet.anu.edu.au/sites/default/files/publications/attachments/2015-05/ WorkingPaper_79_0.pdf).

52 Note that the models presented here are somewhat simplistic because of their two-dimensional nature. There are more complex ways of thinking about catastrophic risk. For the purposes of this book, these models are used to illustrate thinking in an accessible way.

53 For a detailed exploration of the Swiss cheese model and its application see James Reason. 2008. *The Human Contribution: Unsafe Acts, Accidents and Heroic Recoveries*. Farnham: Ashgate Publishing.

54 Adapted from the wikimedia image at https://commons.wikimedia.org/ wiki/File:Swiss_cheese_model.svg by BenAveling, CC BY-SA 4.0 <https://creativecommons.org/licenses/by-sa/4.0>, via Wikimedia Commons. Distributed under the same license.

55 See, for example, Health and Safety Executive. 2008. Optimising hazard management by workforce engagement and supervision. Report prepared by Risk Support Limited (www.hse.gov.uk/research/rrpdf/rr637.pdf).

56 Adapted from J. Aust and D. Pons. 2019. Bowtie methodology for risk analysis of visual borescope inspection during aircraft engine maintenance. *Aerospace* **6**, 110 (https://doi.org/10.3390/aerospace6100110). Published under open access license.

57 GTI Phase 1. 2018. Witness evidence from Commissioner Dany Cotton (London Fire Brigade). Transcript, 27 September, p. 52, lines 2–11.

58 Gill Kernick. 2020. Supply chains and deferring risk. Blog post, Grenfell Enquirer (https://grenfellenquirer.blog/2020/02/01/supply-chains-and-deferring-risk-reflections-on-week-1-of-the-grenfell-tower-inquiry/).

59 Douglas Ready, Carol Cohen, David Kiron and Benjamin Pring. 2020. The new leadership playbook for the digital age. *MIT Sloan Management Review*, January (https://sloanreview.mit.edu/projects/the-new-leadership-playbook-for-the-digital-age/).

60   Ibid, p. 2.

61   Ibid, p. 8 (figure 3: 'Eroding, enduring and emerging leadership behaviors').

62   Ibid, pp. 8, 10.

63   Ibid, p. 2

64   Jeremy Heimans and Henry Timms. 2014. Understanding 'New Power'. *Harvard Business Review*, December (https://hbr.org/2014/12/understanding-new-power).

65   Andrew Day. 2020. *Disruption, Change and Transformation in Organizations: A Human Relations Perspective*, p. 22. Abingdon: Routledge.

66   Daniel H. Pink. 2009. *Drive: The Surprising Truth about What Motivates Us*. New York: Riverhead Books.

67   RSA Animate. 2010. Drive: the surprising truth about what motivates us. YouTube video clip (www.youtube.com/watch?v=uwA97yWz9Uc).

68   Ronald Heifetz, Alexander Grashow and Marty Linsky. 2009. Leadership in a (permanent) crisis. *Harvard Business Review*, July–August (https://hbr.org/2009/07/leadership-in-a-permanent-crisis).

69   Ronald Heifetz, Alexander Grashow and Marty Linsky. 2009. *The Practice of Adaptive Leadership: Tools and Tactics for Changing Your Organization and the World*, p. 19. Boston, MA: Harvard Business Press.

70   Edgar Schein. 2013. *Humble Inquiry: The Gentle Art of Asking instead of Telling*, p. 2. Oakland, CA: Berrett-Koehler.

71   J. R. Ravetz. 1999. What is post-normal science. *Futures* 31, p. 648 (www.andreasaltelli.eu/file/repository/Editorials2.pdf).

72   David J. Snowden and Mary E. Boone. 2007. A leader's framework for decision caking. *Harvard Business Review*, November (https://hbr.org/2007/11/a-leaders-framework-for-decision-making).

73   Adapted from Richard Bolden, Addy Adelaine, Stella Warren, Anita Gulati, Hazel Conley and Carol Jarvis. 2019. Inclusion: the DNA of leadership and change. Report, University of the West of England, p. 15 (https://uwe-repository.worktribe.com/output/852067). (Figure used with permission from Dave Snowden.)

74   Windrush scandal's Wikipedia entry (https://en.wikipedia.org/wiki/Windrush_scandal).

75   Schwab (2015). The Fourth Industrial Revolution – what it means and how to respond.

76   Day (2020). *Disruption, Change and Transformation in Organizations: A Human Relations Perspective*, chapter 9.

NOTES FOR CHAPTER 4

1   Hugh Griffiths QC. 1968. Report of the Inquiry into the collapse of flats at Ronan Point, Canning Town. Report, Ministry of Housing & Local Government, p. 4, paragraph 14.

2   GTI Phase 1 Report, volume 4, p. 607, paragraph 28.54.

3   OpenLearn. 2001. Ronan Point. Report, 26 November (www.open.edu/openlearn/history-the-arts/history/heritage/ronan-point).

4   Norbert J. Delatte. 2009. *Beyond Failure: Forensic Case Studies for Civil Engineers*, p. 418. Reston, VA: American Society of Civil Engineers.

5   Sophie Barnes. 2018. The tower blocks that time forgot. *Inside Housing*, 16 May (www.insidehousing.co.uk/insight/insight/the-tower-blocks-that-time-forgot2-56303).

6   Adam Forrest. 2018. Hundreds of tower blocks across UK at risk of collapse, say experts. *The Independent*, 22 October (www.independent.co.uk/news/uk/home-news/tower-blocks-collapse-risk-grenfell-safety-government-a8592436.html).

7   Barnes (2018). The tower blocks that time forgot.

8   Meriel Jeater. 2016. Three myths you probably believe about the Great Fire of London. Museum of London website, 6 December (www.museumoflondon.org.uk/discover/three-myths-you-believe-about-great-fire-london).

9   The Great Fire of London website (www.fireoflondon.org.uk/story/peoples-lives/).

10 Heather Y. Wheeler. 2018. The Great Fire of London 1666. Totally Timelines website, 27 September (www.totallytimelines.com/the-great-fire-of-london-1666).

11 Jeater (2016). Three myths you probably believe about the Great Fire of London.

12 The Great Fire of London website.

13 Jeater (2016). Three myths you probably believe about the Great Fire of London.

14 Ziauddin Sardar (editor). 2017/9. *The Postnormal Times Reader*, pp. 124–127 (https://postnormaltim.es/sites/default/files/uploads/PostNormalTimesReader(booktext)-USintlepub(25APR2019).pdf).

15 Nassim Nicholas Taleb. 2007. *The Black Swan: The Impact of the Highly Improbable*. New York: Random House.

16 C. Scott Jordan. 2020. A stroll through the menagerie. *Postnormal Times* website, 26 May (https://postnormaltim.es/insights/stroll-through-menagerie).

17 Dan Nosowitz. 2013. Jellyfish shut down massive nuclear power plant. *Popular Science* website, 1 October (www.popsci.com/article/technology/jellyfish-shut-down-massive-nuclear-power-plant/).

18 Martina Lees. 2020. Hidden housing scandal. *The Times*, 2 October (www.thetimes.co.uk/article/hidden-housing-scandal-campaign-safe-homes-for-all-v65h9pcvl).

19 Harry Lambert. 2020. Why weren't we ready? *New Statesman*, 30 March (www.newstatesman.com/politics/uk/2020/03/why-weren-t-we-ready).

20 Bill Gates. 2015. The next outbreak? We're not ready. TED Talk: TED2015 (www.ted.com/talks/bill_gates_the_next_outbreak_we_re_not_ready).

21 World Health Organization. 2019. WHO launches new global influenza strategy. WHO news release, 11 March (www.who.int/news/item/11-03-2019-who-launches-new-global-influenza-strategy).

22 Matthew Bonner, Wojciech Wegrzynski, Bartlomiej K. Papis and Guillermo Rein. 2020. KRESNIK: a top-down, statistical approach to understand the fire performance of building facades using standard test data. *Building and Environment* **169**, 106540, 2020, p. 2 (https://doi.org/10.1016/j.buildenv.2019.106540). Published with permission.

23   Grenfell Action Group. 2016. KCTMO playing with fire. Blog post, 20 November (https://grenfellactiongroup.wordpress.com/2016/11/20/kctmo-playing-with-fire/).

24   Richard Judge and Shirin Elahi. 2021. Foresight review of the future of regulatory systems: regulating in a disruptive world. Lloyd's Register Foundation Report Series, no 2021.1, p. 27 (https://www.lrfoundation.org.uk/en/news/foresight-review-regulation/).

25   Ibid, p. 17–20.

26   Ibid, p. 31. (Reworked and included with the permission of Richard Judge.)

27   Ibid, p. 31.

28   Ibid, p. 29

29   Ibid, pp. 37–42.

30   National Audit Office. 2017. A short guide to regulation. Report, September, pp. 6, 7 (www.regulation.org.uk/library/2017-NAO-A-Short-Guide-to-Regulation.pdf).

31   UK Government. 2013. Legislative process: taking a bill through Parliament. Government website, 20 February (www.gov.uk/guidance/legislative-process-taking-a-bill-through-parliament).

32   Cabinet Office. 2017. Guide to making legislation. Government website, July (https://assets.publishing.service.gov.uk/government/uploads/system/uploads/attachment_data/file/645652/Guide_to_Making_Legislation_Jul_2017.pdf).

33   UK Government. Undated. How legislation comes into force and is amended. (Part of 'Understanding legislation'.) Government website (www.legislation.gov.uk/understanding-legislation#Howlegislationcomesintoforceandisamended).

34   Institute for Government. 2020. Secondary legislation. Institute for Government website (www.instituteforgovernment.org.uk/publication/parliamentary-monitor-2020/secondary-legislation).

35   Harry Yorke. 2020. More than 90 coronavirus laws and rules imposed without Parliamentary scrutiny. The Telegraph, 17 June (www.telegraph.co.uk/politics/2020/06/17/90-coronavirus-laws-rules-imposed-without-parliamentary-scrutiny/).

36   National Audit Office (2017). A short guide to regulation, p. 9.

37   National Audit Office. 2014. Using alternatives to regulation to achieve policy objectives. Report, June, p. 4 (www.nao.org.uk/wp-content/uploads/2014/06/Using-alternatives-to-regulation-to-achieve-policy-objectives-summary.pdf).

38   Dame Judith Hackitt. 2017. Building a safer future – independent review of building regulations and fire safety interim report. Report, December, p. 6 (https://assets.publishing.service.gov.uk/government/uploads/system/uploads/attachment_data/file/668831/Independent_Review_of_Building_Regulations_and_Fire_Safety_web_accessible.pdf).

39   Peter Apps. 2019. Timeline: the road to Grenfell. Inside Housing, 6 November (www.insidehousing.co.uk/insight/insight/timeline-the-road-to-grenfell-63889).

40   Ibid. See 1985 in the timeline.

41   FBU. 2019. The Grenfell Tower fire: a crime caused by profit and deregulation. Fire Brigades Union pamphlet, September.

42   National Audit Office. 2020. Investigation into remediating dangerous cladding on high-rise buildings. NAO website article, 19 June (www.nao.org.uk/wp-content/uploads/2020/06/Investigation-into-remediating-dangerous-cladding-on-high-rise-buildings.pdf).

43   The Fire Safety Bill and the Building Safety Bill are expected to be read into law in 2021.

44   National Audit Office. 2017. A short guide to regulation. NAO website, September, pp. 20–22 (www.nao.org.uk/wp-content/uploads/2017/09/A-Short-Guide-to-Regulation.pdf).

45   Hackitt (2017). Building a safer future – independent review of building regulations and fire safety interim report, p. 3.

46   Philip Parvin. 2007. Friend or foe? Lobbying in British democracy. Discussion Paper, Hansard Society (https://assets.ctfassets.net/u1rlvvbs33ri/1cs8UQoPYg6e2WGUUGoe4U/2e27d2a2254abd3f27cf0f7042bf685c/Publication__Friend-or-Foe-Lobbying-in-British-Democracy-2007.pdf).

47   Sean O'Neill. 2020. Building firm Kingspan 'gamed fire tests in aftermath of Grenfell blaze'. *The Times*, 9 December (www.thetimes.co.uk/article/building-firm-kingspan-gamed-fire-tests-in-aftermath-of-grenfell-blaze-n3f6smwqc).

48   Ibid. See also Peter Apps. 2021. Kingspan director denies attempt to 'mislead' MPs by 'concealing' cladding tests. *Inside Housing*, 23 March (www.insidehousing.co.uk/news/news/kingspan-director-denies-attempt-to-mislead-mps-by-concealing-cladding-tests-70142).

49   National Audit Office (2017). A short guide to regulation, p. 14.

50   Ibid.

51   Regulation.org.uk. 2006. Deregulation 1948–2006. Note on Regulation.org.uk website (www.regulation.org.uk/deregulation-1948_to_2006.html).

52   National Audit Office (2017). A short guide to regulation, p. 4.

53   Regulation.org.uk (2006). Deregulation 1948–2006.

54   Gerard Tubb and Nick Stylianou. 2018. Grenfell: Britain's fire safety crisis. *Sky News*, 4 June (https://news.sky.com/story/long-read-grenfell-britains-fire-safety-crisis-11146108).

55   Ibid.

56   Ibid.

57   *Inside Housing* reporters. 2019. Warning signs: a timeline of major residential fires post-Grenfell. *Inside Housing*, 18 November (www.insidehousing.co.uk/home/home/warning-signs-a-timeline-of-major-residential-fires-post-grenfell-64191).

58   National Fire Chiefs Council. 2010. Timber framed construction. CFOA Position Statement, 23 November (www.cfoa.org.uk/11064).

59   Rowan Moore. 2020. Do you want beautiful, sustainable and safe tall buildings? Use wood. *The Guardian*, 6 June (www.theguardian.com/commentisfree/2020/jun/06/want-beautiful-sustainable-and-safe-buildings-use-wood).

60   Richard Feynman, quoted in John Moriarty. 2016. Viewpoint: *Challenger* and the misunderstanding of risk. *BBC News* website, 1 February (www.bbc.co.uk/news/magazine-35432071).

61   Thanks to Jonathan Evans, the CEO of Ash and Lacy, for his support in writing this.

62   Peter Apps. 2018. The paper trail: the failure of building regulations. *Inside Housing*, 23 March (www.insidehousing.co.uk/news/news/the-paper-trail-the-failure-of-building-regulations-55445).

63   Jonathan Carrington. 2019. 'Class 0' and the end of government's guidance on building regulations. University of Oxford Law Faculty, 13 January (www.law.ox.ac.uk/housing-after-grenfell/blog/2019/01/class-0-and-end-of-governments-guidance-building-regulations).

64   From a conversation with Jonathan Evans, CEO of Ash and Lacy.

65   GTI Phase 1 Report, volume 1, p. 4, paragraph 2.13.a.

66   Apps (2018). The paper trail: the failure of building regulations.

67   Her Honour Frances Kirkham CBE. 2013. Letter re: Lakanal House fire. Letter, 28 March, p. 3 (www.lambeth.gov.uk/sites/default/files/ec-letter-to-DCLG-pursuant-to-rule43-28March2013.pdf).

68   Apps (2018). The paper trail: the failure of building regulations.

69   HM Government. 2010. Fire safety Approved Document B: volume 2 – buildings other than dwellinghouses. Report, p. 95 (https://assets.publishing.service.gov.uk/government/uploads/system/uploads/attachment_data/file/441669/BR_PDF_AD_B2_2013.pdf).

70   Andrew Sparrow. 2017. Cladding on Grenfell Tower is banned on UK high-rises, says Philip Hammond. *The Guardian*, 18 June (www.theguardian.com/uk-news/2017/jun/18/cladding-on-grenfell-tower-banned-in-uk-says-philip-hammond).

71   UK Select Committee on Environment, Transport and Regional Affairs. 1999. Minutes of evidence from examination of witnesses. Report, 20 July, paragraphs 138–139 (https://publications.parliament.uk/pa/cm199899/cmselect/cmenvtra/741/9072016.htm).

72   Lakanal House Inquest. 2013. Evidence from Brian Martin. Transcript, day 40, p. 34, lines 19–21 (www.lambeth.gov.uk/sites/default/files/LakanalTranscriptDay40.pdf).

73   Dr Jonathan Evans has said that: 'The difference in interpretation of MHCLG was purely their internal interpretation designed to effect a change in the use of ACM without having to edit ADB. There is literally no evidence that anybody ever demanded the use of a limited combustibility core ACM on the basis of ADB 12.7. Significantly none of the manufacturers had ever tested the core "filler" material which would have been necessary to demonstrate that it met the "limited combustibility" requirement.' Dr Evans also points out that: 'The Centre for Window and Cladding Technology wrote to Clive Bett's Community and Local Government committee in 2018 to explain that they had met with MHCLG in 2014 and assured them that the core of an ACM panel was not being interpreted as "filler". It is evident therefore that the MHCLG were trying to establish this principle before the Fire without changing ADB, but failed to do so.'

74   Barbara Lane. 2018. Expert report to GTI, 12 April, section 11, p. 6, paragraph 11.2.25.

75   Apps (2018). The paper trail: the failure of building regulations.

76   GTI Phase 2 Module 2 cladding products factsheet (https://assets.
      grenfelltowerinquiry.org.uk/inline-files/Module%202%20-%20Cladding%20
      Products%20Factsheet.pdf).

77   Apps (2018). The paper trail: the failure of building regulations.

78   Peter Apps. 2018. How tweaked guidance led to combustible insulation on high
      rises. *Inside Housing*, 13 September (www.insidehousing.co.uk/insight/insight/
      how-tweaked-guidance-led-to-combustible-insulation-on-high-rises-57877).

79   Peter Apps. 2021. Kingspan used BRE report on failed test as basis for 29 desktop
      studies. *Inside Housing*, 25 February (www.insidehousing.co.uk/news/kingspan-
      used-bre-report-on-failed-test-as-basis-for-29-desktop-studies-grenfell-inquiry-
      reveals-69751).

80   Ibid.

81   UK Government. Undated. How government works. UK government website
      (www.gov.uk/government/how-government-works).

82   University of Portsmouth. 2011. The British constitution. Public policy hub (www.
      sshls.port.ac.uk/hub/public-policy/structures/british-constitution/).

83   Institute for Government. Undated. Civil service. Institute for Government
      website (www.instituteforgovernment.org.uk/publication/whitehall-
      monitor-2020/civil-service).

84   Local Government Association. Undated. What is local government? Local
      Government Association website (www.local.gov.uk/about/what-local-
      government).

85   Benoit Guerin, Julian McCrae and Marcus Shepheard. 2018. Accountability in
      modern government. Report, Institute for Government, October, pp. 4–5 (www.
      instituteforgovernment.org.uk/sites/default/files/publications/Accountability_
      modern_government_WEB.pdf).

86   Ibid, p. 4.

87   Ibid, p. 3.

88   Martin Stanley. Undated. The Westminster model – detail. Civilservant.org
      website (www.civilservant.org.uk/wm-detail.html).

89   Rob Horgan. 2020. Hackitt: engineers must feel 'chronic uneasiness' to improve
      safety. *New Civil Engineer*, 22 April (www.newcivilengineer.com/latest/hackitt-
      engineers-must-feel-chronic-uneasiness-to-improve-safety-22-04-2020/).

90   Guerin, McCrae and Shepheard (2018). Accountability in modern government,
      p. 4.

91   Tom Sasse and Emma Norris. 2019. Moving on. Report, Institute for Government,
      January, p. 4 (www.instituteforgovernment.org.uk/sites/default/files/
      publications/IfG_staff_turnover_WEB.pdf).

92   Gavin Freeguard, Marcus Shepheard, Benoit Guerin, Thomas Pope and Ketaki
      Zodgekar. 2020. Whitehall monitor 2020. Report, Institute for Government, p. 15
      (www.instituteforgovernment.org.uk/sites/default/files/publications/whitehall-
      monitor-2020_1.pdf).

93   Sasse and Norris (2019). Moving on, pp. 9–10.

94   Nicola Hughes and Peter Riddell. 2016. Interview with Kenneth Clarke (part
      of 'Ministers reflect' series). Institute for Government website (www.
      instituteforgovernment.org.uk/ministers-reflect/person/kenneth-clarke/).

95 Jose Torero. 2018. Professionalising fire safety engineering. Speech at the Warren Centre, University of Sydney, 24 July (www.youtube.com/watch?v=7-WPNXjZeO4&t=337s – from 4 minutes 30 seconds to 19 minutes 9 seconds). Transcript available here: https://grenfellenquirer.blog/2019/10/15/best-practice-2-prof-torero-transcript-the-real-failure-of-grenfell-complexity-ambiguity-and-competency/.

96 Judge and Elahi (2021). Foresight review of the future of regulatory systems: regulating in a disruptive world, pp. 3–58.

97 Judge and Elahi (2021). Foresight review of the future of regulatory systems: regulating in a disruptive world, p. 31.

98 Ibid, p. 52.

NOTES FOR CHAPTER 5

1 GTI Phase 2. 2020. Opening statement by Lead Counsel to the Inquiry Richard Millett QC, 27 January, p. 18, lines 9–13.

2 Andrew Hopkins. 2000. *Lessons from Longford*, p. 149. Sydney: CCH Australia.

3 Ibid.

4 Darryl Campbell. 2019. Redline: the many human errors that brought down the Boeing 737 Max. *The Verge*, 2 May (www.theverge.com/2019/5/2/18518176/boeing-737-max-crash-problems-human-error-mcas-faa)

5 Ibid.

6 Ibid.

7 Ibid.

8 Ibid.

9 Ibid.

10 Reuters. 2019. FAA tells U.S. Senate it would need 10,000 new employees, $1.8 billion to assume all certification. *Reuters*, 27 March (www.reuters.com/article/us-ethiopia-airline-congress-faa/faa-tells-u-s-senate-it-would-need-10000-new-employees-1-8-billion-to-assume-all-certification-idUSKCN1R82FT).

11 Dominic Gates. 2019. Flawed analysis, failed oversight: how Boeing, FAA certified the suspect 737 MAX flight control system. *Seattle Times*, 21 March (www.seattletimes.com/business/boeing-aerospace/failed-certification-faa-missed-safety-issues-in-the-737-max-system-implicated-in-the-lion-air-crash/).

12 Campbell (2019). Redline: the many human errors that brought down the Boeing 737 Max.

13 Simon Calder. 2020. Boeing 737 Max: one year after fatal Ethiopian Airways plane crash, did planemaker put profits ahead of safety? *The Independent*, 9 March (www.independent.co.uk/travel/news-and-advice/boeing-737-max-crash-ethiopian-airlines-lion-air-first-anniversary-one-year-a9387661.html).

14 Campbell (2019). Redline: the many human errors that brought down the Boeing 737 Max.

15 C.R. 2019. Why Boeing's shares have not fallen further after the 737 crashes. *The Economist*, 7 April (www.economist.com/gulliver/2019/04/07/why-boeings-shares-have-not-fallen-further-after-the-737-max-crashes).

16 Dominic Rushe. 2020. Boeing puts cost of 737 Max crashes at $19bn as it slumps to annual loss. *The Guardian*, 29 January (www.theguardian.com/business/2020/jan/29/boeing-puts-cost-of-737-max-crashes-at-19bn-as-it-slumps-to-annual-loss).

17 Leslie Josephs. 2020. Boeing's fired CEO Muilenburg walks away with more than $60 million. *CNBC News*, 12 January (www.cnbc.com/2020/01/10/ex-boeing-ceo-dennis-muilenburg-will-not-get-severance-payment-in-departure.html).

18 House Committee on Transportation and Infrastructure. 2020. The design, development & certification of the Boeing 737 Max. Final Committee Report, September, p. 164 (https://transportation.house.gov/imo/media/doc/2020.09.15%20FINAL%20737%20MAX%20Report%20for%20Public%20Release.pdf).

19 Ibid, p. 6.

20 Ibid, p. 13.

21 See https://www.resourcesregulator.nsw.gov.au/__data/assets/pdf_file/0005/332915/Human-Error-Pocket-Tool.pdf, drawing on the work of James Reason and Jens Rasmussen.

22 Reason (1991). *Human Error*, chapter 1.

23 Guerin, McCrae and Shepheard (2018). Accountability in modern government, pp. 32–37.

24 Todd Conklin. 2019. Five principles of human and organizational performance. Blog post from an interview by Jeffrey Dalto, Convergence Training website, 4 August (www.convergencetraining.com/blog/5-principles-of-human-and-organizational-performance-hop-with-dr-todd-conklin).

25 Erik Hollnagel. 2017. *Safety II in Practice: Developing the Resilience Potentials*, p. 6. Abingdon: Routledge.

26 Erik Hollnagel. Undated. Resilience assessment grid. Erikhollnagel.com website (https://erikhollnagel.com/ideas/resilience%20assessment%20grid.html).

27 Ibid.

28 The first time I heard this term was during a speech by renowned safety writer Andrew Hopkins, whose work has influenced me greatly. I would recommend that everybody read his book *Failure to Learn: The BP Texas City Refinery Disaster* (CCH, 2008).

29 Guerin, McCrae and Shepheard (2018). Accountability in modern government, p. 14.

30 Ibid, p. 4.

31 Ibid, p. 12.

32 Ibid, p. 6.

33 Ibid, pp. 19–23.

34 Ibid, pp. 40–41.

35 UK Parliament. Undated. Select Committees. UK Parliament website (www.parliament.uk/about/how/committees/select/).

36 H. W. Harris, J. H. Hunt and J. Thomson. 1987. Overcladding external walls of large panel system dwellings. BRE Report, addendum, p. 118 (www.whatdotheyknow.com/request/404316/response/985060/attach/7/BRE%20LPS%20Overclad.pdf?cookie_passthrough=1).

37   UK Select Committee on Environment, Transport and Regional Affairs. 1999. Evidence of Glyn Evans (Fire Brigades Union). Report on Potential Risk of Fire Spread in Buildings, 20 July, paragraph 4 (https://publications.parliament.uk/pa/cm199899/cmselect/cmenvtra/741/9072004.htm).

38   Ibid, paragraph 18.

39   Ibid, paragraph 19.

40   Carrington (2019). 'Class 0' and the end of government's guidance on building regulations'..

41   Martin Stanley and Julia Wdowin. 2018. Getting regulation right. Bennett Institute for Public Policy, University of Cambridge, December, pp. 12–13 (www.bennettinstitute.cam.ac.uk/media/uploads/files/Getting_regulation_right_jMvOiGb.pdf).

42   Ibid, pp. 19–20.

43   BBC. 2017. Thames Water fined £20m for sewage spill. BBC News website, 22 March (www.bbc.co.uk/news/uk-england-39352755).

44   Josie Co. 2017. Tesco fined £129m by Serious Fraud Office for overstating profits. The Independent, 28 March (www.independent.co.uk/news/business/news/tesco-fined-p. 129-million-serious-fraud-office-overstating-profits-a7653166.html).

45   Stanley and Wdowin (2018). Getting regulation right, pp. 45–46.

46   National Audit Office. 2017. A short guide to regulation. Report, September, p. 21 (www.regulation.org.uk/library/2017-NAO-A-Short-Guide-to-Regulation.pdf).

47   See the building safety page on the Health and Safety Executive website: www.hse.gov.uk/building-safety/index.htm.

48   Draft Fire Safety Bill. 2020. Ministry of Housing, Communities and Local Government. Draft bill, July, paragraph 74 (https://assets.publishing.service.gov.uk/government/uploads/system/uploads/attachment_data/file/906737/Draft_Building_Safety_Bill_Web_Accessible.pdf).

49   The Challenger Space Shuttle disaster's Wikipedia article (https://en.wikipedia.org/wiki/Space_Shuttle_Challenger_disaster).

50   Howard Berkes. 2012. Remembering Roger Boisjoly: he tried to stop Shuttle Challenger launch. NPR News, 6 February (www.npr.org/sections/thetwo-way/2012/02/06/146490064/remembering-roger-boisjoly-he-tried-to-stop-shuttle-challenger-launch?t=1596377343584).

51   Jim Wetherbee. 2016. Controlling Risk: Thirty Techniques for Operating Excellence, pp. 11–17. New York: Morgan James. Published with permission.

52   Ibid, p. 11.

53   Ibid, pp. 11–17.

54   Ibid, pp. 11–14.

55   Ibid, pp. 14–17.

56   Emma Norris and Marcus Shepheard. 2017. How public inquiries can lead to change. Report, Institute for Government, December, pp. 9–12.

57   Ibid, p. 13. Published with permission.

58   Ibid, p. 6.

59   GTI, financial report to 31 March 2019 (https://assets.grenfelltowerinquiry.org.
      uk/inline-files/Grenfell%20Tower%20Inquiry%20financial%20report%20to%2031%20
      March%202019.pdf).

60   Norris and Shepheard (2017). How public inquiries can lead to change, p. 4.

61   JUSTICE. 2020. When things go wrong: the response of the justice system.
      Report, JUSTICE, p. 1–2 (https://justice.org.uk/wp-content/uploads/flipbook/34/
      book.html).

62   Ibid, p. 91.

63   Ibid, p. 3.

64   Peter Apps. 2019. The lost lessons of Lakanal: how politicians missed the chance
      to stop Grenfell. *Inside Housing*, 3 July (www.insidehousing.co.uk/insight/special-
      investigation--the-lost-lessons-of-lakanal-how-politicians-missed-the-chance-to-
      stop-grenfell-61834).

65   Her Honour Frances Kirkham CBE. 2013. Letter re: Lakanal House fire. Letter,
      28 March, p. 3 (www.lambeth.gov.uk/sites/default/files/ec-letter-to-DCLG-
      pursuant-to-rule43-28March2013.pdf).

66   Eric Pickles MP. 2013. Letter re: Lakanal House fire. Letter, 20 May, pp. 2–3
      (www.lambeth.gov.uk/sites/default/files/ec-letter-from-rt-hon-eric-pickles-
      mp.20May2013.pdf).

67   Apps (2019). The lost lessons of Lakanal.

68   Ibid.

69   Ibid.

70   Ibid.

71   Peter Apps. 2019. PM's chief of staff did not act on multiple warnings about
      fire safety in months before Grenfell, new letters show. *Inside Housing*, 13 June
      (www.insidehousing.co.uk/news/pms-chief-of-staff-did-not-act-on-multiple-
      warnings-about-fire-safety-in-months-before-grenfell-new-letters-show-61883).

72   Nathaniel Barker. 2021. Government ministers and officials told to give evidence
      to Grenfell inquiry. *Inside Housing*, 6 January (www.insidehousing.co.uk/news/
      news/government-ministers-and-officials-told-to-give-evidence-to-grenfell-
      inquiry-69096).

73   Christopher Hood. 2010. *The Blame Game*, p. 18. Princeton University Press.

74   Ibid, p. 12.

75   BBC. 2018. Stephen Lawrence murder: a timeline of how the story unfolded. *BBC
      News* website, 13 April (www.bbc.co.uk/news/uk-26465916).

76   Leading article. 2021. Hold builders to account and resolve this housing scandal.
      The Times, 31 January (www.thetimes.co.uk/article/hold-builders-to-account-and-
      resolve-this-housing-scandal-l7v82vh8s).

NOTES FOR CHAPTER 6

1   Diane Coyle, Gill Kernick, Owen Garling, Martin Stanley, Flora Cornish, David Wales
      and David Slater. 2020. Policy lessons from catastrophic events. Bennett Institute
      Workshop Report, May, p. 38 (www.bennettinstitute.cam.ac.uk/media/uploads/
      files/REPORT_Policy_Lessons_from_Catastrophic_Events_-_FINAL_005.pdf).

2   Kernick Gill. 2020. The danger of the narratives we use to silence: Grenfell and the Rebel Residents. Blog, Bennett Institute for Public Policy, 29 July.

3   G. Morse. 2019. The lessons from Ladbroke Grove. *Rail* 889, p. 82.

4   Nippin Anand. 2020. Conflicts within and without: the *Costa Concordia* case. Nippinanand.com website, 18 May (https://amchamtt.com/resources/Documents/Goal%20conflicts%20-%20costa%20concordia-1_NippinAnand.pdf).

5   Ibid, p. 66.

6   House of Commons Transport Committee. 2019. Road safety: driving while using a mobile phone. Report, 22 July, p. 6 (https://publications.parliament.uk/pa/cm201719/cmselect/cmtrans/2329/2329.pdf).

7   Christopher Bucktin. 2016. Driver on mobile phone killed Jacy Good's parents and left her fighting for her life – now she wants change. *The Mirror*, 15 September (www.mirror.co.uk/news/world-news/victim-mobile-phone-driver-who-8844913).

8   The integral model is loosely based on the work of philosopher Ken Wilbur and has been adapted and utilized by JMJ Associates in its safety leadership and cultural consulting work. Published with permission from JMJ Associates.

9   Sidney Dekker. 2017. *The Safety Anarchist*, p. 12. Abingdon: Routledge.

10   Stanley and Wdowin (2018). Getting regulation right, chapter. 5.

11   Ibid, p. 7.

12   House Committee on Transportation and Infrastructure (2020). The design, development and certification of the Boeing 737 Max, p. 3.

13   Ibid, p. 6.

14   Ibid, p. 14.

15   Ministry of Housing, Communities & Local Government. 2017. Expert panel appointed to advise on immediate safety action following Grenfell fire. UK Government press release, 27 June (www.gov.uk/government/news/expert-panel-appointed-to-advise-on-immediate-safety-action-following-grenfell-fire).

16   Alexi Mostrous. 2017. Grenfell Tower inquiry chief accused of conflict of interest. *The Times*, 4 August (www.thetimes.co.uk/article/grenfell-tower-inquiry-chief-sir-ken-knight-accused-of-conflict-of-interest-b5c86wmtw).

17   Mayor of London website. 2019. Mayor appoints new London Fire Commissioner. Press release, 10 December (www.london.gov.uk/press-releases/mayoral/andy-roe-to-lead-london-fire-brigade).

18   Health and Safety Executive. 2021. HSE announces new Chief Inspector of Buildings. Press release, 16 February (https://press.hse.gov.uk/2021/02/16/hse-announces-new-chief-inspector-of-buildings/).

19   Stanley and Wdowin (2018). Getting regulation right, chapter 5.

20   Ibid, p. 9.

21   Ibid, p. 32.

22   Ibid, p. 32.

23   Ibid, p. 34.

24   Ibid, p .35.

25   Peter Apps. 2020. Six key factors in the failure of the Grenfell Tower refurbishment. *Inside Housing*, 6 August (www.insidehousing.co.uk/insight/six-key-factors-in-the-failure-of-the-grenfell-tower-refurbishment-67309).

26   Stanley and Wdowin (2018). Getting regulation right, p. 47.

27   Megan Reitz, Viktor O. Nilsson, Emma Day and John Higgins. 2019. Speaking truth to power at work. Report, Hult Research, Summer (http://page.hult.edu/rs/900-NUY-491/images/Speaking_Truth_to_Power_Report_2019_Final.pdf).

28   Ibid, p. 24.

29   Esther Webber and Eleni Courea. 2020. Dozens of Tory MPs set to refuse unconscious bias training. *The Times*, September 21 (www.thetimes.co.uk/article/dozens-of-tory-mps-set-to-refuse-unconscious-bias-training-sfnrm895g).

30   Lee Rowley. 2020. Slaying the strange beast of unconscious bias training. *The Times*, 16 December (www.thetimes.co.uk/article/slaying-the-strange-beast-of-unconscious-bias-training-vs67rvfnt).

31   Martin Stanley. Undated. Understanding the Civil Service website. The Westminster Model (www.civilservant.org.uk/wm-summary.html).

32   Rajeev Syal. 2020. The growing list of civil servants frozen out while Johnson's ministers remain. *The Guardian*, 26 August (www.theguardian.com/politics/2020/aug/26/the-growing-list-of-civil-servants-frozen-out-while-johnsons-ministers-remain).

33   Tracie Jolliff. 2019. Speaking truth to power, we have some work to do on inclusion. NHS Leadership Academy, 27 August (www.leadershipacademy.nhs.uk/blog/speaking-truth-to-power/).

34   Martin Stanley. 2019. Fire safety – still no one listens. Blog, UKcivilservant, 20 June (https://ukcivilservant.wordpress.com/2019/06/20/fire-safety-still-no-one-listens/).

35   UK Government. 2018. Consultation principles. UK Government website (https://assets.publishing.service.gov.uk/government/uploads/system/uploads/attachment_data/file/691383/Consultation_Principles__1_.pdf).

36   Stanley (2019). Fire safety – still no one listens.

37   GTI Phase 2. 2020. Witness evidence from Simon Lawrence (project manager for Rydon). Transcript, 21 July, p. 83, lines 7–16.

38   Ibid, 22 July, p. 162, lines 20–23.

39   Ibid, 22 July, p. 153, lines 21–23.

40   Ibid, 21 July, p. 160, lines 2–9 and p. 164, lines 1–24.

41   Ibid, 22 July, p. 89, lines 24–25 and p. 90 lines 1–3.

42   Ibid, 22 July, p. 68, lines 9–10.

43   Ibid, 22 July, p. 72–93.

44   Eddy Daffarn and Francis O'Connor. 2016. KCTMO – playing with fire! Blog, Grenfell Action Group, 20 November (https://grenfellactiongroup.wordpress.com/2016/11/20/kctmo-playing-with-fire/).

45   GTI Phase 1. 2018. Witness evidence from Commissioner Dany Cotton (London Fire Brigade). Transcript, 27 September, p. 52, lines 2–11.

46   GTI Phase 1 Report, volume 4, p. 607, paragraph 28.55.

47   LFB. 2019. London Fire Commissioner to step down. LFB website, 6 December (www.london-fire.gov.uk/news/2019-news/december/london-fire-commissioner-to-step-down/).

48 George Stephens. 2019. Public outcry as London fire fighters blamed. *EuroWeekly News*, 30 October (www.euroweeklynews.com/2019/10/30/public-outcry-as-london-fire-fighters-blamed/).

49 GTI Phase 1 Report, volume 4, p. 784, paragraphs 34.5.

50 UK Government. 2019. Civil Service diversity and inclusion dashboard. Online tool, 11 September (www.gov.uk/government/publications/civil-service-diversity-inclusion-dashboard/civil-service-diversity-and-inclusion-dashboard).

51 Ibid.

52 Denise Wilson (CEO of Hampton-Alexander Review), quoted by Ian Coyle. 2020. Diversity in the boardroom: where does the UK stand? Blog, Barclay Simpson, 3 March (www.barclaysimpson.com/blogs/diversity-in-the-boardroom-where-does-the-uk-stand-06331646931).

53 Coyle (2020). Diversity in the boardroom: where does the UK stand?

54 Coyle, Kernick, Garling, Stanley, Cornish, Wales and Slater (2020). Policy lessons from catastrophic events, p. 38.

55 Adapted from Jeremy Souder and Jennifer S. Myers. 2016. Medical errors and patient safety. *Aneskey*, 7 July (https://aneskey.com/medical-errors-and-patient-safety/).

56 David Berger. 2021. Up the line to death: covid-19 has revealed a mortal betrayal of the world's healthcare workers. *thebmjopinion*, 29 January (https://blogs.bmj.com/bmj/2021/01/29/up-the-line-to-death-covid-19-has-revealed-a-mortal-betrayal-of-the-worlds-healthcare-workers/).

57 Ibid.

58 Royal College of Nursing. 2020. Second PPE survey of UK nursing staff. Survey, May, p. 3 (www.rcn.org.uk/professional-development/publications/rcn-second-ppe-survey-covid-19-pub009269).

59 Charlie Haynes and James Clayton. 2020. Coronavirus: doctors 'told not to discuss PPE shortages'. *BBC News*, 15 May (www.bbc.co.uk/news/uk-52671814).

60 James McKay. 2020. Hancock suggests NHS staff are overusing protective equipment. *Nursing Notes*, 12 April (https://nursingnotes.co.uk/news/hancock-suggests-nhs-staff-overusing-protective-equipment/).

61 UK Public Accounts Select Committee. 2020. Readying the NHS and social care for the Covid-19 peak. Summary, 29 July (https://publications.parliament.uk/pa/cm5801/cmselect/cmpubacc/405/40503.htm#_idTextAnchor000).

62 Locality. 2020. We were built for this. Report, June, p. 10 (https://locality.org.uk/wp-content/uploads/2020/06/We-were-built-for-this-Locality-2020.06.13.pdf).

63 Ibid, p. 7.

64 Julian McCrae. 2020. No, Britain isn't in the middle of a culture war – and our discussions with voters proved it. *Prospect*, 4 February (www.prospectmagazine.co.uk/politics/no-britain-isnt-in-the-middle-of-a-culture-war-and-our-focus-groups-prove-it).

65 Jon Snow. 2017. I know nothing – but I've experienced a lot. MacTaggart Lecture, reported in *inews*, 23 August (https://inews.co.uk/news/uk/jon-snow-speech-full-i-know-nothing-ive-experienced-lot-86607). Reprinted with permission.

NOTES FOR CHAPTER 7

1   RR James Jones KBE. 2017. The patronising disposition of unaccountable power: report into the suffering of the Hillsborough families. UK Government, 1 November, p. 6, paragraphs 4–5 (https://assets.publishing.service.gov.uk/government/uploads/system/uploads/attachment_data/file/656130/6_3860_HO_Hillsborough_Report_2017_FINAL_updated.pdf).

2   Hackitt (2018). Building a safer future – independent review of building regulations and fire safety final report, p. 6.

3   Industry Safety Steering Group. 2020. Building safety. Report, UK Government, p. 4 (https://assets.publishing.service.gov.uk/government/uploads/system/uploads/attachment_data/file/906951/The_Industry_Safety_Steering_Groups_report_for_the_Secretary_of_State_and_the_Minister_for_Building_Safety.pdf).

4   Aerossurance. 2016. Chernobyl: 30 years on – lessons in safety culture. Report, 26 April (http://aerossurance.com/safety-management/chernobyl-30-years-on/).

5   Richard Gray. 2019. The true toll of the Chernobyl disaster. *BBC News*, 26 July (www.bbc.com/future/article/20190725-will-we-ever-know-chernobyls-true-death-toll).

6   See International Atomic Energy Agency's 'Frequently asked Chernobyl questions' pages (undated) at www.iaea.org/newscenter/focus/chernobyl/faqs.

7   International Safety Advisory Group. 1992. The Chernobyl accident: updating INSAG1: INSAG 7. Report, International Atomic Energy Agency, Vienna, p. 84.

8   Tom Lowe. 2020. Hackitt warns industry to change now to survive new safety regulator. *Building Design*, 14 October (www.bdonline.co.uk/news/hackitt-warns-industry-to-change-now-to-survive-new-safety-regulator/5108442.article).

9   Eddie Daffarn. 2021. GTI hearing, 12 April, p. 242, lines 20–25 and p. 243, lines 1–3.

10 Lexico definition of 'context' (www.lexico.com/definition/context).

11 Jones (2017). The patronising disposition of unaccountable power, p. 3.

12 Ibid, p. 6.

13 Ibid, p. 6.

14 BBC. 2019. Hillsborough: timeline of the 1989 stadium disaster. *BBC News* website, 28 November (www.bbc.co.uk/news/uk-england-merseyside-47697569).

15 Ibid.

16 Jim Edwards. 2012. See *The Sun*'s front-page apology. *Business Insider*, 13 September (www.businessinsider.com/the-suns-front-page-on-hillsborough-2012-9?r=US&IR=T).

17 Richard Moriarty, Lauren Veevers and Tom Newton Dunn. 2012. Hillsborough the real truth. *The Sun*, 12 September (www.thesun.co.uk/archives/news/915727/hillsborough-the-real-truth/).

18 BBC (2019). Hillsborough: timeline of the 1989 stadium disaster.

19 BBC. 2016. Hillsborough inquests: fans unlawfully killed, jury concludes. *BBC News* website, 26 April (www.bbc.co.uk/news/uk-england-36138337).

20 BBC (2019). Hillsborough: timeline of the 1989 stadium disaster.

21   Ibid.

22   More than thirty-two years after the disaster, on 19 April 2021, the trial of two former South Yorkshire police officers and the force's lawyer at the time of Hillsborough began. They were charged with perverting the course of justice over the amendment of police statements about the tragedy. See David Conn. 2021. Hillsborough police face trial accused of perverting the course of justice, *The Guardian*, 18 April (www.theguardian.com/uk-news/2021/apr/18/hillsborough-police-face-trial-accused-of-perverting-course-of-justice).

23   Jones (2017). The patronising disposition of unaccountable power.

24   Ibid, p. 7.

25   Ibid, p. 65.

26   Ibid, pp. 80–1.

27   JUSTICE. 2020. When things go wrong: the response of the justice system. Report, p. 86 (https://justice.org.uk/wp-content/uploads/flipbook/34/book.html).

28   David Conn. 2017. The scandal of Orgreave. *The Guardian*, 18 May (www.theguardian.com/politics/2017/may/18/scandal-of-orgreave-miners-strike-hillsborough-theresa-may).

29   Jones (2017). The patronising disposition of unaccountable power, pp. 27–28.

30   Sidney Dekker. 2014. *Field Guide to Understanding Human Error*, p. xi. Farnham: Ashgate Publishing.

31   Martin Farrer. 2019. Historian berates billionaires at Davos over tax avoidance. *The Guardian*, 30 January (www.theguardian.com/business/2019/jan/30/historian-berates-billionaires-at-davos-over-tax-avoidance).

32   Fire Protection Association. 2020. HCLGC estimates £15bn fire safety repair costs. FPA website, 12 June (www.thefpa.co.uk/news/hclgc-estimates-15bn-fire-safety-repair-costs).

33   Alice Lilly, Gemma Tetlow, Oliver Davies and Thomas Pope. 2020. Whitehall monitor: the cost of Covid-19. Institute for Government, 23 September (www.instituteforgovernment.org.uk/publications/cost-covid-19).

34   Amy Walker. 2020. Andy Burnham trying to hold us over a barrel on lockdown says Raab. *The Guardian*, 16 October (www.theguardian.com/politics/2020/oct/16/andy-burnham-trying-to-hold-us-over-a-barrel-on-tier-3-covid-lockdown-says-raab).

35   Daniel Kahneman. 2012. *Thinking, Fast and Slow*, p. 27. Penguin.

36   Ibid, pp. 20–32.

37   Ibid, pp. 22–23.

38   Ibid, p. 25.

39   Ibid, p. 118.

40   Ibid, p. 243.

41   Ibid, p. 333.

42   Ibid, p. 333.

43   Gokhan Aydin. 2017. Thinking fast, thinking slow and thinking together. *The Circle*, 14 June (http://thecrcl.ca/thinking-fast-thinking-slow-thinking-together/).

44   Edgar Schein and Peter A. Schein. 2017. *Organizational Culture and Leadership*, 5th edition, p. 183. Wiley.

45   Robert Booth. 2020. Boris Johnson's pick to help lead Grenfell Inquiry linked to cladding firm. *The Guardian*, 16 January (www.theguardian.com/uk-news/2020/jan/16/benita-mehra-grenfell-inquiry-boris-johnson-appoints-engineer-with-links-to-cladding-firm).

46   Rhiannon Curry. 2019. Gavin Barwell lands board appointment at major housing association. *Inside Housing*, 16 December (www.insidehousing.co.uk/news/news/gavin-barwell-lands-board-appointment-at-major-housing-association-64545).

47   Onora O'Neill. 2002. Reith Lectures 2002: a question of trust. Lecture 4: trust and transparency. BBC website (http://downloads.bbc.co.uk/rmhttp/radio4/transcripts/20020427_reith.pdf).

48   David Collins. 2020. Dominic Cummings was 'spotted on riverside path in Barnard Castle'. *Sunday Times*, 31 May (www.thetimes.co.uk/article/dominic-cummings-was-spotted-on-riverside-path-in-barnard-castle-szwdjpbc8).

49   Daisy Fancourt, Andrew Steptoe and Liam Wright. 2020. The Cummings effect: politics, trust, and behaviours during the Covid-19 pandemic. *The Lancet*, 6 August (www.thelancet.com/journals/lancet/article/PIIS0140-6736(20)31690-1/fulltext).

50   Jill Rutter. 2020. Video clip on Twitter, Tortoise Media, 26 May (https://twitter.com/tortoise/status/1265254118635057153).

51   Tim Shipman. 2020. They are tied together, but is the Dominic Cummings and Boris Johnson show over? *The Times*, 31 May (www.thetimes.co.uk/article/they-are-tied-together-but-is-the-dominic-cummings-and-boris-johnson-show-over-9qgxxdlvz).

52   Will Clothier. 2020. The Dominic Cummings saga has gripped the public in a way we've never seen before. *The Times*, 1 June (www.thetimes.co.uk/article/the-cummings-saga-has-gripped-the-public-in-a-way-we-ve-never-seen-before-hdh9qrmlo).

53   Onora O'Neill. 2002. The Reith Lectures: a question of trust. BBC Radio 4 (www.bbc.co.uk/programmes/p00ghvd8).

54   See, for example, IAmBirmingham. 2018. 'Sickening' video emerges of group burning effigy of Grenfell Tower on bonfire. YouTube video (www.youtube.com/watch?v=e8akk-nZtuk).

55   BBC. 2019. Man cleared over burning Grenfell effigy film. *BBC News*, 22 August (www.bbc.co.uk/news/uk-england-london-49435117).

56   Glenn Geher. 2019. The psychology of 'othering'. *Psychology Today*, 6 April (www.psychologytoday.com/us/blog/darwins-subterranean-world/201904/the-psychology-othering).

57   Jones (2017). The patronising disposition of unaccountable power, p. 54.

58   IAEA. 2002. *Safety Culture in Nuclear Installations: Guidance for Use in the Enhancement of Safety Culture*, p. 3. Vienna: International Atomic Energy Agency.

59   Edgar H. Schein. 2016. *Organizational Culture and Leadership*, p. 2. Wiley.

60   Kwasi Adjekum. 2014. Safety culture perceptions in a collegiate aviation program: a systematic assessment. Report, April, p. 47.

61   Schein (2016). *Organizational Culture and Leadership*, p. 20.

62   Coyle, Kernick, Garling, Stanley, Cornish, Wales and Slater (2020). Policy lessons from catastrophic events, p. 18.

63   Amy Edmondson. 1999. Psychological safety and learning behaviour in work
      teams. *Administrative Science Quarterly*, June, appendix, p. 382 (https://web.
      mit.edu/curhan/www/docs/Articles/15341_Readings/Group_Performance/
      Edmondson%20Psychological%20safety.pdf).

NOTES FOR CHAPTER 8

1   David Snowden. 2020. Self-destructive tendencies. *Cognitive Edge*, 3 September,
      (https://www.cognitive-edge.com/self-destructive-tendencies/).
2   GTI Phase 1. 2018. Witness evidence by Hanan Wahabi. Transcript, 8 November,
      p. 188, lines 1–4.
3   Jones (2017). The patronising disposition of unaccountable power, p. 3.
4   Judith Butler, as cited in Andrew Day. 2020. *Disruption, Change and
      Transformation in Organizations: A Human Relations Perspective*, p. 116. Abingdon:
      Routledge Publishing.
5   HSE. 2020. Work-related stress, anxiety or depression statistics in Great Britain,
      2020. Report, March (www.hse.gov.uk/statistics/causdis/stress.pdf).
6   Stormzy. 2018. Rise up: the #Merky story so far. Extract quoted in *GQ Magazine*,
      30 October (www.gq-magazine.co.uk/article/stormzy-book-rise-up-extract).
7   Snowden (2020). Self-destructive tendencies.
8   Karl E. Weick and Kathleen M. Sutcliffe. 2011. *Managing the Unexpected: Resilient
      Performance in an Age of Uncertainty*, pp. 9–15. Wiley.
9   Daniel Renwick. 2019. We walk in silence. Poem (https://www.facebook.com/
      watch/?v=1060648657469643). Published with permission.
10   Rebecca Solnit. 2010. *A Paradise Built in Hell: The Extraordinary Communities That
      Arise in Disaster*. Penguin.
11   Rebecca Solnit. 2019. How change happens. *Lit Hub*, 3 September (http://lithub.
      com/Rebecca-solnit-progress-is-not-inevitable-it-takes-work).